SOUTH KOREA SINCE 1980

This book examines the changes in politics, economics, society, and foreign policy in South Korea since 1980. Starting with a brief description of its history leading up to 1980, this book deals with South Korea's transition to democracy, the stunning economic development achieved since the 1960s, the 1997 financial crisis and the economic reforms that followed, and concludes with the North Korean nuclear crisis and foreign relations with regional powers. The theoretical framework of this book addresses how democratization affected all of these dimensions of South Korea. For instance, democratization allowed for the more frequent alternation of political elites from conservative to liberal and back to conservative. These elites initiated different policies for dealing with North Korea and held different views on South Korea's role in its alliance with the United States. Consequently, ideological divides in South Korean politics became more stark and the political process more combative.

Uk Heo is Professor of Political Science at the University of Wisconsin–Milwaukee. He is a Korean native and has widely written on Korean politics and security. His work has appeared in *Journal of Politics*, *Political Research Quarterly*, *British Journal of Political Science*, *International Studies Quarterly*, *Journal of Conflict Resolution*, *Comparative Politics*, *Comparative Political Studies*, *Journal of Peace Research*, *International Interactions*, *Armed Forces and Society*, *Asian Survey*, and others. He is a former president of the Association of Korean Political Studies.

Terence Roehrig is Associate Professor of National Security Affairs at the U.S. Naval War College. He is the author of two books, *From Deterrence to Engagement: The U.S. Defense Commitment to South Korea* (2006) and *The Prosecution of Former Military Leaders in Newly Democratic Nations: The Cases of Argentina, Greece, and South Korea* (2002), and a co-editor of *Korean Security in a Changing East Asia* (2007). Professor Roehrig has published numerous articles and book chapters on North Korea's nuclear weapons program, Korean and East Asian security issues, deterrence theory, the U.S.–South Korea alliance, human rights, and transitional justice. Professor Roehrig is a former president of the Association of Korean Political Studies.

THE WORLD SINCE 1980

This new series is designed to examine politics, economics, and social change in important countries and regions over the past three decades. No prior background knowledge of a given country will be required by readers. The books are written by leading social scientists.

Volumes published

Brazil Since 1980; Francisco Vidal Luna and Herbert S. Klein

Europe Since 1980; Ivan T. Berend

Israel Since 1980; Guy Ben-Porat, Yagil Levy, Shlomo Mizrahi, Ayre Naor, and Erez Tzfadia

Japan Since 1980; Thomas Cargill and Takayuki Sakamoto

Mexico Since 1980; Stephen Haber, Herbert S. Klein, Noel Maurer, and Kevin J. Middlebrook

Russia Since 1980; Steven Rosefielde and Stefan Hedlund

The United States Since 1980; Dean Baker

Volumes in preparation

Britain Since 1980; Roger Middleton

China Since 1980; Ross Garnaut

France Since 1980; Timothy Smith

India Since 1980; Sumit Ganguly and Rahul Mukherji

Iran Since 1980; Ali Ansari

Turkey Since 1980; Sevket Pamuk and Yesim Arat

SOUTH KOREA
SINCE 1980

Uk Heo

University of Wisconsin–Milwaukee

Terence Roehrig

U.S. Naval War College

CAMBRIDGE
UNIVERSITY PRESS

CAMBRIDGE UNIVERSITY PRESS
Cambridge, New York, Melbourne, Madrid, Cape Town, Singapore,
São Paulo, Delhi, Dubai, Tokyo, Mexico City

Cambridge University Press
32 Avenue of the Americas, New York, NY 10013-2473, USA

www.cambridge.org
Information on this title: www.cambridge.org/9780521743532

First published 2010

Printed in the United States of America

A catalog record for this publication is available from the British Library.

Library of Congress Cataloging in Publication data

Heo, Uk, 1962–
South Korea since 1980 / Uk Heo, Terence Roehrig.
    p.   cm. – (The world since 1980)
Includes bibliographical references and index.
ISBN 978-0-521-76116-1 – ISBN 978-0-521-74353-2 (pbk.)   1. Korea (South) – History –
1988–2002.   2. Korea (South) – Politics and government – 1988–2002.   3. Korea (South) –
Economic conditions – 1988–   4. Democratization – Korea (South) – History – 20th
century.   5. Korea (South) – History – 2002–   6. Korea (South) – Politics and government –
2002–   7. Korea (South) – History – 1960–1988.   8. Korea (South) – Politics and
government – 1960–1988.   I. Roehrig, Terence, 1955–   II. Title.   III. Series.
DS922.462.H46   2010
951.9504′4–dc22   2010000988

ISBN 978-0-521-76116-1 Hardback
ISBN 978-0-521-74353-2 Paperback

Contents

This book is dedicated to our parents,
Man-sik Heo, Sun-ok Chang,
and Richard and Shirley Roehrig.

1

Politics, Economics, and Foreign Relations before 1980

As Park Chung-hee sat down for dinner on October 26, 1979, with some of his closest advisors, he was facing one of his most difficult decisions as president of South Korea. Protests calling for political reform and democracy were intensifying throughout the country, and many feared the demonstrations would get out of control. Should the government crack down on the demonstrators or begin a process of bringing political change to the country? During dinner, a heated argument ensued during which Kim Jae-kyu, the head of the Korean Central Intelligence Agency (KCIA), received severe criticism from those in attendance for his handling of the demonstrations. Kim Jae-kyu stormed out of the room and returned after a few minutes with a .38 revolver in his pocket, having told his own security detail to shoot President Park's guards if shots rang out. Suddenly Kim Jae-kyu rose from his place, pointed the gun at Cha Ji-chul, the head of Park's security guards, and shouted to Park, "How can you have such a miserable worm as your adviser?"[1] Kim squeezed off two shots at close range, first at Cha Ji-chul and then at Park himself, before the gun jammed. With Park lying wounded on the floor, Kim grabbed a gun from one of his men and shot Park again, finishing the job. Cha Ji-chul ran away to another room, but Kim chased him down and shot him to death. By this time, Kim's security guards had opened fire on President Park's men and killed five of them.[2] Later, Kim maintained that he had killed President Park to end the dictatorship and bring

---

[1] D. Oberdorfer, *The Two Koreas: A Contemporary History* (New York: Basic Books, 1997), 110.
[2] Ibid., 109–10.

1

democracy back to South Korea.[3] Park's death brought an abrupt end to eighteen years of military rule. The public was shocked and dismayed by the tragic death of a leader who had ruled as a dictator but had brought the country out of poverty. Yet, with the end of this long period of authoritarian rule, many South Koreans also looked forward to beginning the process of democratization.

In many respects, understanding the complexities and achievements of South Korea since 1980 begins with the leader who immediately preceded that year, President Park Chung-hee. Until Park's rule from 1961 through 1979, South Korea struggled economically and was unable to achieve a per-capita gross domestic product (GDP) greater than $100. Even North Korea's economy had better success. After President Park's policies, planning, and leadership, along with much hard work by the South Korean public, South Korea's economy grew beyond most people's wildest imagination. Yet his rule and the prosperity it spawned came at a high price. The government suppressed civil rights and liberties and often dealt severely with dissenters, and people worked long, hard hours to stoke the engine of economic growth. People were willing to work so hard because they could envision a better life for their children and took great pride in the strides their country was making as it rose from the poverty of the 1950s. This book begins with a brief portrait of the man who began this journey into modernity for South Korea. His life is a reflection of the achievements and the costs the country has experienced in becoming the nation it is today.

Park Chung-hee was born on September 30, 1917, near Daegu in Gyeongsang province, the youngest of eight children in a poor farming family. Park's father had participated in a peasant rebellion (*Tonghak* uprising) and was subsequently arrested, although he later received a pardon just prior to his scheduled execution.[4] By this time, Korea was part of the Japanese Empire, having been formally annexed in 1910 after Tokyo emerged victorious over regional rivals in the Sino–Japanese (1894–5) and Russo–Japanese (1904–5) Wars. After high school, Park attended normal school to become a teacher but soon tired of this career. In 1940, following a brief stint of teaching, Park entered the Manchukuo Military Academy; by that time Manchukuo,

---

[3] A. Nahm, *Korea: Tradition and Transformation: A History of the Korean People* (Elizabeth, N.J.: Hollym International, 1988), 463–4.

[4] J. Kie-Chiang Oh, *Korean Politics: The Quest for Democratization and Economic Development* (Ithaca, N.Y.: Cornell University Press, 1999), 49–50.

also known as Manchuria, was a puppet state under Japanese control. Park excelled in his studies and was chosen to attend Japan's Army Staff College in Tokyo, where he graduated third in his class in 1944. He was assigned to the Kwangtung Army in Manchuria, where he served under the Japanese name Okamoto Minora during the closing months of the war. Thus, while many in Park's generation were fighting against the Japanese, he served with the Japanese Army until the end of the war.

When the war ended, Park left the Japanese Army and returned to Korea, where he joined the Korean Constabulary. Soon after, he enrolled in the Korean Military Academy, where he graduated in 1946 as part of the second class at the institution under U.S. occupation.[5] Park rose steadily in the ranks in the next two years until his unit was sent to quell a military mutiny in the Yosu-Sunchon region. Park and his brother were accused of conspiring with the mutineers and being communists with Park leading a communist cell at the Korean Military Academy.[6] Although these reports are unconfirmed, Park allegedly provided the government with a list of officers and enlisted personnel who were co-conspirators to spare himself from execution.[7] Although Park had to leave the military, with the outbreak of the Korean War in 1950 he returned to the army as a commissioned officer, becoming an expert in logistics and rising to the rank of brigadier general by the war's end in 1953.

After the war, Park soon became disenchanted with the state of the country and the military. Having led a very austere life, Park was troubled by the corruption and greed he saw among civilian leaders and high-ranking military officers. Park and others with similar beliefs also became increasingly concerned with personnel issues and the possibility that they might be forced out of the army.

In the early-morning hours of May 16, 1961, Park Chung-hee and a group of senior officers launched a coup to seize control of the government. The coup was relatively bloodless, and, soon after, Park

[5] B. Cumings, *Korea's Place in the Sun: A Modern History* (New York: W. W. Norton, 1997), 350.

[6] Oberdorfer, *The Two Koreas*, 32.

[7] Oberdorfer, *The Two Koreas*, 32; C. Kim, *The Korean Presidents: Leadership for Nation Building* (Norwalk, Conn.: EastBridge, 2007), 98; Cumings, *Korea's Place in the Sun: A Modern History*, 350; and G. Brazinsky, *Nation Building in South Korea: Koreans, Americans, and the Making of a Democracy* (Chapel Hill: University of North Carolina Press, 2007), 113–14.

began his plan to restructure and revitalize the South Korean economy. In January 1962, Park announced the first of several Five-Year Economic Plans that brought significant government involvement to the economy and gradually boosted South Korean growth and living standards. Later chapters will discuss his economic plans and achievements in greater detail. As the economy showed progress, however, Park expected loyalty, cooperation, and hard work while tolerating little dissent. Later, the authoritarian character of the regime decreased for a time, but, in 1972, Park pushed through a new constitution that returned to the days of draconian rule. The new constitution also contained provisions that allowed Park to rule for life, and it appeared he was determined to do so. By the late 1970s, many had concluded that Park may have stayed in office too long and that it was time for him to move on. Park's assassination brought his regime to a sudden end.

Park Chung-hee rose from humble beginnings to become the most powerful man in South Korea, beginning the country's climb to a top-fifteen global economic power. In part, Park's time in office (1961–79) was a bridge for South Korea from its largely agrarian, feudal past to the modern, industrialized state it is today, laying the foundation for the economic takeoff that continued from 1980 and beyond. Although Park laid the foundation for South Korea's economic success, political liberalization and reform were another matter. Park ruled with a tightly clenched fist, and those who opposed his rule felt his wrath, often through the agency he created, the KCIA. Thus, Park's legacy is a mixed affair. His leadership brought economic growth and prosperity, but often they came at a high price. South Koreans view him with admiration and gratitude but also question his authoritarian tendencies and determination to rule for life. Although the country would experience eight more years of military rule following another coup, Park's regime marks an important transition point for South Korea's political and economic modernization since 1980.

Introduction to Korea

Koreans have a long, proud history. Most of that history occurred as a united country; division of the peninsula into North and South following World War II represents only a small part of Korea's past.

Korea has had the unfortunate geographic fate of being in a tough neighborhood surrounded by some of Asia's most powerful countries. It has often been fought over or fought through by the regional powers as their rivalry for power played out. Consequently, Korea's history has often been an effort to maintain its sovereignty and territorial integrity, a task that has frequently been difficult.

Korea also has a long history of centralized authority and autocratic rule, first through the many years of the Korean monarchy, then by the thirty-five-year occupation by Japan, and, finally, by more than twenty-five years of military rule in South Korea after World War II before it finally transitioned to democracy in 1987. The South Korean social system is rooted in Confucianism, which created a hierarchical political and social structure that made obedience to higher authority paramount. Thus, when South Korea began its transition to democracy, it had no democratic heritage or institutions on which to draw, beginning most of this difficult journey from scratch.

We begin this book with a review of Korea's early history, examining the important events and forces that helped to shape Korea's future.

Early Korean History

According to tradition, the Korean nation began with the birth of Tan'gun, who was conceived from parents who were the god Hwan-ung and a mother who was a bear turned woman. According to Korea's founding myth, Tan'gun established the first Korean kingdom, Kojoson, sometime during the Bronze Age; Koreans often place the start of Kojoson at 2333 B.C.

From Kojoson, the Kingdom of Koguryo emerged in approximately 37 B.C. Koguryo occupied most of present-day North Korea along with the current Chinese provinces of Liaoning and Jilin. The remainder of the peninsula was dominated by two other kingdoms, Silla in the southeast beginning in approximately 57 B.C. and Baekche in the southwest in approximately 18 B.C. This is the period known to Koreans as the "Three Kingdoms" period. The relationship of Koguryo to China remains a matter of contention between China and both Koreas. For Koreans, Koguryo's ties to Korean history is a core element of their national identity, and recent Chinese efforts to claim

Koguryo history is viewed as threatening to many Koreans, in both North and South.[8]

In 660 A.D., Silla began an effort to unify the peninsula under its rule. First, it seized Baekche; later, in an alliance with China's Tang Dynasty, Silla conquered Koguryo at a time when the northern kingdom was weakened by a divisive succession struggle. By 668 A.D., Silla successfully unified the peninsula, creating the precursor to the modern Korean state.[9]

Silla kings ruled for almost three hundred years, providing a long period of stable government and cementing the concept of a single, unified Korean state. During these years, the kingdom embraced Buddhism and saw an extended period of cultural and artistic growth. By the late 800s, however, Silla rule began to unravel, and regional leaders who resembled those of the old "Three Kingdoms" period began to reemerge.[10] In 918, the northern state of Goryeo succeeded in bringing about the fall of what was left of the Silla Dynasty and unified the peninsula under its rule. The Goryeo Dynasty ruled from 918 to 1392, and its name became the source of the Western name of Korea. During this extended period of peace, Buddhism and the arts, in particular celadon pottery, flourished. By the 1200s, Goryeo came under pressure from the Mongol onslaught and fell in 1259. For the next hundred years, Mongol rulers dominated the peninsula but were finally expelled in 1356. The strength and cohesion of the Goryeo Dynasty was not the same, however, and, in 1392, it fell to a new order, the Chosun Dynasty, which ruled Korea for the next five hundred years.

Chosun Dynasty: 1392–1910

The Chosun Dynasty, also known as the Yi Dynasty for its founder, Yi Seong-gye, was ruled by a series of kings until 1910, when it ended with the Japanese occupation. These monarchs often engaged in factional power struggles within the kingdom while battling

---

[8] For a more detailed discussion of this issue, see T. Roehrig, "History as a Strategic Weapon: The South Korean and Chinese Struggle for Koguryo," *Journal of Asian and African Studies* 45, no. 1 (February 2010): 5–28.

[9] See C. J. Eckert, K. Lee, Y. Lew, M. Robinson, and E. Wagner, *Korea: Old and New, A History* (Cambridge, Mass.: Harvard University Press, 1990), 42–67.

[10] Cumings, *Korea's Place in the Sun: A Modern History*, 39.

external enemies on their borders. While dealing with these internal and external challenges, Koreans also managed to make advances in science, painting, pottery, and literature. A significant achievement was the creation of its own written language, *hangul*, in 1443 to replace the reliance on Chinese characters. It was also a period of rising Korean nationalism, fueled by the multitude of external challengers. The social structure became ever more rooted in Confucianism as adopted from China, so that, according to one historian, "Korea became more Confucian than Confucian China as its influence permeated every aspect of the life of the nation."[11] Confucian tenets meant that Korea had a rigid, hierarchical socioeconomic structure dominated by the *yangban* elites at the top. The *yangban* comprised approximately 10 percent of the population.

The decline of the Chosun Dynasty began in the late sixteenth century with the renewal of internal power struggles and factional rivalries. In addition, Korea was plagued by several invasions. The first attacks were launched by Japan in the late 1500s. In 1592, Japanese leader Toyotomi Hideyoshi intended to attack China by going through Korea. Hideyoshi had recently emerged victorious from a bloody civil war and needed further military campaigns to ensure his generals remained occupied. The Korean army was no match for Japan, lacking modern weaponry and an effective military organization, and Japanese forces advanced as far north as Pyongyang. Eventually, Korean opposition, naval victories by Admiral Yi Sun-shin, and Chinese intervention forced a Japanese retreat to a small foothold in southeast Korea. After peace talks between China and Japan failed, in 1597 Japan launched a second campaign but with the goal focused more on conquering Korea than on subduing China. This time, however, Koreans and a Ming Dynasty relief army were ready. Japanese forces made little headway, and, after Hideyoshi's death in 1598, they withdrew completely from the peninsula. Although Korea succeeded in driving out Hideyoshi's army, the eight years of war had had a devastating effect on Korea and its people, as much of the peninsula had been destroyed during the invasions.[12]

These invasions were followed in 1627 and again in 1636 by more from the Manchus in Manchuria. The Manchus were seeking to oust the Chinese Ming Dynasty, and Korea, as a Chinese vassal, was a

---

[11] Nahm, *Korea: Tradition & Transformation: A History of the Korean People*, 95.

[12] K. Lee (trans. E. Wagner and E. Shultz), *A New History of Korea* (Seoul: Ilchokak Publishers, 1984), 209–15.

threat to its southern border. Eventually, Korea succumbed to Manchu forces, agreeing to become a Manchu vassal and pay tribute. In 1644, the Manchus conquered the Ming Dynasty, and Korea remained a vassal of the new Chinese empire.

By the late 1800s, Korea became caught in the rivalry of the regional powers in East Asia: China, Japan, and Russia. For years, China had been the dominant power in the region and maintained a "big brother–little brother" relationship with Korea called *sa dae ju ui*. Rooted in Confucianism and power politics, this hierarchical relationship had Korea, the little brother, provide tribute and loyalty, while in return China, the big brother, furnished protection and left Korea alone. This relationship maintained Korean security as long as China remained the dominant power in the region, which it did for many years. In the 1800s, Chinese power began a steady decline that occurred in conjunction with the incursion of European powers and the rise of Japan and Russia. During the last forty years of the Chosun Dynasty, control of Korea was a central element of the competition between Japan, China, and Russia. Korea's ruler, King Kojong, saw many areas of Asia fall under foreign domination and hoped that a growing relationship with the United States might save the peninsula from a similar fate; however, he gravely overestimated Washington's interests in Korea and its willingness to protect it. The U.S. government simply did not see the region as sufficiently important for its interests.[13]

In the end, the regional rivalry resulted in two wars for control of Korea and Northeast Asia. The first was the Sino–Japanese War (1894–5). According to one scholar, "The war delivered a coup de grace to the expiring traditional international order in the Far East: It shattered Chinese hegemony and demonstrated to an astonished West that Japan had become a modern great power."[14] China's defeat and the resulting Treaty of Shimonoseki forced China to relinquish control of Korea and cede Taiwan, the Pescadores, and the Liaotung Peninsula to Japan. After the treaty was concluded, Russia convinced France and Germany to join Moscow in pressuring Japan to return the Liaotung Peninsula. The Japanese victory liberated Korea from Chinese suzerainty, but Korean independence was short-lived.

---

[13] H. Conroy and W. Patterson, "Duality and Dominance: A Century of Korean-American Relations," in *Korean-American Relations, 1866–1997*, ed. Y. Lee and W. Patterson (Albany: State University of New York Press, 1999), 2–4.

[14] S. C. M. Paine, *The Sino-Japanese War of 1894–1895: Perceptions, Power, and Primacy* (Cambridge: Cambridge University Press, 2005), 3.

With the end of Chinese hegemony, the regional struggle continued between Russia and Japan, particularly over control of Manchuria and Korea. The rivalry culminated in the Russo–Japanese War (1904–5), which produced a series of disastrous Russian defeats on land and at sea, leaving Japan as the dominant power in the region.[15] The Japanese victory shocked the world, demonstrating that a rising power in Asia could defeat one of the traditional powers of Europe. To ensure this position over the Korean Peninsula, Japan also obtained agreements with the United States and Great Britain that recognized Washington's and London's interests in Asia in return for Japan's interests in Korea.

Soon after Japan's victory, Tokyo coerced Korean authorities to sign the Eulsa Treaty, which established Korea as a Japanese protectorate and formalized Japan's formal control over the peninsula. The treaty entered into force upon obtaining the signature of five Korean cabinet ministers. Eventually, five did sign the agreement, believing Korea had no choice but to succumb to Japanese pressure. King Kojong refused to sign, however, and today the five signatories are viewed as traitors by many in Korea. Under the terms of the agreement, Japan assumed control over all external matters, especially foreign affairs and trade. Methodically, Japanese authorities, led by the first Resident-General Ito Hirobumi, established control over all elements of Korean affairs. King Kojong made several secret appeals to western leaders in an effort to wrest Korea from Japanese domination. The West was not interested, however, and in August 1910 Korea was formally annexed, becoming part of the Japanese empire.[16]

Japanese Occupation: 1910–1945

For the next thirty-five years, Koreans endured a brutal occupation by Japan.[17] In an effort at cultural assimilation, Japan forced Koreans

---

[15] For more detailed treatments of this conflict, see D. Warner and P. Warner, *The Tide at Sunrise: A History of the Russo-Japanese War, 1904–05* (New York: Routledge, 2004) and R. Connaughton, *Rising Sun and Tumbling Bear: Russia's War with Japan* (London: Cassell, 2004).

[16] See C. I. Eugene Kim and Kim Han-kyo, *Korea and the Politics of Imperialism, 1876– 1910* (Berkeley: University of California Press, 1967) and P. Duus, *The Abacus and the Sword: the Japanese Penetration of Korea, 1895–1910* (Berkeley: University of California Press, 1998).

[17] See G. Shin, *Ethnic Nationalism in Korea: Genealogy, Politics, and Legacy* (Stanford, Calif.: Stanford University Press, 2006) and A. Dudden, *Japan's Colonization of Korea: Discourse and Power* (Honolulu: University of Hawaii Press, 2005).

to take Japanese names, revere the Shinto religion and the Japanese emperor, and use the Japanese language in schools and within the government. Japanese authorities also confiscated land from those who could not prove ownership, creating many more tenant farmers. Many farmers had difficulty producing formal documents because their land holdings had been in their families for generations. Korean agricultural production rose during the occupation, but much of it was diverted to Japanese consumers. The Japanese occupation also brought some economic development and expanded industrial production through the investment of large Japanese corporations, *zaibatsu*, such as Mitsui and Mitsubishi. Japan built a modern infrastructure of roads, railroads, ports, and bridges while expanding Korea's industrial base. These efforts were not undertaken for Korea's benefit, but rather to aid Japan's war effort, and all of this came at a steep price for Korea and its people.[18]

By 1936, Japan was on a full war footing and used Korea to support this effort. Koreans were taken to Japan to work in factories and mines as the Japanese labor pool shrank to fill the ranks of the armed forces. It is estimated that two thousand and twenty thousand Koreans, respectively, who were forced to work in Japan were killed at Nagasaki and Hiroshima with the dropping of the atomic bombs.[19] As the war dragged on, an increasing portion of the Korean rice crop was shipped to Japan, and Koreans were drafted into the Japanese Army. Finally, the Japanese military forced women and girls from Korea as well as from China, the Philippines, and other locations into sexual slavery for the Japanese armed forces. An estimated two hundred thousand to four hundred thousand women and girls were forced to be what were euphemistically referred to as "comfort women."[20]

In assessing the Japanese occupation, Bruce Cumings noted:

> This colonial experience was intense and bitter, and shaped postwar Korea deeply. It brought development and underdevelopment, agrarian growth and deepened tenancy, industrialization and extraordinary dislocation, political mobilization and deactivation; it spawned a new

---

[18] K. Lee, *A New History of Korea*, 346–61.

[19] M. Hane, *Modern Japan: A Historical Survey*, 2nd ed. (Boulder, Colo.: Westview Press, 1992), 413.

[20] See Y. Yoshimi, *Comfort Women* (New York: Columbia University Press, 2001) and M. Stetz and B. Oh, eds., *Legacies of the Comfort Women of World War II* (Armonk, N.Y.: ME Sharpe, 2001).

role for the central state, new sets of Korean political leaders, communism and nationalism, armed resistance and treacherous collaboration; above all, it left deep fissures and conflicts that have gnawed at the Korean soul ever since.[21]

Liberation and Division

As World War II came to an end, Koreans believed their liberation was finally at hand. It was not to be as Koreans had hoped, however. The first indication occurred at the 1943 Cairo Conference among Franklin Roosevelt, Winston Churchill, and Chiang Kai-shek when they met to discuss the war in Asia. In the resulting "Declaration of Cairo," the allies, "mindful of the enslavement of the people of Korea, are determined that in due course Korea shall become free and independent."[22] "In due course" was the key phrase, as these leaders presumed that, before gaining its independence, Korea would need a period of trusteeship following the war. Later, Roosevelt estimated that a trusteeship lasting approximately twenty to thirty years would be appropriate.[23] Koreans were upset when Washington and Moscow announced a trusteeship plan for the peninsula.

The dropping of the atomic bombs on Japan brought World War II to an end earlier than Washington had anticipated. Consequently, U.S. planners had made few preparations for the eventual fate of Korea. In hasty deliberations, U.S. military officials developed a proposal to have U.S. forces accept the Japanese surrender south of the 38th parallel, while the Soviets would accept the surrender north of that line. The United States hoped Stalin would accept the proposal because the Red Army was already in Manchuria, and it would be weeks before the U.S. military could arrive in Korea. Moreover, designating the 38th parallel as the dividing line placed Seoul, the Korean capital, in the U.S. zone. The Soviets could have easily rejected the proposal, but, much to Washington's surprise, Stalin accepted the offer. It is also

[21] Cumings, *Korea's Place in the Sun*, 148.

[22] "Final Text of the Communiqué," November 26, 1943, *Foreign Relations of the United States, Conferences at Cairo and Teheran, 1943*, 449. Hereafter, the series of *Foreign Relations of the United States* will be referred to as *FRUS*.

[23] "Bohlen Minutes for the February 8, 1945 meeting at Yalta between Roosevelt and Stalin," *FRUS, Conferences at Malta and Yalta, 1945*, 766–71.

important to note that Washington had no intention of maintaining a permanent division of the peninsula.

For two years, the United States and the Soviet Union conducted negotiations to reunify the two occupation zones, but to no avail. Despite multiple efforts, Cold War hostility impeded progress, and, in frustration, Washington turned the problem over to the United Nations (UN) for a solution. On November 14, 1947, the UN adopted a resolution that called for reuniting the two Korean zones and holding elections to establish a single government. Moscow and Pyongyang refused to abide by the decision and did not hold elections. The South did hold elections in May 1948, and, on August 15, 1948, the Republic of Korea (ROK) came into being under its first president, Syngman Rhee (Korean name – Yi Sung-man). Soon after, Moscow established a separate government in the North, the Democratic People's Republic of Korea (DPRK), on September 9, 1948, under the leadership of Kim Il-sung.

Syngman Rhee and the Republic of Korea

South Korea's first president, Syngman Rhee, spent most of the thirty-five years of the Japanese occupation in the United States, where he tirelessly promoted the cause of Korean independence.[24] While abroad, Rhee was elected to head the Korean Provisional Government (KPG) in 1919. The KPG was the Korean government-in-exile during the occupation and was based in China. Eventually, the KPG fragmented, and factions vied for control of whatever government was going to follow the defeat of the Japanese. When World War II ended, Rhee returned to Korea and began to ingratiate himself with U.S. occupation authorities in an effort to outmaneuver his rivals for control of South Korea's government. Rhee's efforts with U.S. officials were aided by his command of the English language, as he had obtained a master's degree in history from Harvard University and a doctorate in political science from Princeton University.

When Rhee came to office in 1948, South Korea faced a host of serious challenges. Few South Koreans had any experience or training in democracy. From 1392 to 1910, Korea was governed by Chosun

---

[24] For more detailed discussions of Syngman Rhee, see R. Oliver, *Syngman Rhee: The Man Behind the Myth* (New York: Dodd, Mead, 1954) and R. Allen, *Korea's Syngman Rhee: An Unauthorized Portrait* (Rutland, Vt.: Tuttle, 1960).

Dynasty kings through a strong bureaucracy that centralized author-ity in the hands of the Korean monarchs. This era was followed by thirty-five years of Japanese occupation that allowed Koreans few opportunities to participate in government. Thus, for more than five hundred and fifty years, Korea had little chance to develop the val-ues, practices, and institutions of democratic governance. Rhee had to build South Korea's democracy from scratch, creating the necessary state structure, bureaucracy, and political institutions for a functioning democracy. Rhee had little personal experience in government and in managing a large administrative entity, however. As John Oh notes,

> It was presumed that Rhee would have learned about democratic pol-itics and observed American democracy in operation at close range for a few decades, and that he would conduct his presidency in the style of American chief executives. Such a hope in the euphoric days of the inauguration of the republic, however, tended to ignore the weight of the traditional political culture in Korea, Rhee's own origins and per-sonality, and the political realities that divided Korea was then facing.[25]

Despite hopes that South Korea was beginning its path toward democ-racy, Rhee ruled more like an autocrat than a democrat, centralizing power in the executive branch and ruling more like a king of old. Rhee was quick to dismiss government ministers who displeased him and rewarded officials for loyalty rather than achievement. Cabinet changes were so common during the Rhee years that the average stay of a cabinet minister was between ten and eleven months.[26]

The country also faced many serious economic problems. South Korea was desperately poor, with inflation rates rising out of control. A large segment of the population lacked adequate food, clothing, and shelter, particularly in urban areas. In the division of the peninsula, South Korea received much of the productive farmland, but most of the mineral resources and the industrial base that Japan had built remained in the North. The government had to revitalize an econ-omy that had long been subservient to Japan and ravaged by World War II. To address some of these problems, the government required money. Given the decrepit state of the ROK economy, however, the government had few resources for investment or public services to address a long list of desperate needs.

[25] Oh, *Korean Politics*, 31.
[26] S. Kim, *The Politics of Military Revolution* (Chapel Hill: University of North Carolina Press, 1971), 21.

During these early years, South Korea faced serious internal security challenges, particularly from pro-communist groups upset with the South's reluctance to embrace communism. Rhee was a staunch anti-communist, maintaining, "Communism is akin to cholera; it is impossible to compromise or cooperate with it; the only choices are to surrender to communist totalitarian control or oppose it."[27] Rhee had little other ideology or vision, however, to guide his administration. He was ruthless in rooting out political opposition and often used communism as the excuse for their removal. In 1947 and 1948, South Korea was rocked by numerous rebellions and guerrilla attacks from groups that often had communist leanings. North Korea successfully infiltrated agents into the South to help organize opposition to U.S. and South Korean authorities. A considerable share of the resistance, however, stemmed from indigenous sources, such as villagers who were unhappy with local Korean officials and the lack of progress in improving the economy.[28] On April 3, 1948, even before the formal creation of South Korea, communist guerrillas attacked police and government officials on the island of Cheju off South Korea's southern coast. By the time police and the military imposed order in the following year, twenty thousand to sixty thousand had been killed. In response to the Cheju rebellion, President Rhee sent the 14th Regiment to subdue the guerrillas. Before departing for Cheju from the port city of Yosu, the regiment mutinied on October 9, 1948, killing many of their officers, local police, and government officials as they seized control of the city. The next day, the mutineers marched on the neighboring city of Sunchon, but troops loyal to the government intercepted and defeated the force.

In response to the unrest at Cheju and Yosu, the National Assembly passed the National Security Law (NSL) in December 1948. The stated goal of the NSL was to "suppress anti-State acts that endanger national security and to ensure [the] nation's security, people's life and freedom."[29] Under the guise of "anti-state acts," the law essentially outlawed communism and support for North Korea along with criticism of the ROK government and the constitution. Police were given wide latitude and almost unlimited power to enforce the NSL. Authorities used the law to remove those who were determined to

[27] As quoted in C. Kim, *The Korean Presidents*, 33.
[28] Oh, *Korean Politics*, 35, and Cumings, *Korea's Place in the Sun*, 217–19.
[29] The text of South Korea's National Security Law is available at http://www.hartford-hwp.com/archives/55a/205.html (accessed August 10, 2009).

overthrow the state. It was also used to muzzle any opposition to the regime and did little to support civil rights and liberties.

With the formal division of Korea in 1948, the North and South each proclaimed that it was the legitimate authority on the peninsula and declared its determination to reunify the country. Throughout the late 1940s, the two Koreas had conducted numerous raids across the 38th parallel to destabilize the opposing regime. Rhee pleaded with U.S. authorities to provide him with tanks and planes to defend the ROK against a large-scale DPRK invasion, but Washington feared that these weapons would embolden Rhee to attack the North. Rhee had bragged that, if given the proper support, he could seize Pyongyang in three days and defeat North Korea in two weeks.[30] Consequently, while the Soviet Union supplied the DPRK with heavy weapons, South Korea received mainly defensive weapons and small arms. Rhee also begged for a formal security guarantee, but the Truman administration was not willing to go that far. U.S. leaders understood the importance of maintaining South Korea's security and demonstrating the U.S. commitment to that goal. Washington believed the primary threat to South Korea was subversion and infiltration, not an invasion from the North. U.S. public support for a large defense budget and overseas commitments was dwindling, increasing pressure to withdraw U.S. forces from Korea. Consequently, in June 1949, the United States withdrew its last combat units from South Korea.[31] Given the powerful nationalism on both sides of the demilitaritized zone (DMZ), the number of cross-border raids, mutual antagonism, and conflicting ideology, continued hostility between North and South Korea was inevitable.

The Korean War: 1950–1953

On June 25, 1950, North Korean forces rolled across the 38th parallel, determined to reunify the peninsula by force.[32] ROK forces could do

---

[30] D. Rees, *Korea: the Limited War* (New York: St. Martin's Press, 1964), 16.

[31] T. Roehrig, *From Deterrence to Engagement* (Lanham, Md.: Lexington Books, 2006) 30, 115–21.

[32] For more detailed studies of the Korean War, see W. Steuck, *Rethinking the Korean War: A New Diplomatic and Strategic History* (Princeton, N.J.: Princeton University Press, 2002) and B. Cumings, ed., *Child of Conflict: The Korean-American Relationship, 1943–1953* (Seattle: University of Washington Press, 1983).

little to stop the advance, and DPRK troops overran Seoul in three days, forcing Syngman Rhee and the ROK government to flee south. U.S. leaders assumed that the attack came at the instigation of the Soviet Union. President Truman maintained that the attack by North Korea made "it plain beyond all doubt that Communism has passed beyond the use of subversion . . . and will now use armed invasion and war."[33] Documentary evidence available since the end of the Cold War demonstrated, however, that Kim Il-sung was the chief proponent of the invasion, and it took a great deal of effort on Kim's part to convince Stalin that an attack could succeed if executed quickly before the United States would intervene.[34]

With the Soviet Union boycotting the proceedings over the seating of the People's Republic of China, the UN Security Council passed resolutions to come to the South's aid.[35] By August 1950, North Korea had advanced to control most of the peninsula except for an area surrounding the southeastern city of Pusan. In a daring military operation in mid-September 1950, U.S./UN forces led by General Douglas McArthur landed at the west coast port city of Inchon, approximately fifty kilometers from Seoul, in an effort to flank the North Korean army. The invasion was a huge success, and within weeks, DPRK troops were retreating back across the 38th parallel.

At this point, U.S./UN leaders faced a decision. The initial goal of coming to South Korea's aid was to restore the border at the 38th parallel. With the overwhelming success of U.S./UN forces, leaders saw an opportunity to roll back communism in the North and reunite the two Koreas. In the end, it was an opportunity leaders believed they could not pass up. U.S./UN forces headed north and, by October 1950, captured the North Korean capital of Pyongyang. As U.S. troops continued up the peninsula, however, Washington received warnings from Beijing that continuing the offensive to the Yalu River would provoke Chinese intervention in the war. U.S. leaders did not heed the warnings. On November 25, 1950, three Chinese divisions poured across the border, stalling the U.S./UN offensive and pushing the

---

[33] "Truman's Statement on the Korean War, June 27, 1950," in H. Commager, ed., *Documents in American History*, vol. II (New York: Appleton-Century-Crofts, 1962), 560–1.

[34] See K. Weathersby, "To Attack or Not Attack? Stalin, Kim Il Sung, and the Prelude to War," *Cold War International History Project Bulletin 5* (Spring 1995).

[35] Eventually, sixteen countries fought under the UN flag in Korea: Australia, Belgium, Canada, Colombia, Ethiopia, France, Greece, Luxembourg, the Netherlands, New Zealand, the Philippines, South Africa, Thailand, Turkey, the United Kingdom, and the United States.

troops back down the peninsula in bloody fighting during a bitter Korean winter. Eventually, Chinese and North Korean forces captured Seoul, but UN troops were able to retake the city in March 1951. Thus, Seoul was overrun four times in the course of the war.

By July 1951, the battle lines solidified into a stalemate, approximating the war's starting point at the 38th parallel. Truce talks began at Kaesong and later were moved to Panmunjom. On July 27, 1953, North Korea, China, and the United States signed the armistice agreement that ended hostilities, but South Korean President Rhee refused to sign the armistice, believing the war should not end until the peninsula was reunified under his control. The war dealt a devastating blow to Korea and its people. Some estimates project that between one and two million Koreans were killed during the conflict, with well over $3 billion in property damage.

South Korean Politics and the Rhee Years

As the Korean War progressed, Rhee faced his own domestic political struggles. To win the next election, he needed to alter the constitution. In 1948 he was elected by the National Assembly, but, by 1952, it was appearing increasingly unlikely that he would have the votes there to win a second term. To solve this problem, Rhee intimidated the legislature into passing a constitutional amendment that enabled a direct popular election of the president – an election he had a good chance of winning. The measure also increased the powers of the presidency. His ability to intimidate the opposition in the National Assembly through arrests and detention were quite effective. Five weeks before the vote on these constitutional amendments, Rhee detained many of those who opposed the changes but released most of these representatives two days later, sending a clear message of the need to support his plan. For the final vote, the National Assembly lacked a quorum, so Rhee released on bail any members still being detained and escorted them to the assembly chamber to cast a vote. Not surprisingly, the amendments passed unanimously, 163 to 0, with three abstentions. Soon after, the charges against most of the assembly representatives were dropped.[36] Rhee won another election in 1956, but by 1958, his support was fading throughout ROK society. Consequently, Rhee

---

[36] G. Henderson, *The Politics of the Vortex* (Cambridge, Mass.: Harvard University Press, 1968), 167–8.

resorted to even more draconian measures to silence the opposition and quiet a hostile ROK press.

It was also clear that there were significant levels of corruption during the Rhee years. The United States provided massive amounts of military and economic aid but did little to monitor its use, allowing unscrupulous government officials and senior military leaders to divert funds for personal gain. One example of the corruption involved U.S. funding to pay civilian workers for construction projects. Rather than use the money to pay workers, ROK officers pocketed the funds and had military recruits do the work after the day's training schedule with no payment for the labor.[37] Rhee also had little expertise or interest in economic development, and his economic ministers were similarly inexperienced and untrained in economic policy making. Despite twelve years in office, the Rhee government never instituted a nationwide economic policy. During the early years of Rhee's administration, U.S. aid accounted for one-third of South Korea's budget, yet the ROK economy showed relatively little progress during the Rhee years; per-capita income in 1953 was $67 and by 1959 had risen to only $81.[38]

By the late 1950s, South Koreans were increasingly unhappy with their president, and it was unlikely that Rhee would win the upcoming 1960 presidential election, but Rhee, already eighty-five years old, won with an amazing total of nearly 89 percent of the vote. It was obvious to all that he could not have won such a decisive victory without massive fraud perpetrated by the police and the Internal Affairs Ministry. The Ministry sent instructions to police chiefs specifying the winning margin that was expected for Rhee party candidates in their respective districts. Police chiefs who did not produce the required number of votes were fired or transferred.[39] After the election, demonstrations erupted throughout South Korea calling for Rhee to resign. The protests gained intensity when the body of a high school student washed up on shore in Masan with fragments from a tear gas canister in his head, a likely casualty when police were called in to quell demonstrations in the city. As protests increased, Rhee imposed martial law and used the police to stop the demonstrations. When this failed to end the disturbances, he dispatched the military to

---

[37] Ibid., 348–9.
[38] Oh, *Korean Politics*, 34–35.
[39] Oh, *Korean Politics*, 40, and Han Sung-joo, *The Failure of Democracy in South Korea* (Berkeley: University of California Press, 1974), 25–8.

impose order, but the military refrained from enforcing martial law or confronting the demonstrators, and the situation continued to deteriorate. After receiving counsel from some of his cabinet ministers and the U.S. ambassador in Seoul, Rhee reluctantly left office on April 26, 1960, to spend the rest of his life in exile in Hawaii.

The years under Syngman Rhee (1948–60) were supposed to be the beginning of a democratic South Korea; however, Rhee governed more like a monarch of the past, making little effort to develop the institutions and procedures of a democracy. Instead, rigged elections, a muzzled press, and corrupt politics were commonplace. Unfortunately, in the years ahead, democracy would take an even worse beating.

An Interim Year: Chang Myon and the Second Republic (1960–1961)

With Rhee gone, many of the forces in South Korean politics that had been stifled were now able to participate in the political process. After Rhee's departure, South Korea's system changed to a parliamentary one, in large measure to shift the power that had accumulated in the executive branch back to the National Assembly. Elections held in July 1960 brought the Democratic Party, Rhee's opposition, to power and, with it, Chang Myon as prime minister. At the outset, this new government faced a host of difficult challenges.

First, the Democratic Party was severely fragmented, making it difficult to achieve consensus in formulating policy.[40] The resulting gridlock prevented the government from moving on important problems, particularly in improving the dismal economy. To make matters worse, South Korean society was deeply polarized, so that those on the left and right had great difficulty working together and possessed little tolerance for dissenting viewpoints. Thus, Han Sung-joo writes, "Korea lacked the proper pluralistic social base, governmental and administrative structure was too centralized, and the majority of the people lacked a democratic political culture."[41] Consequently, the Chang Myon Government was ineffective, appearing disorganized and inept.

[40] Eckert et al., *Korea Old and New: A History*, 356–8.
[41] S. Han, *The Failure of Democracy in South Korea*, 2–5.

Second, students who had played an important role in bringing down the Rhee government believed they should continue to be active players in ROK politics. Student demonstrations continued on a regular basis, and occasionally students marched into the National Assembly in an effort to push the legislature into taking action. Of great concern to some ROK leaders were the calls students and others on the left made for reunification with the North. Some student groups were proposing a meeting with their North Korean counterparts to discuss possible steps for moving toward reunification. North Korea was quick to exploit this opportunity in its propaganda and state-run media.

Third, the executive branch had already seen its power curtailed in response to the Rhee years. As a result, Chang had far less ability to bring order to this chaotic period. Addressing all of these political issues as well as pulling the South Korean economy out of the doldrums required strong leadership, which Chang was lacking. He was well-educated and smart but often moved too cautiously. He lacked the resolve and personal charisma to fight through the factionalism and make the political process work. Moreover, Chang received little sympathy in the ROK press, which blasted him regularly for his poor leadership and policies. Many segments of the South Korean populace were becoming increasingly nervous for the future of the country and were slowly losing faith in Chang and his administration.[42]

One group in particular that had long been disenchanted with civilian rule was the ROK military. Prior to Rhee's departure, coup plans were already under consideration but were put on hold with his exit.[43] The increasingly chaotic state of South Korean politics, however, pushed some in the military over the edge.

Park Chung-hee and Military Rule: 1961–1979

Early on May 16, 1961, the military seized control of the ROK government and ousted Chang Myon and his administration. The coup leaders consisted of a small group of mid-career officers, mainly colonels and lieutenant colonels, led by Major-General Park Chung-hee. Park was the highest ranking of the coup leaders and was

---

[42] Henderson, *The Politics of the Vortex*, 180 and S. Kim, *The Politics of Military Revolution*, 28.

[43] Henderson, *The Politics of the Vortex*, 356.

well-known for his honesty, integrity, and clean record from the corruption of the Rhee years.

There were several reasons why these officers decided to seize control of the government. First, they were concerned with the state of
the political system. Politics and the government were in disarray, the
National Assembly was often paralyzed, and there seemed to be little
anyone could do about it. In short, from the military's perspective,
civilian democracy was not working well, and the military needed to
bring order to this chaos.

Second, the coup leaders believed the government had an ineffective record of managing the economy, and corruption was rife among
civilian politicians and senior military officers. These officers were
convinced they could do a better job and save the country from the
political and economic morass created by civilian leadership. According to one scholar, these officers had a "messianic, self-styled patrio-
tism that despised civilian politics and believed that direct, extremist
action could perfect the world."[44] When the political and economic
house was put back in order, the leaders pledged to return to the
barracks. Thus, Park maintained that the "military revolution" was
necessary to establish a "true, free democracy in Korea – certainly
not for the establishment of a new dictatorship and totalitarianism."
Consequently, Park maintained Korea would

> have to resort to undemocratic and extraordinary measures in order to
> improve the living conditions of the masses . . . one cannot deny that
> people are more frightened of poverty and hunger than totalitarian-
> ism. . . . The purpose of this revolution is to reconstruct the nation and
> establish a self-sustaining economy, and its essential purpose is to restore
> to all the people the political and economic systems which had become
> the possession of a few privileged classes.[45]

Third, the coup was not only a revolt against civilian government
but also against senior military officers whom their juniors viewed
as corrupt and motivated by their own self-interest rather than by a
desire to protect the nation. Prior to the coup in September 1960,
sixteen junior officers, including Kim Jong-pil, demanded that the
army chief of staff remove many of the senior officers tainted by
corruption and the politics of the Rhee years. Senior military leaders
refused to take action and arrested these officers for insubordination.

[44] Ibid., 183.
[45] As quoted in Oh, *Korean Politics*, 51–2.

Any hope of change in the ROK military and politics was unlikely, as these corrupt officers had too big a stake in the status quo. The senior officer corps had risen from the politicization of the military during the Rhee years, when promotions were given more for loyalty and political connections than for merit. Moreover, many of the seniors were relatively young and likely to delay promotions for those below for some time. Thus, a coup would help to clean out the upper ranks of corrupt, undeserving officers and open positions for those who were more selfless and deserving.[46]

In the early days following the coup, Park ruled through the Supreme Council for National Reconciliation, a military junta formed after the takeover. He dissolved the National Assembly, declared martial law, and arrested or purged thousands in the military and in government. Although Park had had ties to the Communist Party in the past, he was now a strong anti-communist who took harsh measures against anyone suspected of leftist leanings. The government banned countless politicians from participating in politics and imposed strict censorship on the press. To enforce these new measures, Park created the KCIA and tasked it with maintaining a close watch on domestic and international opponents of the government.

In 1963, Park resigned his commission under strong U.S. pressure and ran in the presidential election as a civilian. He tried to renege on his promise to hold elections, arguing that another four years of military rule was necessary to bring order and stability. U.S. pressure was significant, however, as aid from Washington accounted for 50 percent of the ROK budget and 70 percent of defense expenditures.[47] In the months leading up to the election, Park had withheld the actual date for voting to make it more difficult for the opposition to organize. In mid-August, Park suddenly announced that the elections would take place on October 15, which gave the opposition parties only two months of advanced notice. Despite this maneuver, the opposition still made a strong showing and narrowly lost to Park's party, the newly formed Democratic Republican Party. Park ran again in 1967, winning once more in a close vote. According to the ROK Constitution, this should have been President Park's last term. Instead, he pushed through an amendment ending the two-term limit, allowing him to run again in 1971. With the help of the KCIA and large sums of

[46] Henderson, *Politics of the Vortex*, 356, and S. Kim, *The Politics of Military Revolution*, 36–7.
[47] Carter et al., *Korea Old and New*, 361–2.

money from Korean corporations, President Park was able to defeat challenger Kim Dae-jung, winning 53 percent of the vote compared to Kim's 45 percent.

Throughout the first ten years of Park's rule, the authoritarian nature of the regime waned as the years passed. Restrictions on the press and opposition parties gradually weakened, and President Park tolerated some degree of dissent. In 1972, however, the Park regime became decidedly more authoritarian. In October 1972, President Park again declared martial law and dissolved the National Assembly while banning political parties and closing all colleges and universities. The following month, he institutionalized this authoritarian shift with a national referendum that ratified the new *Yushin* Constitution. *Yushin* means "revitalizing" in Korean, a term that was borrowed from Japan's 1868 Meiji Restoration. The *Yushin* Constitution greatly expanded the powers of the executive branch, including the power to appoint and dismiss cabinet members and the prime minister, suspend civil liberties, rule by emergency decree, and appoint one-third of National Assembly members. The new constitution essentially made Park president for life because, in addition to the removal of term limits, the president was now selected by the National Conference for Unification, an electoral college group whose membership the administration controlled to ensure repeated election.

What factors caused President Park to impose the harsh *Yushin* Constitution? First, Park was becoming increasingly unhappy with the disruptive nature of democratic politics and the difficulty of controlling the process to produce the outcomes he desired. Dissent was rising and critics becoming more outspoken, despite Park's efforts to stifle the opposition. Moreover, new dissident leaders such as Kim Dae-jung and Kim Young-sam were gaining popularity and helping to energize the resistance. The opposition's strength was growing, making it exceedingly more difficult to win through the ballot box.

Second, an expansion of presidential powers allowed Park to have firmer control over the South Korean economy, including labor and business. Worker unrest was rising, and Park wanted to move the ROK economy into new sectors such as steel, chemicals, shipbuilding, and automobile production.

Finally, Park also feared the impending direction of the ROK–U.S. alliance. In 1969, President Richard Nixon put forth the Nixon Doctrine, which stated that the United States would maintain all of its treaty commitments in Asia and provide economic and military assistance if needed. In the future, however, Washington would expect allies to furnish the personnel for their own defense.[48] Soon after, Nixon announced his intention to withdraw the 7th Infantry Division from Korea. Park also worried about improving U.S. relations, with China and the Soviet Union putting South Korea in a precarious position among these Cold War adversaries and within Washington's Asia policy. The centralization of power afforded by the *Yushin* Constitution provided Park with the tools to deal with these uncertain times. The *Yushin* Constitution marked the beginning of the 4th Republic and remained in effect until the end of Park's presidency in 1979.

When Park launched the coup, one of his concerns was the decrepit ROK economy. Because he had seized power illegally, economic growth provided legitimacy for his rule. In addition, Park chaffed at South Korea's economic dependence on the United States, particularly when Washington pressured him to democratize. Economic development was one way to address all of these concerns while helping to improve South Korea's security through a thriving economy. In this effort, Park was successful, generating economic growth rates that often exceeded 10 percent and made South Korea one of the rising "dragons" of Asia. South Korea's economic growth will be addressed in more detail in Chapters 4 and 5.

Although ROK economic performance rose under Park's leadership, it came at a steep price. Many South Koreans worked long, hard hours for low wages, willing to accept the hardships for the hope of a brighter future and proud of the nation's progress. As the years passed and working conditions deteriorated, some tried to form unions, but the government allowed only state-sponsored unions and labor associations while suppressing any independent organizations.

The Park administration also continued to impede civil liberties and human rights, arresting thousands under the NSL for allegedly criticizing the government or being a communist. Emergency Measure No. 9 was particularly harsh, making it a crime to criticize the president or the law itself. Arbitrary arrests, lengthy detentions, and the use of torture to produce a confession were commonplace.[49] One of the chief enforcers of this repression was the KCIA, which had a complex and clandestine network of agents positioned throughout South Korean society and abroad in an effort to track down critics of

---

[48] R. Nixon, "American Policy in the Pacific: Informal Remarks of President Nixon with Newsmen at Guam," July 25, 1969, *Public Papers of the President, 1969*, 545–9.
[49] Eckert et al., *Korea Old and New*, 369.

the government. One of the high-profile examples of these activities occurred in August 1973, when KCIA agents abducted Kim Dae-jung from his Tokyo hotel room and took him to Seoul. Kim was slated for execution when Washington intervened and demanded his release. Several days later, Kim was dropped off on a street near his home, alive but severely beaten.[50]

The End of the Park Chung-hee Regime

As the *Yushin* period wore on, support for Park began to decrease dramatically. Increasingly, the number of followers of key dissidents like Kim Dae-jung and Kim Young-sam grew along with demonstrations and unrest among South Korean workers. Park continued to have strong support from business leaders and could always invoke the threat from North Korea in calls for national unity and support for his regime. Using the threat from the North was not difficult, given Pyongyang's harsh rhetoric and provocative actions. Indeed, North Korean operatives made two attempts on Park's life, the first occurring in January 1968 when a North Korean guerrilla unit attempted, unsuccessfully, to kill Park at the Blue House. The second attempt came on August 15, 1974, when a North Korean agent tried to shoot Park while he was giving a speech but missed and killed Park's wife instead. DPRK provocations also included large numbers of incidents along the DMZ and numerous infiltration attempts. These provocations generated support for the regime, but discontent was mounting, and by the end of the 1970s, the unrest forced President Park into a corner.

Park's regime and political future reached a crossroads in August 1979 that grew out of a labor dispute known as the YH Incident. The incident began when textile workers, mostly women, began a sit-in protest at their factory, the YH Trading Company, over large-scale layoffs. The government sent in riot police to break up the demonstrations, severely beating many of the women. Protestors fled to the headquarters of opposition party leader Kim Young-sam to seek safety, but the beatings continued, resulting in the death of Kim Kyung-sook, one of the workers, and the arrests of many of the protestors.[51] Other large demonstrations followed in October at Pusan

---

[50] Oh, *Korean Politics*, 60.
[51] S. Kim, *The Politics of Democratization in Korea: The Role of Civil Society*, chap. 4.

National University and Kyungnam University in Masan. Thousands gathered at these events, which were composed of mainly students and disgruntled workers protesting against Park and the *Yushin* system.

As the unrest grew, it became clear to Park and his advisors that something had to be done or the protests would spiral out of control. Park faced a difficult decision: crush the protests or back down and seek a compromise. Park's advisors disagreed about how to respond, and Kim Jae-kyu, head of the KCIA, killed the president at a dinner meeting, bringing the Park regime and the 4th Republic to an end.

When news broke of President Park's assassination, the country was stunned but showed little outward grief at his passing. According to one ROK official, "his time had come."[52] Today, memories of Park's rule evoke ambivalence among South Koreans. The Park regime was harsh and autocratic but was also the beginning of South Korea's phenomenal economic rise. He built the foundation for South Korea to shift from a poor, agrarian country to a modern, industrial, and technologically advanced state. South Korea's gross national product skyrocketed from $2.3 billion in 1962 to $64 billion in 1980, more than a 2,500 percent increase.[53] Park's political legacy continued in the work of his daughter, Park Geun-hye, a leader in the conservative Grand National Party (GNP). In the 2007 election, she came close to obtaining the party's presidential nomination and remains a force in ROK politics.

After Park's assassination, an emergency cabinet meeting named Prime Minister Choi Kyu-ha as interim president in accordance with the *Yushin* Constitution. He promptly declared martial law and designated Army Chief of Staff General Cheung Sung-hwa as martial law commander. Government officials were unsure if the assassination had been the work of Kim Jae-kyu alone or if there had been a broader conspiracy that involved others in the KCIA or the military. Although there was little concern that North Korea was immediately involved, many feared that Pyongyang might try to exploit the power vacuum. North Korea had been involved in at least two other assassination attempts, so this was not a far-fetched possibility. Choi also repealed Emergency Measure No. 9 and released many of the dissidents who were under arrest or serving prison terms. Rather than undertake the

---

[52] As quoted in Oberdorfer, *The Two Koreas*, 113.
[53] Korean Culture and Information Service, "Economic Growth," http://www.korea.net/korea/kor_loca.asp?code=R01 (accessed August 9, 2009).

contentious process of revising the *Yushin* Constitution, Choi chose to retain it, allowing his successor to take on this task.

On December 6, 1979, Choi was elected to the presidency, and inaugurated on December 12, but his time in office would not last long. Although many thought South Korea was beginning its transition to democracy, one more chapter of military rule lay ahead. By spring 1980, it was clear that South Korea's transition to democracy would have to wait a few years.

Conclusion

Prior to the 1980s, it was evident that Koreans had little experience with democracy. From the Chosun Dynasty to the Japanese occupation and on through the semifeudal rule of Syngman Rhee and the military regime of Park Chung-hee, South Koreans were governed largely by an authoritarian system. Power was concentrated in the state, and authorities allowed little popular participation or the development of the institutions necessary for democratic government. With Park's passing, South Korea was poised to make the transition to democracy, but the country would have to endure one more round of military rule before making that journey.

2

From Dictatorship to Democracy

The assassination of Park Chung-hee shocked the country and came at a difficult time. After years of solid growth, the economy was in the midst of a steep decline that was due in large measure to the 1979 oil price shock, the second in the decade, that once again doubled the price of oil. In addition, South Korea's debt skyrocketed, and banks were reluctant to provide additional loans that were desperately needed to get through this period. With the shaky economy and uncertain political times following Park's assassination, banks were unsure that South Korea offered a stable investment opportunity. Inflation rose to more than 30 percent, and labor disputes increased, adding to the economic uncertainty.[1] The new government of President Choi Kyu-ha faced some daunting problems, and he had little time to produce results. In the end, he did not prove up to the task and failed to be the strong, decisive leader South Korea needed to weather this storm.

Return to Military Rule: Chun Doo-hwan and the Rolling Coup

While Choi Kyu-ha was working to solidify the new civilian government in the wake of Park's assassination, others had been planning a different course of action. In 1979, Major General Chun Doo-hwan was appointed to head the Defense Security Command (DSC), the most powerful of South Korea's military intelligence agencies. Because the DSC had jurisdiction in dealing with military coups and revolts, Chun was given the responsibility of investigating Park's murder. With the

---

[1] C. Kim, *The Korean Presidents*, 160.

investigation as a pretext to move against the military leadership and the government, Chun and his allies used the DSC to instigate what one scholar called a "multistage military coup."[2] This rolling coup began on December 12, 1979, a day often referred to as the "12–12 incident" by South Koreans.

The first stage of the coup began with a mutiny in the army led by Major General Chun. On December 12, Chun sent a detachment to interrogate and ultimately arrest Army Chief of Staff and martial law commander Cheung Sung-hwa, alleging his involvement in Park's assassination. The charge was false, but Chun used the allegation to remove the senior commander and take control of the military chain of command. Kim Jae-kyu, the KCIA director who had shot Park, had already been arrested. He was later convicted and executed. With the assistance of other army units, Chun seized the Ministry of National Defense and Army Headquarters in addition to shutting down most media outlets. Some of the units used in the mutiny included units that left front-line positions on the DMZ and those of the Ninth ROK Division stationed around Seoul, which was commanded by Major General Roh Tae-woo, Chun's old friend and 1955 classmate at the Korean Military Academy.

There was another motive for the arrest of General Cheung. After Park's assassination, rumors surfaced that General Cheung was planning to remove or reassign several generals, including Chun, who were viewed as "ambitious and troublesome" by senior military leaders. According to the rumors, Chun was likely to be reassigned to the East Coast Security Command, a post that would remove him from the political center in Seoul and exile him to a backwater command, effectively ending his army career. As army chief of staff and martial law commander, Cheung had the power to carry out these actions, forcing Chun and his allies to act first. General Cheung was eventually convicted, reduced to the rank of private, stripped of all pay and benefits, and forced to serve some prison time. In 1997, however, ROK courts reversed his conviction.

Chun now controlled the military and, for all intents and purposes, dictated to a weak civilian government from behind the scenes. The U.S. ambassador to South Korea at the time was William Gleysteen, Jr., who remarked in a report to Washington, "We have been through

---

[2] S. Kim, "State and Civil Society in South Korea's Democratic Consolidation," *Asian Survey XXXVII*, no. 12 (December 1997): 1138.

a coup in all but name. The flabby façade of civilian constitutional government remains but almost all signs point to a carefully planned takeover of the military power positions by a group of 'Young Turk' officers."[3] President Choi was largely a figurehead and exercised no control over the military. Similar to Park's coup, the 12/12 mutiny was also based on generational divisions within the armed forces. Chun's allies were members of the eleventh, twelfth, and thirteenth classes at the Korean Military Academy, whereas most senior officers were members of the eighth class. With the mutiny complete, Chun proceeded to make numerous personnel changes through reassignment and retirement to remove those loyal to General Cheung and replace them with his own followers. Throughout the next few months in early 1980, Chun maintained that he had no intention of taking control of the government, but it was far from clear whether he would honor that pledge, and he bided his time.

In April 1980, Chun made the next move to advance his control over the government by prodding President Choi first to promote him to lieutenant general and then to name him director appointee of the KCIA. Control of this office provided Chun with an important new power base. Taking this position was illegal for Chun unless he resigned from the military, but he refused to do so. If there had been doubts about Chun's ambitions, this move signaled that he was determined to seize control of the entire ROK government. In the wake of these actions, widespread protests flared, and, on May 14, 1980, a massive demonstration of tens of thousands composed mainly of students and workers occurred in Seoul. During the previous months, Choi had pledged his support for democracy and released many dissidents who had been in detention, including Kim Dae-jung along with many students, journalists, and religious leaders. Many anticipated a revived opposition movement, a "Seoul Spring," but Chun could not let this challenge to his authority stand.

On May 17, President Choi declared full martial law in an effort to halt the demonstrations from spreading, a move that essentially turned the reins of government over to Chun as martial law commander. Chun clamped down on student demonstrations and closed the colleges and universities. In addition, he shut down the National Assembly along with the headquarters of most political parties, arrested student leaders, outlawed labor strikes, arrested the three Kims – Kim

---

[3] Oberdorfer, *The Two Koreas*, 117–19.

Dae-jung, Kim Young-sam, and Kim Jong-pil – the chief opposition leaders, and banned all political activity.[4] ROK military leaders believed the harsh response was justified to save the country from escalating unrest and anarchy and, as some feared, to prevent a possible opening for a North Korean invasion.

Although these actions quieted most of the protests in Korea, demonstrations continued in Kwangju, a city located in South Cholla province (*Chollanam-do*) in the southwest portion of the Korean Peninsula. Kwangju was the political home of Kim Dae-jung and for years had been a base of opposition to the Park government. Consequently, Park punished the region by withholding economic investment. For South Cholla province, a transition to democracy meant not only political reform but also the chance to share more fully in the country's growing prosperity.

On May 18, 1980, Chun sent troops, mainly special forces with little training in controlling demonstrations, to stop the unrest in Kwangju. When the soldiers entered the city, they badly beat some of the demonstrators, resulting in many deaths. One press account depicted the scene as follows:

> What followed is all but impossible to describe: an army attack – a pincer attack on civilians. Military trucks crammed with heavily armed paratroopers with fixed bayonets lurched into sight at both ends of Gumnam-ro [a street that was the site of demonstrations] simultaneously. The paras [paratroopers] jumped out and waded into the crowd from both ends of the street, working toward the middle – striking out with heavy-duty clubs, left, right, left, right . . . with no regard to who was there, male or female, young or old. The soldiers went for headshots with their big clubs. Gumnam-ro – moments before the scene of a peaceful sit down demo [demonstration] – was transformed in a matter of seconds into hell on earth.[5]

According to one estimate, more than one hundred people were killed, and one reporter noted, "'What the hell is the military up to?' 'How could a national army do this to fellow Koreans?' Rank incomprehension was overtaken by a sense of outrage."[6] Fuming at

---

[4] Eckert et al., *Korea Old and New*, 374.

[5] C. Kim, "Days and Nights on the Street," in *The Kwangju Uprising: Eyewitness Press Accounts of Korea's Tiananmen*, ed. Henry Scott-Stokes and Lee Jai Eui (New York: M.E. Sharpe, 2000), 8–9.

[6] T. Anderson, "Remembering Kwangju," *The Kwangju Uprising*, 48, and C. Kim, "Days and Nights on the Street," *The Kwangju Uprising*, 8–9.

the indiscriminant use of force, the students were joined by other citizens who fought back using weapons from local armories and police stations to drive out the soldiers. Failing to subdue the demonstrators, the troops withdrew, creating a perimeter around the city. During the next few days, U.S. officials pushed Chun for some accommodation or negotiated settlement but realized they had little leverage.[7] The students and townspeople waited for a week for the government's response, wondering if this challenge to Chun's leadership would be permitted and would generate an attempt to compromise. It was not long before they had their answer.

On May 27, 1980, Chun sent twenty thousand troops from elite units in the South Korean army, many from the 20th ROK Division, to retake Kwangju. Chun simply could not tolerate this test to his authority. The poorly armed group of students and citizens was no match for some of the best troops in the ROK army, and the city was retaken with brutal force. Initial government reports cited that only two were killed in the clash, but subsequent government estimates stated that two hundred demonstrators died at Kwangju. Other groups, however, have estimated the number killed to be closer to two thousand in what South Koreans refer to as the "Kwangju massacre," an event likened to China's Tiananmen Square.[8] For Koreans, these events remained a source of considerable bitterness and made it nearly impossible for Chun Doo-hwan to establish any sort of legitimacy for his rule. Throughout his time in office, there would remain a lingering sense of anger and a desire to hold him and his compatriots accountable for what happened at Kwangju.

A dimension of these events that continues to be a sore spot for some South Koreans is U.S. involvement, or, more importantly, a lack thereof, in Chun's actions at Kwangju. Many South Koreans believed the United States should have intervened to halt the Kwangju massacre. After the mutiny, U.S. officials were uncertain about what would follow and how they should respond. Washington was clearly unhappy with Chun's actions but was reluctant to impose economic sanctions for fear of making an already bad ROK economy worse. U.S. officials also decided not to make a political statement by canceling a scheduled defense ministers' meeting for fear of jeopardizing South Korean security. Washington feared it could have another "Iran" on

---

[7] W. Gleysteen, Jr., *Massive Entanglement, Marginal Influence: Carter and the Korea in Crisis* (Washington, D.C.: Brookings Institution Press, 1999), 127–43.

[8] Oberdorfer, *The Two Koreas*, 129, and Cumings, *Korea's Place in the Sun*, 378.

its hands. In 1979, the regime under the Shah of Iran, a strong U.S. ally in the region, fell and was replaced by a radical government under the Ayatollah Khomeini that was hostile to Washington. U.S. officials worried that a radical, anti-U.S. government similar to Iran could come to power in Seoul that would jeopardize U.S. security interests and the ROK–U.S. alliance if Washington pushed too hard. Recognizing the security concerns, the Carter administration sent a carrier battle group to warn North Korea not to exploit the events. Washington hoped that Chun would eventually moderate his behavior and refrain from any further disruptions to the civilian government. When Chun was appointed director of the KCIA and demonstrations exploded across South Korea, it was clear, according to Brazinsky, that "U.S. policymakers now faced a decision that they had desperately wanted to avoid making. They had to either abandon their objective of promoting gradual political liberalization or run the risk of jeopardizing security by supporting the protestors."[9] Ultimately, Washington resolved to err on the side of security, deciding that the ROK military should bring law and order to the country before moving toward political liberalization. In a message to Secretary of State Edmund Muskie, U.S. ambassador to Korea, William Gleysteen, Jr., noted that, in discussions with South Korean officials, he had indicated that the United States would not oppose "contingency plans to maintain law and order, if absolutely necessary by reinforcing the police with the army."[10] U.S. officials did not intend to condone the use of excessive force and told Chun and other ROK military leaders on many occasions to avoid such use of force. Chun took the nuanced U.S. response as approval, however, and cracked down on protests throughout the country.

Another dimension of U.S. involvement was the use of the 20th ROK Division in the assault. The ROK government was required to notify the Combined Forces Command (CFC), the ROK–U.S. command organization that was led by the U.S. four-star general who commanded U.S. Forces Korea, of the movement of any ROK units that fell under CFC authority. The 20th Division was such a unit, and a few days prior to moving on Kwangju, South Korean authorities informed the CFC of the plan to move units of the 20th Division away from positions along the DMZ for operations in Kwangju.

---

[9] G. Brazinsky, *Nation Building in South Korea: Koreans, Americans, and the Making of a Democracy* (Chapel Hill: University of North Carolina Press, 2007), 234.
[10] Ibid., 235.

General John Wickham had left for the United States on May 14 for a scheduled meeting in Washington, however, and, on May 16, the ROK military notified the CFC of their intent to move units of the 20th Division. Because Wickham was gone, the ROK Deputy Commander accepted the notification in his stead.[11] Although U.S. officials believed there was little they could do and essentially acquiesced to Chun's actions, Washington did not approve the movement of ROK troops to Kwangju. CFC arrangements required only that ROK authorities notify the CFC commander, so ROK officials did not seek or receive approval to move elements of the 20th Division. In contrast, during the 12/12 incident, Chun had failed to notify the CFC commander of the units he was moving to assist in the coup, so he was in violation of CFC protocol. In the end, CFC Commander Wickham described the U.S. predicament this way:

> The American mission was over a barrel, because our basic objective was to protect the ROK from invasion. That left us obliged to accept the realities of the Korean political apparatus, with all of its warts, and to work with it as best we could. Our leverage was limited because of our security commitment, and because the Koreans, particularly the military, were increasingly intolerant of U.S. intervention in their domestic affairs.[12]

U.S. actions and apparent lack of support for South Korean democracy generated a lot of criticism among some quarters in South Korea and helped stoke anti-Americanism, especially among students.[13] The South Korean college students' belief that moving a military division required permission from the CFC instead of simply notification prompted large-scale protests against the United States.

Chun Doo-hwan and the Fifth Republic (1980–1988)

With the protests subdued, Chun moved to further solidify his hold on power. In August 1980, he promoted himself to the rank of four-star general and then resigned his commission in preparation to run for

---

[11] Oh, *Korean Politics*, 80.

[12] J. Wickham, *Korea on the Brink: From the "12/12 Incident" to the Kwangju Uprising, 1979–1980* (Washington, D.C.: National Defense University Press, 1999), 147.

[13] Oh, *Korean Politics*, 78–9, and J, Fowler, "The United States and South Korean Democratization," *Political Science Quarterly* 114, no. 2 (Summer 1999): 265–88.

the presidency. Soon after, Choi Kyu-ha resigned from the presidency, and, on August 27, 1980, Chun was elected to the post by the National Conference for Unification, the electoral college system that Park had instituted under the *Yushin* system. Given Chun's control over the membership of the council, his election victory was a certainty. On September 1, 1980, Chun Doo-hwan was inaugurated as president of the ROK. Subsequently, Chun revised the constitution, retaining the election process of the *Yushin* system. He added a presidential term limit provision, however, of one seven-year term, and early in his administration, he maintained his commitment to following this mandate. In February 1981, Chun was elected again, this time under a new constitution that would begin his seven-year term and the Fifth Republic. The new election process was not a nation-wide popular vote, a procedure Chun could not have won, but was another electoral college process that gave considerable advantage to Chun's newly formed Democratic Justice Party.

After solidifying his power, Chun turned to addressing the economic problems he inherited from the Park regime. Chun had little training and experience in leading the economy, so he brought in many well-trained technocrats to guide ROK economic policy. He followed economic issues but left much of the economic strategizing to his advisors. Based on this advice, Chun restructured the bureaucracy, reduced inflation and government spending, and attracted more foreign direct investment. These issues will be discussed in detail in Chapter 4. After approximately two years, the economy began to stabilize and continued its phenomenal rise, with South Korea becoming a major player in heavy industry, automobiles, shipbuilding, and high-technology sectors such as semiconductors. South Korea also applied for and received the bid to host the 1988 Summer Olympic Games in Seoul. Many hoped that the attention of the games would provide further stimulus to the economy and help showcase the South Korean economic miracle to a worldwide audience.

During Chun's rule, he continued to maintain a tight grip on power and heavy control over the media, banning more than 150 periodicals and dismissing numerous journalists from their positions. Chun also launched a "purification campaign" (*Jeonghwa*) to clean up society by purging dissidents and corrupt officials while cracking down on other types of crime. Eventually, he did relax some elements of authoritarian rule, including softening the national security laws and abolishing the midnight-to-4:00 A.M. curfew. Despite these accomplishments, the country was never able to forget the coup and the Kwangju incident, so the legitimacy of his rule was always in doubt. Most South Koreans could not forget what he had done and harbored continuing resentment throughout his administration.

Early in his tenure, Chun received a big boost from the new Reagan administration when, on February 2, 1981, he was the first foreign leader to visit the Reagan White House. After several years of tense ROK–U.S. relations with the Carter administration, the visit was not only a strong show of support for Chun but also for the ROK–U.S. alliance. The visit was also a quid pro quo for sparing the life of convicted and soon-to-be executed dissident Kim Dae-jung. Kim had been convicted and sentenced to death on September 17, 1980, for allegedly plotting the Kwangju uprising. Reagan officials worked behind the scenes to reverse the sentence, but Chun made it clear that a state visit was the price for commuting Kim Dae-jung's death sentence. Reagan later returned the favor when he visited South Korea in November 1983.

Transition to Democracy

Throughout his term, President Chun Doo-hwan insisted that he would honor the new constitution's limit of one seven-year presidential term. Given the constitutional manipulation of previous presidents, South Koreans had reason to be skeptical that he would honor his pledge. Even if Chun allowed elections to occur as required, the election process favored Chun's ruling party, so whoever received its nomination was likely to be the next president. As Chun's term approached its end and he remained committed to stepping down, the opposition turned its attention to electoral reforms and constitutional revisions. Most importantly, opponents wanted to end the electoral college and replace it with an election by direct popular vote. South Korea's opposition became further energized in spring 1986 with the fall of Philippine leader Ferdinand Marcos. Perhaps it would be South Korea's turn to remove an authoritarian leader.

In 1986, the government formed the Special Constitutional Revisions Committee and began negotiations with opposition groups to change the electoral system and make other modifications to the constitution. The talks dragged on for several months, but, on April 13, 1987, Chun shocked the country by announcing that he was suspending all talks to revise the constitution. He argued that the revision process could not be completed in time before the December 1987 elections. Instead, he maintained that the deliberations should continue under a new administration after Seoul hosted the Olympics in fall 1988. To make matters worse, Chun announced soon after that the appointment of his friend and former army General Roh Tae-woo as the candidate for his ruling Democratic Justice Party. Thus, not only had Chun ended any chance for political reform, but also his nomination of Roh ensured that the Blue House, the executive office and presidential residence, would be filled by another military man.

With constitutional and election reforms off the table, protests intensified in the spring of 1987. The protests were fed by the growing *minjung* (common people) movement, a diverse combination of beliefs including Marxism, nationalism, Catholic liberation theology, anti-economic dependency, and a peace movement.[14] The movement began in the 1970s, and by the late 1980s was a dominant force in the drive for democratization. The intellectual energy of the movement came from students and faculty at universities, but its proponents called for all the common people who were oppressed to rise up and reclaim their destiny that had been dominated by military dictators, big business, and foreign powers.[15] As the unrest escalated, it appeared Chun would face the same dilemma Park Chung-hee had faced in fall 1979 – crack down on the demonstrators or seek some sort of compromise. Given Chun's temperament and previous actions, most were expecting further repression.

On June 29, 1987, presidential candidate Roh Tae-woo preempted Chun's decision and announced that he was willing to adopt many of the opposition's demands. Outlined in an eight-point plan, Roh Tae-woo maintained that "the Constitution should be expeditiously amended, through agreement between the government party and the opposition, to adopt a direct presidential election system, and presidential elections should be held under a new Constitution to realize a peaceful change of government in February 1988." In addition, Roh concluded "that a presidential election system must be adopted at this juncture in order to overcome social confusion and achieve national reconciliation. The people are the masters of the country and

[14] Oh, *Korean Politics*, 88.
[15] See N. Lee, *The Making of Minjung: Democracy and the Politics of Representation in South Korea* (Ithaca, N.Y.: Cornell University Press, 2007).

the people's will must come before everything else."[16] The remaining points in Roh's plan called for revising the election law to allow for more free and fair elections, the release of political detainees except those who have committed treason or violent crimes, the amnesty and release of Kim Dae-jung, protecting basic human rights (including a "drastic extension of habeas corpus"), promoting a free press, greater autonomy for colleges and universities, protection and nurturing of political parties, and social reforms to "build a clean and honest society," such as stepped-up efforts to reduce crime and corruption. Although this point remains disputed, apparently Roh saw the growing opposition and believed he had to break from the government's position to save his own political future. A few days later, Chun reversed his position and allowed the constitution revisions committee to continue its work.

Roh's announcement was a shock; most had prepared for a new round of crackdowns and the imposition of martial law with possibly more violent demonstrations. Chun's acceptance of Roh's proposal appeared equally surprising. Why did President Chun change his mind and allow the process of revising the constitution to go forward? Several factors seem to have played a role.

First, the Olympic Games to be held in September 1988 were fast approaching. All of South Korea was looking forward to hosting this event that would showcase the economic progress the country had made in the last thirty years. With the international media focused on South Korea, the last thing anyone wanted, including President Chun, was to have massive street protests and tear gas canisters flying about as riot police attempted to bring order. There was even discussion within the International Olympic Committee of canceling or moving the games from South Korea because of the potential for unrest. President Chun had no desire to jeopardize South Korea's opportunity to be the center of attention on the international stage during this historic sporting event.

Second, the United States played an active role in pressing President Chun to take a more moderate course. During Chun's rolling coup and the violence at Kwangju, many in South Korea had criticized U.S. military and political officials for not doing enough to

---

[16] Roh Tae-woo, "Special Declaration for Grand National Harmony and Progress Towards a Great Nation By the Chairman of the Democratic Justice Party," June 29, 1987, 19, in *Working a Political Miracle: Sweeping Democratic Reforms* (Seoul: Korean Overseas Information Service, 1987).

promote democracy and restrain Chun's actions. Although U.S. officials believed there was little they could have done at that time, in this instance, Washington exerted considerable pressure on Chun. President Ronald Reagan, who had welcomed Chun to the White House in February 1981, sent a personal letter to Chun calling for restraint. This was followed by visits from Under Secretary of State Edward Derwinksi and Assistant Secretary of State Gaston Sigur that called for moderation, negotiations, and restraint in using force to settle the issue.[17]

Third, whereas past protests going back to the days of Syngman Rhee were composed largely of students, increasingly the demonstrations were drawing from a broader cross-section of ROK society, particularly members of South Korea's more affluent middle class. The result was what Sunhyuk Kim called a "grand democratic alliance" that was pushing for democracy. According to Kim, "as economic development exceeded a certain level, the middle class became more and more impatient with their postponed political rights. Although the middle class did not form their own organizations, they actively supported students, workers, and churches during the democracy movement in 1987."[18] In the past, the government had few qualms about suppressing the student demonstrations. Crushing these protests was far more difficult when participants included businessmen and housewives along with others from the middle class. Given this broad degree of support, one scholar noted there were indications that the military was "unhappy with the prospect of taking yet again a direct role in politics, a role that would undoubtedly have led to severe domestic and international pressure."[19]

Finally, there may have been one other dimension that was part of Chun's and Roh's calculations. It was clear that the pressure for democratization was growing and the ability to resist the tide becoming ever more difficult to stop. It appears that Chun and Roh may have collaborated, seeing an opportunity where they would be able to compromise with the opposition, keep the ruling party in power, and secure Roh's

---

[17] O. Masao, "South Korea's Experiment in Democracy," in James Cotton, *Korea Under Roh Tae-woo* (Canberra, Australia: ANU Printery, 1993), 11.

[18] S. Kim, "Civil Society in South Korea: From Grand Democracy Movements to Petty Interest Groups?" *Journal of Northeast Asian Studies* 15, no. 2 (Summer 1996): 90–3.

[19] J. Cotton, "From Authoritarianism to Democracy in South Korea," in J. Cotton, *Korea Under Roh Tae-woo* (Canberra, Australia: ANU Printery, 1993), 33.

victory in the upcoming presidential election. The two likely possi-
bilities for an opposition candidate were the leading dissidents, Kim
Dae-jung and Kim Young-sam. A victory for the opposition required
uniting behind only one of these candidates. Which of the Kims would
be willing to step aside for the sake of a unified opposition? These two
Kims were strong leaders who had long struggled against past military
governments, but they were also rivals. Both may have had a difficult
time standing on the sideline and supporting the other in the election. If the Kims failed to reach an accommodation, there was a good
chance they would split the opposition vote, allowing Roh Tae-woo
to triumph in the end. In fact, Kim Dae-jung was included, by name,
in the June 29 statement that he should be granted an amnesty and
have his civil rights restored to encourage him to compete for the
presidency.[20] If this assessment proved correct, Chun and Roh could
mollify the opposition and remain in power.

1987 Presidential Elections

On December 16, 1987, South Koreans went to the polls to vote for
the first time under their new constitution. Approved by the voters
in October 1987, the new constitution used a direct popular vote and
expressly prohibited the armed forces from participating in politics.
Article 5 maintained that "the Armed Forces are charged with the
sacred mission of national security and the defense of the land and
their political neutrality must be maintained" along with the military
staying on the sidelines.[21] Despite the opposition's long-awaited hopes
for a direct popular election, the results turned out as Chun and Roh
had hoped. When the votes were counted – and there were many
to count, with more than 89 percent voter turnout – Roh won the
election with only 36.6 percent of the popular vote. As the ruling
party had anticipated, neither of the Kims could agree to step aside,
so they split the opposition vote, with Kim Young-sam receiving 28
percent and Kim Dae-jung receiving 27 percent (see Table 1). Had
the two been able to combine the opposition vote under a single
candidate, it is likely their total would have produced a comfortable
margin to defeat Roh Tae-woo.

[20] Oh, *Korean Politics*, 98–102.
[21] Constitution of the Republic of Korea, http://www.ccourt.go.kr/home/english/
welcome/republic.jsp.

Table 1. *1987 Presidential election results*

Roh Tae-woo	36.6%
Democratic Justice Party	
Kim Young-sam	28.0%
Reunification Democratic Party	
Kim Dae-jung	27.0%
Party for Peace and Democracy	
Kim Jong-pil	8.1%
New Democratic Republican Party	

Roh Tae-woo was sworn in on February 25, 1988, to begin South Korea's Sixth Republic. Although South Korea had made the transition to democracy, it now faced the challenges of consolidating that transition while developing the political institutions and civil society necessary to further deepen democratization. President Roh was elected in a free and fair election, and South Koreans were happy to have a democracy, yet, for many, the results were bittersweet. South Korea still had a former general at the helm with clear ties to Chun Doo-hwan, Kwangju, and the military regimes of the past. Many were also disenchanted with the two Kims because they could not set aside their rivalry and ambition for the cause of reform. Some even argue that, because of Roh's ties to the military, democracy did not actually begin until the next presidential election in 1992 that brought Kim Young-sam to the Blue House. Despite these concerns, this was indeed the beginning of South Korea's transition to democracy.

Roh Tae-woo and the Sixth Republic

With the election settled, Roh moved on to the business of running the country, and he had a difficult job ahead. President Roh had been freely elected, but many questions remained regarding his role in the previous regime along with his involvement in the Kwangju incident and the 12/12 mutiny. Indeed, Chun had gone to great lengths to see that Roh was elected to protect himself and Roh from any investigations of these past issues. Thus a cloud continued to hang over Roh's administration.

In addition to these questions, Roh also faced some other serious political obstacles. Roh had been elected with less than 37 percent

Table 2. *1988 National Assembly election results*

Party	District seats	Proportional seats	Total seats
Democratic Justice Party	87	38	125
Party for Peace and Democracy	55	16	71
Republican Democratic Party	46	13	59
New Democratic Republican Party	27	8	35
Independents			9
			299

of the popular vote, hardly a ringing endorsement for his leadership. In a few months, parliamentary elections made matters worse when Roh's Democratic Justice Party lost numerous seats to opposition candidates from three parties and failed to maintain a majority in the National Assembly. In an election fraught with many irregularities including vote buying, bribery, hostage taking, and assaults, the April 1988 elections created what South Koreans referred to as *yoso yadae* – small ruling party, large opposition (see Table 2). Now Roh's weak presidency also faced strong opposition in the National Assembly and had a difficult time obtaining the necessary votes to implement his agenda.

Despite these difficulties, Roh inherited a strong economy with GDP growth rates that averaged approximately 10 to 11 percent. The country was thriving and continued to demonstrate its prowess as one of the rising economies in Asia. Roh also faced two competing economic pressures that could be potential problems, however. On the one hand, the middle class, which had been a strong player in the democratic transition, wanted to see continued economic growth along with peace, stability, and an end to internal political unrest. On the other hand, workers believed that they had tolerated low wages and long hours for far too long and now deserved a greater share of South Korea's economic prosperity. Moreover, they were willing to hit the streets again to obtain what they felt they had earned. Consequently, there was strong pressure from below to set aside the earlier priority of "growth first" for a more equitable distribution of wealth, not only for workers but also for farmers and others who believed they deserved a greater share of South Korea's boom economy. As a result, there were frequent strikes and much labor unrest that helped to pull the ROK economy into a steep decline by the end of 1989.

Finally, Roh's administration was the beneficiary of all that comes from hosting a successful round of the Olympic Games. During the Chun years, Roh served as minister of the newly created Ministry of Athletics that was in charge of planning the games. South Korea underwent a building spree that included constructing numerous Olympic facilities in Seoul and the surrounding area, upgrading and extending the subway system, cleaning up the Han River, and organizing the infrastructure necessary for a successful event. South Korea believed that this event would put the country's economic miracle on a world stage, displaying the progress it had made as the "miracle on the Han River," and generate further momentum for its economy. The games opened on September 17, 1988, and ROK officials received high marks for their skill in hosting the event. South Koreans still take great pride in having sponsored the Olympics, and the nationalism it generated bolstered the public's confidence in the Roh Tae-woo administration.

In January 1990, the political landscape took another interesting twist when Kim Young-sam, Kim Jong-pil, and Roh Tae-woo, the leaders of the Reunification Democratic Party, the New Democratic Republican Party, and the ruling Democratic Justice Party, respectively, joined forces to form a grand coalition named the Democratic Liberal Party (DLP). Kim Young-sam, the long-time dissident, was roundly criticized for "selling out" to the ruling party, although the move all but assured him of the DLP nomination in the upcoming December 1992 election. President Roh was now forced to work with a former adversary, but the merger provided his party with a solid majority in the National Assembly.

1992 Presidential Elections

As was expected from the three-party merger, the ruling DLP nominated Kim Young-sam, who was challenged once again by Kim Dae-jung, now running under the banner of the Millennium Democratic Party. In the past, there had often been a question of whether the military would intervene in the election or nullify the results if an unacceptable candidate was the victor. This was a particular concern should Kim Dae-jung, a candidate the military despised, run. This time, however, there were few worries the military would interfere; the Ministry of Defense and the Joint Chiefs of Staff made it clear they would accept whoever won.

The election became even more interesting when Chung Ju-yung, former chair of Hyundai Corporation, one of South Korea's largest family-owned business conglomerates or *chaebol*, decided to enter the contest. Chung entered the race arguing that South Koreans should have an alternative to the two Kims who had so far failed to win several presidential elections. With his wealth and business background, many in the U.S. press compared him to Ross Perot, who was running as an independent party candidate in the 1992 U.S. election with Bill Clinton and George H. W. Bush. Despite the attention Chung received and the personal wealth he was able to spend, Chung was not a major challenger to either of the Kims.

The campaigns of both Kims featured huge mass rallies attended by thousands. Kim Young-sam also expended considerable funds for his campaign, money that later would be alleged to have come from Roh Tae-woo's campaign coffers. Kim Young-sam is also credited with running an excellent campaign; when the results were tallied, he received 41.4 percent of the vote to Kim Dae-jung's 33.4 percent. Chung Ju-yung finished a distant third with 16.1 percent, bringing an end to his political ambitions (see Table 3). This was Kim Dae-jung's third effort at seeking the presidency, as he had lost in 1971 and 1987. After the election, he announced his retirement but returned to politics just prior to the next election.

On February 25, 1993, Kim Young-sam was sworn into office as the next president of the Sixth Republic. Although some remained upset with him for having joined the ruling party, his victory meant that, for the first time in more than thirty years, South Korea had a president who had not been a general. Moreover, the second free and fair election under a direct popular system, along with the peaceful passing of power to another administration, was further indication of the progress South Korea had made in its consolidation of democracy.

Table 3. *1992 Presidential election results*

Kim Young-sam	41.4%
Democratic Liberal Party	
Kim Dae-jung	33.4%
Millennium Democratic Party	
Chung Ju-yung	16.1%
Unification National Party	

Holding the Military Leaders Accountable for the Past

One final issue remains in this examination of the ROK's transition to democracy. South Korea was one of many countries in the 1970s and 1980s that had made the transition to democracy from authoritarian rule. These regimes ranged from communist, one-party states to countries ruled by the military. Often, these governments were responsible for horrible violations of human rights, including kidnapping, illegal detention, rape, torture, and execution. The old regime, particularly if it was a military government that came to power in a coup d'état, may also have been guilty of violating the constitution by illegally seizing power. When making the transition, the new democracy faced a difficult decision: prosecute the former leaders and risk disrupting the transition, particularly problematic if the former regime was a military one, or move on from the past to allow old wounds to heal.

South Korea's decision was decidedly mixed.[22] Early in the Roh Tae-woo administration, proponents of prosecution exerted considerable pressure on the government to investigate Chun and the "irregularities" of the past. Roh complied with these desires but only reluctantly; he did as little as possible in an effort to protect his old friend. Before turning over power, military regimes often enact measures that protect them from prosecution and retribution afterward. ROK military leaders did not do so, believing there was no need because Roh would be able to protect them and resist any efforts to prosecute. Moreover, Roh had a stake in this as well, as he would also be a target of any investigation because of his involvement in Kwangju and with Chun's regime.

To address these concerns, Roh formed a committee to investigate the allegations, especially those regarding the Kwangju incident. The committee's report acknowledged that Kwangju was not a communist plot as Chun had claimed but rather an effort to bring democracy to South Korea. Later, the government apologized for its severe response to the demonstrators and provided medical care and employment assistance to those affected by Kwangju. The report, however, went no further and did not call for more investigations or prosecutions.

---

[22] For detailed treatment of South Korea's efforts to prosecute its past military leaders, see T. Roehrig, *The Prosecution of Former Military Leaders in Newly Democratic Nations: The Cases of Argentina, Greece, and South Korea* (Jefferson, N.C.: McFarland, 2002), chaps. 6 and 7.

When the opposition gained control of the National Assembly in the April 1988 elections, it had the votes and the power to push for a more intensive investigation. Allegations of corrupt financial dealings by Chun, his family – including his wife and brother – and cronies of the regime added further motivation to opening up more extensive investigations. Thus, with the National Assembly now under control by the opposition, it was likely that pressure would build for a detailed inquiry to look into the "irregularities" of the past, despite Roh's efforts to thwart these moves.

With the conclusion of the October 1988 Olympic Games, the National Assembly launched a series of hearings into the allegations of corruption during the Chun years. Chun was accused of skimming money from the Ilhae Foundation, an organization that was created after the 1983 Rangoon Bombing to help the families of those killed in the tragedy. The foundation later became a research institute and received most of its funding from business leaders who often felt coerced to contribute lest they lose favor with the government. The public also learned of the Samchung Reeducation Camp that Chun used to incarcerate criminals. More than thirty-nine thousand people were sent to the camp during Chun's time in office, including some who were political dissidents. For the first time in ROK history, the hearings were televised live and captivated viewers, producing ratings that surpassed those of the Olympics. The public was outraged by what they saw, and calls for holding Chun and his family accountable increased dramatically.

As public anger grew, sentiment within the National Assembly began to shift, from simply calling for a full accounting of Chun's misdeeds and an apology, to greater interest in imposing punishment. Even the Roh administration began to see that, for the matter to be settled, Chun would have to make a gesture of apology and return some of the money he had acquired. After resisting these pressures and threatening to reveal information that would embarrass and implicate Roh, Chun relented. On November 23, 1988, Chun went on national television to give a formal apology to the country.[23] In addition, he agreed to return close to $17 million in personal assets, political funds, his home, and a ski resort condominium among other possessions as a sign of his contrition. Following the televised apology, Chun and his

---

[23] "Chun Apologizes for Misdeeds Under His Rule," *Korea Newsreview*, November 26, 1988, 4.

wife, Lee Soon-ja, left their home in Seoul for Packdamsa, a secluded Buddhist monastery in northeast South Korea.

Although these events appeared to settle some of the angst about Chun's financial dealings, momentum continued for looking into the 1979 mutiny and the Kwangju massacre. In another effort to mollify growing anger, on December 31, 1989, Chun testified before the National Assembly. In a nationally televised session, Chun answered 125 questions that he had received in advance. His answers were often vague, and little was learned that most did not already know. Many times during the testimony, Chun was interrupted with epithets such as "lies" and "murderer" shouted from the gallery and from legislators.[24] Eventually, Chun found it impossible to finish and left before completing his answers. Later that day, Chun convened a news conference and read the remainder of his answers to reporters. In the end, few were satisfied with his responses.

When Kim Young-sam won the presidency in 1992, calls resumed for further investigations into "irregularities of the past." Despite his history as a leader of the opposition, Kim Young-sam was now president of the ruling party, and he made clear his position that it was time to move on. While maintaining that Chun's December 12 mutiny was a "coup-like incident" and that Kwangju was a pro-democracy demonstration, not a communist plot, he argued that "we should not forget the atrocities. But let's forgive them to achieve national reconciliation."[25]

Protests waned for a time, but in two years they grew in size and intensity. Their efforts received a boost from an unexpected quarter. In 1994 and 1995, several tragic accidents occurred in South Korea, including the explosion of an underground gas line, a bridge collapse, and the collapse of the Sampoong Department Store in Seoul. Investigators blamed these tragedies on poor quality construction and corruption that fed calls for investigating relations between business and government. Consequently, investigations began again, but this time they focused on potential corruption in the Chun and Roh administrations. In October 1995, evidence surfaced that Roh had accumulated a huge political slush fund during his administration composed largely of donations from big business that were likely given under

[24] J. Shim, "Old Testimony, Fresh Fury," *Far Eastern Economic Review*, January 11, 1990, 8–9.
[25] "Kim Vows to Restore Honor of Kwangju Citizens," *Korea Newsreview*, May 22, 1993, 4.

pressure to ensure favorable treatment from the government. It was also alleged that Roh had received large sums from Chun's war chest during his run for office and, in turn, had given Kim Young-sam sizeable amounts for his campaign. These allegations were the undoing of Chun and Roh.

On October 27, 1995, Roh admitted to accepting $654 million during his administration and, on November 16, was arrested for taking close to $365 million from some of South Korea's most prominent businessmen. Police also arrested these business leaders, including the chairmen of South Korea's top companies such as Samsung and Daewoo, for giving the bribes. On December 3, 1995, Chun was arrested on charges of mutiny and treason for the December 12 incident. With Roh already in custody, authorities included him on the indictment for the 1979 military mutiny. In January 1996, prosecutors added Chun to the bribery indictments, charging him with amassing a fund from business leaders that was even larger than Roh's at $1.2 billion. The indictments charged that $270 million were bribes with the remainder provided as general campaign contributions. Both Chun and Roh acknowledged receiving the money but maintained that the funds were solely campaign donations and not bribes to buy favors. Chun claimed these allegations were a "political maneuver." Soon after his arrest, he went on a hunger strike to protest the political nature of these proceedings and President Kim Young-sam's failure to protect him from prosecution. Indeed, many South Koreans were keenly aware of President Kim's apparent flip-flop of advocating that the issue be left to the "judgment of history" to now supporting prosecutions. Moreover, it also seemed likely that President Kim shared some responsibility in the accusations given the three-party merger and the likelihood he received campaign contributions from Roh. Despite the suspicion, Kim was able to dodge further scrutiny.

With the trials already beginning on these charges, on January 23, 1996, prosecutors added the final indictments, charging Chun, Roh, and six other accomplices in the military with treason in connection with Chun's seizure of power in May 1980. According to these indictments, Chun and Roh mobilized troops without President Choi's approval, surrounded the capitol building, and coerced the cabinet to expand martial law throughout the entire country. These units also arrested politicians and dissidents without the approval of the president or the Army Chief of Staff who served as the martial law commander and disrupted sessions of the National Assembly. Finally, and most seriously, the charges included the events at Kwangju, although Chun was not charged with giving direct orders to open fire on demonstrators.

The trials began in December 1995 in Seoul District Court before a three-judge panel. The proceedings lasted for close to seven months, with convictions coming down in July 1996 followed by the imposition of sentences on August 26, 1996. The court found Chun and Roh guilty on all counts. Because Chun was the leader of the December 12 mutiny and the "rolling coup," he was sentenced to death and assessed a fine of $283 million to ensure he had no remaining assets from his slush fund. The court sentenced Roh to serve twenty-two and a half years in prison and to pay a $355 million fine. In addition, thirteen of the fourteen that also stood trial with Chun and Roh were convicted, receiving sentences that ranged from four to ten years. Concerning Kwangju, the Court did not convict Chun, Roh, and the other defendants of murder for ordering the soldiers to open fire on the demonstrators. During the proceedings, Chun had argued that any order to shoot was given by local commanders and involved self-defense. Consequently, he maintained the shootings were accidental and not a result of an order to kill. The Court maintained it could not find sufficient evidence to the contrary and refrained from convicting on these counts.[26] The nine business leaders who stood trial for paying bribes were also convicted, but they received suspended sentences. The Court feared that forcing them to serve jail time would have a negative impact on an already struggling economy. All of the defendants appealed the verdicts, and, although sentences were reduced, all of the convictions were upheld. The Court reduced Chun Doo-hwan's death sentence to life in prison, and Roh Tae-woo's sentence was reduced to seventeen years.

Throughout the trials, speculation was rife that President Kim Young-sam would pardon the offenders before his term ended. On December 18, 1997, two days after South Koreans elected his successor, Kim Dae-jung, both Kims agreed to pardon Chun Doo-hwan, Roh Tae-woo, and the others who had been convicted in these prosecutions. When Kim Dae-jung was inaugurated as the next ROK president on February 25, 1998, Chun and Roh were in attendance at the ceremony.

[26] Oh, *Korean Politics*, 177, and "Chun Denies 'Double Chain of Command' in Kwangju Massacre: Court to Hear Witnesses From Thursday," *Korea Times*, June 18, 1996.

Conclusion

The eighties and early nineties was a difficult period for South Korea as
it began its transition to democracy, worked to consolidate democracy,
and prosecuted two of its former presidents for corruption, mutiny,
and treason, yet South Korea's fledgling democracy endured while the
country also came to terms with its past. While going through all of the
political upheaval of this period, the economy continued to grow and
cemented South Korea as one of the world's rising economic powers.
By the end of the decade, however, South Korea faced serious economic challenges and an ongoing crisis with North Korea regarding
its nuclear ambitions. Despite these challenges that lay ahead, South
Korea now confronted them as one of the world's new democracies.

3

Democratic Consolidation and Social Change

On February 25, 1998, long-time dissident leader Kim Dae-jung was inaugurated as president. The election of President Kim had significant political implications in South Korean history. This lateral power transfer was the first in modern South Korean politics. Prior to the victory of Kim Dae-jung, candidates from the ruling party always won the presidential election. Thus, this power transition was the first time an opposition candidate won the election, an important indication that South Korea was becoming a stable democracy. Also, President Kim Dae-jung was different from his predecessors. He was the first president from Cholla Province, the southwestern part of South Korea, and he had a progressive, left-wing political orientation, by contrast with his predecessors, who were conservative, right-wing leaders from the southeastern Kyongsang Province. As a result, significant changes followed in his administration. In this chapter, we discuss political and social changes during the Kim Dae-jung administration in the context of the democratic consolidation process in South Korea.

Domestic Politics during the Kim Dae-jung Administration

Although South Korea experienced the transition to democracy in 1987, there were no clear political cleavages in South Korean society that led to distinct, institutionalized political parties. The chief explanations for this situation are grounded in the legacy of Confucianism and the Korean War. Confucianism emphasizes harmony and discourages division. The Korean War, the first conflict between the Korean people since Silla's unification of the country in 668 A.D., was a result of differences in political ideology. Because of the tragic Korean War experience, Koreans have been hesitant to develop parties based on political ideologies.[1]

Despite the lack of clear political cleavages linked to ideology, there were differences in the patterns of voting behavior between various regions: urban versus rural areas and Kyongsang versus Cholla Provinces. Prior to the transition to democracy, urban voters traditionally supported the opposition parties, whereas rural voters backed the governing party because the authoritarian government rewarded rural districts for electoral support with government subsidies. Because city dwellers were less in need of the government's financial assistance, the inducements for votes worked better in rural areas. This pattern, however, started changing as South Korea democratized because the ruling party no longer relied on rural voters for electoral support. Instead, regionally based personalism became an important characteristic of South Korean elections. After democratization, political leaders created their own parties according to personal loyalty to the candidate rather than to a specific party ideology. These leaders viewed political parties as campaign vehicles for winning presidential elections instead of seeing them as political institutions. Thus, they used political parties to exploit regional and personal ties for political gains.[2]

In the 1997 presidential election, Kim Dae-jung's chief rival was Lee Hoi-chang, the ruling party candidate. Lee served as prime minister during the Kim Young-sam administration and was known for his clean, uncorrupted image. Because Kyongsang province always provided strong support to the ruling Grand National Party (GNP), having allowed it to win easily in all previous presidential elections, Lee Hoi-chang was expected to prevail.

Opinion poll results before the election were very close, however, and eventually Kim Dae-jung won the election for several reasons. First, prior to the presidential nomination, Lee Hoi-chang's popularity soared because of his untainted image. Because the South Korean people were tired of corrupt politics, Lee Hoi-chang's reputation for intolerance of corruption appealed to the public. This image was severely tarnished after allegations were made regarding exemptions for his two sons from South Korea's compulsory military service. Despite the untruth of the allegations, people's perception that he was

---

[1] B. Kim, "Korea's Crisis of Success," in *Democracy in East Asia*, ed. L. Diamond and M. Plattner, 113–32 (Baltimore, Md.: Johns Hopkins University Press, 1988).

[2] U. Heo and H. Stockton, "Elections and Parties in South Korea Before and After Transition to Democracy," *Party Politics* 11 (2005): 675–89.

Table 4. *1997 Presidential election results*

Candidate and party	Percentage of the popular vote cast
Kim Dae-jung National Congress for New Politics	40.27
Lee Hoi-chang Grand National Party	38.75
Lee In-je People's New Party	19.21

different from other politicians significantly changed and his popularity dropped. Second, Lee Hoi-chang could not rid himself of responsibility for the 1997 financial crisis, as he had served as prime minister during the Kim Young-sam administration. Because the presidential election was held shortly after the financial crisis broke out, the issue dominated the contest. Third, Lee In-je, who lost to Lee Hoi-chang in the GNP's nomination competition, defected and created a new party to enter the presidential race. As a result, there were two candidates representing conservatives, which split the vote and helped Kim Dae-jung win the election. Fourth and finally, Kim Dae-jung allied with Kim Jong-pil to gain votes in Choongchung Province, the political home of Kim Jong-pil. This political arrangement was based on Kim Dae-jung's promise that, if he was elected, his government would change the current presidential system to a parliamentary structure. Because Kim Jong-pil believed that the parliamentary system would aid his party, the United Liberal Democrats (ULD), because of their small size and limited regional support, he viewed the alliance to be mutually beneficial. Thus, he withdrew his candidacy and endorsed Kim Dae-jung. All these factors helped Kim Dae-jung win the election, although the margin of victory was slim, as shown in Table 4.

Although a small number of votes determined the race, the 1997 presidential election was crucial in terms of transferring power to the opposition party, and it also introduced changes in the election process, voting behavior, and election law. For the first time in South Korean history, the election introduced a series of televised debates among the three leading candidates. With this change, voters were able to see the positions of the candidates on controversial issues and their ability

to articulate their political views. Moreover, television debates significantly reduced campaign costs by replacing the traditional expensive,
massive outdoor rallies.[3]

Another noticeable change concerned Lee In-je's decision to run
for the presidency after losing the GNP party nomination. This led to
new legislation by the National Assembly to ban candidates who lost
their party nomination from running for the presidency under a new
party. This law made the presidential party nomination competition
more meaningful and legitimate.

Despite all these positive developments, candidates also continued
old and questionable political tactics, such as making unconfirmed
accusations. During the campaign, Kang Sam-jae, secretary-general
of the ruling GNP, publicly accused Kim Dae-jung of holding a $67
million slush fund and called for an investigation. Another source
accused Kim Dae-jung of receiving funds from North Korea.[4]

Unconfirmed accusations were not limited to Kim Dae-jung. There
were accusations of wrongdoing regarding the military service waiver
of Lee Hoi-chang's two sons along with follow-up meetings of two
GNP lawmakers and Lee Hoi-chang's confidants to cover up the illegal
behavior. This claim significantly damaged Lee Hoi-chang's image and
his chances in the election, although no evidence of wrongdoing was
found.

Another dark side of the election was an illegal effort to raise funds
for the ruling GNP, called *Sepung* ("Wind from the National Tax
Service"). To support Lee Hoi-chang, his brother and some lawmakers
in the GNP pressured some *chaebol*, including Samsung, Hyundai, and
LG, by suggesting that they might be audited by the National Tax
Service if they did not raise $80 million for his campaign fund. These
actions violated campaign finance laws, and because a portion of the
money was delivered as a truckload of cash, the GNP was later mocked
as the truckload rate party (*Chattegi-Dang*).

Although Kim Dae-jung won the presidential election, the GNP
still enjoyed a majority in the National Assembly and was hostile
toward President Kim and his agenda. President Kim's party, the
National Congress for New Politics (NCNP), was the largest party
in a coalition that also included Kim Jong-pil's ULD. Despite the
honeymoon period, the GNP refused to confirm Kim Jong-pil as

---

[3] S. Jin, "Aftermath of Presidential Debate on TV," *Chosun Ilbo*, December 16,
1997.
[4] Oh, *Korean Politics*, 1999, 230.

prime minister. As a result, Kim Jong-pil was appointed as acting prime minister, and the new cabinet had a delayed start. Moreover, President Kim Dae-jung attempted to improve the laws on campaign finance and political parties by creating the Political Reform Committee (PRC) in the National Assembly. However, the GNP did not cooperate, and the PRC achieved nothing except reducing the number of seats in the National Assembly to 273 because of public pressure.[5]

To break the GNP majority in the National Assembly, President Kim Dae-jung threatened opposition lawmakers using the Prosecutor's Office and the National Tax Service for suspected violation of various laws. There also was a significant increase in illegal wiretapping from 2,400 in 1996 during the Kim Young-sam administration to 3,580 in just the first six months of 1998.[6] By September 1998, seven months after President Kim's inauguration, the number of lawmakers affiliated with the ruling coalition increased from 121 to 158. With a majority in the National Assembly, the ruling coalition passed sixty-six bills in fifteen minutes in January 1999 and six more in eight minutes in May.[7] After that, there was no communication or compromise between the ruling coalition and the opposition GNP throughout President Kim Dae-jung's tenure.[8]

In 1999, other political scandals disappointed the Korean people. The so-called Furgate scandal involved Choi Soon-young, the owner of the Shindonga Group, and the prosecutor-general, Kim Tae-joung. Choi Soon-young was arrested in 1998 and charged with capital flight. According to South Korean law, capital flight – taking large sums of capital abroad – was against the law because it drained the country of badly needed investment capital. While the case was being investigated, Choi's wife bribed Kim Tae-joung's wife by buying her an expensive fur coat, implicitly asking her to persuade her husband to go easy on Choi. The opposition party disclosed this scandal and requested an investigation by independent counselors because the scandal involved the prosecutor-general, and evidence surfaced that

[5] After South Korea experienced a financial crisis and was saved by the international monetary fund's (IMF's) bailout program, the whole country underwent structural reforms. As a result, there was strong public pressure to reduce the size of the National Assembly. The number of seats in the National Assembly returned to 299 after the 2000 election, however.

[6] *Korea Herald*, October 19, 1998.

[7] *Korea Herald*, May 7, 1999.

[8] C. Kim, *The Korean Presidents*.

the Prosecutor's Office attempted to cover it up.[9] In addition, GNP lawmaker Chung Hyung-keun disclosed a document with evidence of government involvement in controlling the media through ties to the Korean Intelligence Service. The GNP also revealed that the Korean Intelligence Service illegally monitored opposition party activities from a base in the National Assembly building.[10] These scandals significantly tarnished the reputation of longtime democratic activist President Kim Dae-jung and his party.[11]

The political alliance between Kim Dae-jung and Kim Jong-pil also started to unravel because President Kim failed to keep his promise to change the presidential system to a parliamentary structure. President Kim Dae-jung and his party were not interested in amending the Constitution to change the existing presidential system. Moreover, the ruling coalition could not change the Constitution without the GNP's cooperation because an amendment required a two-thirds vote for approval. President Kim was also more interested in the forthcoming National Assembly election. Thus, the NCNP and ULD postponed a discussion of changing the Constitution until after the election.[12] Although the discord that occurred between Kim Dae-jung's NCNP and Kim Jong-pil's ULD concerned changing the government system, it was also expected because of differences in their political ideologies. The NCNP was a liberal, progressive party, whereas the ULD was conservative.

For the upcoming election, President Kim adopted *dongjin jungchek* (eastward policy) to gain more support in Kyongsang Province. Regionalism had dominated elections since the transition to democracy, and Kyongsang Province had always supported the GNP. Thus, *dongjin jungchek* started with a reassessment and an embrace of the late President Park Chung-hee because in Kyongsang province he was still respected and considered one of the best leaders in South Korean history as a result of the phenomenal economic growth during his tenure. President Kim even proposed a government-financed memorial park project for the late President Park Chung-hee. This was a bold move,

---

[9] Y. Youn, "South Korea in 1999: Overcoming Cold War Legacies" *Asian Survey* 40 (2000): 164–71.

[10] N. Kristof, "A Locked Door Is Broken and Seoul Lawmakers Have a Spy Furor," *New York Times*, January 4, 1999.

[11] H. Kim, "The 2000 Parliamentary Election in South Korea," *Asian Survey* 40 (2000): 894–913.

[12] C. Kim, *The Korean Presidents.*

Table 5. *2000 National Assembly election results*[13]

Party	District seats	Proportional seats	Total seats
Grand National Party	112	21	133
Millennium Democratic Party	96	19	115
United Liberal Democrats	12	5	17
Democratic People's Party	1	1	2
New Korea Party	1	0	1
Independents	5	0	5
			273

considering that Kim Dae-jung was one of the most persecuted victims of Park Chung-hee's authoritarian rule.[14] President Kim also expanded welfare policies and formed a new party for the election to improve the image of the ruling NCNP. The outcome was the creation of the Millennium Democratic Party (MDP) three months prior to the election to replace the NCNP. Despite these concerted efforts, the election results were disappointing for the ruling coalition. The MDP won 115 seats and the ULD only 17. The opposition GNP won 133 seats, relegating the ruling MDP party to minority status in the National Assembly (see Table 5).[15]

Three factors account for the results of the 2000 National Assembly election. First, the image of President Kim Dae-jung fighting for democracy and clean government was severely tainted by scandals and the use of old political tactics such as wiretapping, luring opposition party members to defect their parties and join the MDP, and passing laws quickly and in secret without the presence of opposition party lawmakers. To the South Korean public, the Kim administration was just as corrupt as previous governments. Second, President Kim's *dongjin jungchek* to gain more support from Kyongsang Province was not successful because the people there doubted President Kim's sincerity, and thus regionalism continued to dominate the

[13] The 2000 National Assembly election was held under the new legislation, which reduced the number of seats from 299 to 273.

[14] The government's financial support was limited. As a result, the project did not make progress.

[15] K. Kang and S. Walker, "The 2000 National Assembly Elections in South Korea," *Electoral Studies* 21 (2002): 480–5.

election.[16] Finally, the Kim Dae-jung government introduced a significantly enhanced social welfare program, yet did not increase revenue to finance the reforms, leaving unanswered the question of how this policy change would affect the national economy.[17]

Despite the regionalism that dominated voting patterns, a change occurred in the 2000 election concerning the role of civil society and its impact on election outcomes. During the campaign period, the Citizens' Coalition for Economic Justice (CCEJ) published a voter's guide that included a list of 167 politicians who should not be elected because of their involvement in corruption scandals, opposition to reform policies, or appeals to regionalism for political gain. Moreover, 460 civil society groups organized *Chongseon Yondai* (The Citizens' Alliance for the 2000 National Assembly Election) and released a list of politicians who should not be nominated. After candidates were nominated, the *Chongseon Yondai* finalized a list of eighty-six candidates who should not be elected and campaigned against twenty-two of them. The campaign against select politicians by *Chongseon Yondai* significantly affected the election results, and only seven of the twenty-two politicians against whom *Chongseon Yondai* campaigned were elected.

The origin of civil society in South Korea goes all the way back to the Japanese colonial period, when harsh Japanese colonial rule led to the creation of a highly resistant civil society. These organizations were created to fight for liberation from Japanese colonial rule. When colonial rule ended after Japan lost World War II, civil society quickly expanded to represent labor and peasant interests. Communists were actively involved in forming these organizations for political purposes, although they were not in full control of them. Conservatives also organized groups in response to left-wing organizations. The political landscape changed quickly, however, after the United States Army Military Government in Korea (USAMGIK) took over the government and banned left-wing organizations because of their communist ties. The Syngman Rhee government instituted anti-communist campaigns, and throughout his tenure (1948–60) Rhee limited the organization and activity of civil society.[18]

---

[16] H. Kim, "The 2000 Parliamentary Election in South Korea," 2000.

[17] C. Kim, *The Korean Presidents.*

[18] S. Kim, *The Politics of Democratization in Korea: The Role of Civil Society* (Pittsburgh: University of Pittsburgh Press, 2000).

Corruption and ineffectiveness of the government, however, gave way to the reemergence of civil society toward the end of the 1950s. In 1959, unions banded together to form the Korea Trade Union Council (KTUC). When Park Chung-hee came to power through a military coup, however, he kept tight control of dissident groups in civil society. After the transition to democracy, though, the number of civil society groups soared. By 2006, 5,556 civil society organizations were registered, including the CCEJ, the People's Solidarity for Participatory Democracy, and the Korean Federation for Environmental Movements.[19]

With the increased number of these organizations, their role in politics rose dramatically. For instance, they pressured the government to prosecute individuals who persecuted democracy activists or were involved in corruption scandals. Many civil society groups played a key role in pressing for the prosecution of former Presidents Chun Doo-whan and Roh Tae-woo.[20] Enhanced activities of South Korean civil society helped deepen democracy by facilitating political development and promoting citizen participation in the policy-making process. Yet its deep involvement in politics and strong positions on one side of an issue made it difficult for the government to implement certain policies.

The outcome of the 2000 National Assembly election led to changes in relations between the ruling coalition parties. Because the ULD had won only seventeen seats, it lost the status of a floor-negotiating group, which requires a minimum of twenty seats. Maintaining this status is important in South Korea because government subsidies are provided only to parties with the status of a floor-negotiating group. Thus, the ULD urged the MDP to reduce the minimum seat requirement by changing the law. The GNP strongly opposed the move and publicly protested against it. Eventually, the MDP abandoned the change, which led to a sour relationship between the MDP and the ULD.[21] Then a political comedy occurred. To placate the ULD, three MDP lawmakers joined the ULD so that it could maintain its

---

[19] D. Cho, "Nation Witnesses Upsurge of Civil Organizations," in *Social Change in Korea*, ed. K. Kim and the *Korea Herald* (Seoul: Jimoondang, 2008), 196–210.

[20] S. Kim, "Civil Society in Democratizing Korea," in *Korea's Democratization*, ed. S. Kim (New York: Cambridge University Press, 2003), 81–106.

[21] Y. Ha, "South Korea in 2000: A Summit and the Search for New Institutional Identity," *Asian Survey* 41 (2001): 30–9.

floor-negotiating group status. This is a good example that demonstrates South Korea's lack of mature democratic institutions and how
political leaders used parties for their own political gain.

After the election, there were a series of policy-reform blunders.
In his Liberation Day speech on August 15, 1999, President Kim
introduced initiatives addressing a national pension, an unemployment support system, education, and health insurance reform. With
this ambitious agenda, the government hastily carried out the policies
but soon began to face some unexpected problems.[22] For instance,
the health care reform introduced by the government included differentiation between over-the-counter and doctor-prescribed drugs.
Doctors were outraged and went on strike, and the entire medical system malfunctioned for six months. The reason for the doctors' strike
was complex, but part of the reason was as follows: With the increase
in hospitals and people's preference for them, individual doctors who
practiced medicine in their offices became concerned about their loss
of business. Moreover, the South Korean health care system pays doctors relatively low fees for their services. To supplement their income,
doctors took rebates from pharmaceutical companies by prescribing
and selling their products. This system had existed for a long time, and
the new law jeopardized doctors' incomes.[23] To fix the problem, the
government increased doctors' fees paid by the national health care
system, which nearly bankrupted the national health plan.

The national pension plan was another policy blunder. The plan
included all South Korean citizens, but generous benefits for small contributions created a serious deficit problem. Hasty education reform
also showed a lack of sound policy implementation. Lee Hae-chan, the
Kim government's first education minister, assumed there was significant corruption in education. His anticorruption measures, along with
a reduction in the retirement age from sixty-five to sixty, humiliated
teachers.[24] Within a year, schools suffered from a shortage of teachers,
and the quality of education has continued to drop. For instance, in
1988, 13 percent of students responded that students chat and disrupt
class. This number increased to 48 percent in 2008. Because many

---

[22] J. Burton, "Series of Policy Blunders Hit South Korea," *Financial Times*, May 23,
2001.

[23] B. Cho, "Differentiation between Over-the-counter Drugs and Doctor-prescribed
Drugs and Social Conflicts," *Journal of Korean Bioethics Association* 1 (2000): 201–29.

[24] The retirement age for teachers has been changed again to sixty-two because of
the shortage of teachers.

students take classes at private tutoring institutions, they tend not to focus in school classes, which has become a serious problem for public education.[25]

In 2002, the December 19 presidential election dominated domestic politics. The MDP adopted an American-style primary as a party candidate selection method to allow citizen participation in the process. Approximately seventy thousand party members and randomly selected citizens took part in the primary, which occurred in several major cities. The primary started with several important candidates, but only two were left at the end of the voting: Roh Moo-hyun and Lee In-je. Roh Moo-hyun was a former human rights lawyer who never attended college but was highly respected for his personal integrity.[26] Although he was from Kyongsang Province, he received strong support from Cholla Province, the strong hold of the MDP. Perceiving Roh Moo-hyun's popularity in Cholla Province as a sign of Kim Dae-jung's endorsement, Lee In-je withdrew and Roh Moo-hyun became the party nominee.[27]

Roh Moo-hyun was genuinely popular among the younger generation, particularly the so-called 386 generation – those who were in their thirties, went to college in the 1980s, and were born in the 1960s. Because Roh was actively involved in the democracy and labor movements, many of the 386 generation who led the democracy movement in the 1980s shared Roh's political views. Moreover, many in this age group were impressed by Roh's political integrity when he refused to join Kim Young-sam in the 1992 three-party merger with Roh Tae-woo. This political move by Kim Youn-sam was harshly criticized by democracy activists. By contrast, Roh Moo-hyun's refusal to join Kim Young-sam intrigued many young people and drew them into his camp.

During the campaign, Roh's supporters formed an Internet-based group, *Roh Sa Mo* (Gathering of those who love Roh Moo-hyun), which played a key role in delivering Roh's message to the public and publicizing Roh's campaign activities.[28] The *Roh Sa Mo* had more than

---

[25] Y. Kim. "Students Chat, 13 Percent in 1988 – 48 Percent in 2008." *Chosun Ilbo*, October 27, 2009.

[26] In South Korea, there is no formal education requirement for taking the bar exam.

[27] H. Lee, "South Korea in 2002: Multiple Political Dramas," *Asian Survey* 43 (2003): 64–77.

[28] *Roh Sa Mo* was initially created directly after the 2000 National Assembly election by followers of Roh Moo-hyun. Prior to the election, he insisted on running in

seventy thousand members, and more than three thousand "netizens" visited the Web site, which showed video clips and audio broadcasts every day. The site also raised more than $7.7 million from more than two hundred thousand individuals.[29] In addition, *Roh Sa Mo* created a cyberspace forum to discuss political issues and raised funds from the younger generation who tended to be apathetic about politics. Roh himself sometimes became involved in lively online debates of political issues, which significantly increased his popularity.[30]

As the campaign progressed, however, Roh Moo-hyun's popularity started to decline because of his controversial statements, anti-American stance, and attempts to obtain endorsements from both Kim Young-sam and Kim Dae-jung despite his being an MDP candidate. For instance, when he was asked if he wanted to visit the United States if elected, he said, "I have never been to the United States. I will not go to the United States to have my picture taken for Korean domestic political purposes."[31] In addition, he pursued Kim Young-sam's support, but his efforts to get Kim's endorsement were seen as old political tactics that tarnished his image. Furthermore, a corruption scandal involving President Kim Dae-jung's sons and confidants led to declining public support for the MDP, which also affected Roh's popularity. President Kim's second son, Kim Hong-up, was found guilty of taking bribes, and his youngest son, Kim Hong-gul, and his oldest, Kim Hong-il, were involved in influence-peddling cases for money. The opposition party also charged that President Kim Dae-jung and his three sons owned real estate worth $10 million despite the fact that none of them had an income-generating job. President Kim's long-time confidant, Kwon No-gap, was also charged with bribery and manipulating stock prices using inside information and influence peddling.[32]

Roh's main opponent in the general election was Lee Hoi-chang, the GNP candidate. As Roh's popularity declined, the MDP started

his hometown, Pusan, to fight against regionalism, although his chance for getting elected there as an MDP candidate was slim because Pusan was a GNP stronghold. Those who were impressed by Roh's political integrity created an Internet-based gathering to support Roh in an organized manner.

[29] S. Yun, "Political Participation in the Internet Era," in *Political Change in Korea*, ed. the *Korea Herald* and the Korean Political Science Association (Seoul: Jimoondang, 2008), 203–10.

[30] H. Lee, "South Korea in 2002: Multiple Political Dramas," 2003.

[31] Interview with *Pyonghwa* (Peace) Radio, April 26, 2002.

[32] H. Lee, "South Korea in 2002: Multiple Political Dramas," 2003.

attacking Lee Hoi-chang for living in his relative's luxurious apartment without paying rent. Another accusation of wrongdoing was made regarding Lee's son's military waiver. Kim Dae-up, an illegal military service waiver broker, claimed that Lee's wife paid $20,000 to government officials so that her sons could avoid military service. He also said some GNP lawmakers and Lee's confidants had a meeting to cover up their wrongdoings. Litigation started, and long after the presidential election ended, the Supreme Court ruled that there was no evidence of foul play and sentenced Kim Dae-up to twenty-two months in prison for perjury. Although this allegation had a limited effect on the election outcome, it showed that South Korea still has a long way to go in terms of having a mature democratic system.

Another candidate in the election was Chung Mong-jun, the youngest son of the late Chung ju-yung, the founder of Hyundai group. Because of South Korea's success in the 2002 FIFA (Federation of International Football Association) World Cup soccer competition and Chung's role as co-chair of the Korean Organizing Committee for the tournament and vice-president of the FIFA, his popularity surged. Capitalizing on his fame, Chung created his own party, People's Unity of the 21st Century, and ran for the presidency. Because of Roh's low popularity, some members of the MDP proposed that Chung Mong-jun should be considered as the MDP nominee.

In the meantime, an incident that had occurred in June 2002 resurfaced and had a tremendous impact on the presidential election. During a U.S. military exercise on June 13, 2002, a U.S. armored vehicle accidentally killed two teenage girls. After the incident, the United States Forces Korea (USFK) command issued a statement of regret but failed to formally apologize, arguing that the view of the road was blocked. The Korean people were outraged and thousands went to the streets. As protests intensified, U.S. officials, including top military commanders and the ambassador, extended their apologies for the incident.[33] When the two U.S. soldiers involved in the accident were acquitted in December in a U.S. military court, however, thousands of people protested again, and anti-American sentiment rose sharply.[34]

[33] D. Kirk, "Koreans Protest U.S. Military's Handling of a Fatal Accident," *New York Times*, August 4, 2002

[34] Russel Honore, commanding general of the 2nd Infantry Division at that time, wrote in his book that the initial statement by the U.S. Forces' Press Secretary trying to explain the incident was a mistake. The South Korean people expected an apology for the teenaged girls' death. When the statement did not include

Table 6. *2002 Presidential election results*

Roh Moo-hyun	48.91%
Millennium Democratic Party	
Lee Hoi-chang	46.59%
Grand National Party	

Because of his previous anti-American political stance, Roh's popularity started to rise.

Because Roh and Chung Mong-jun were competing for essentially the same voters – those who did not support Lee Hoi-chang – they devised a plan to determine who would run against Lee Hoi-chang. They agreed to have one television debate followed in the subsequent days by a public opinion poll. The winner of the poll would be the winning candidate. When Roh came in with 46.8 percent to Chung's 42.2 percent, Chung withdrew his candidacy and joined Roh's campaign. The two still had important differences, however, because of sharply different backgrounds. Roh came from a poor family and, as an attorney, often represented labor, whereas Chung was from a *chaebol*-owner family and shared interests with management. A few hours before the end of the official campaign period, Chung abruptly withdrew his endorsement of Roh, ending an awkward relationship.

When the votes were counted, Roh won by a small margin of 2.3 percent, as shown in Table 6. After losing his second presidential election, Lee Hoi-chang announced his retirement from politics. The election had several important political implications. For the first time, parties used an American-style primary to select their nominees. This new system allowed citizens to participate in the presidential candidate selection process, pushing South Korea's political development one step further.

Unlike in previous elections, the generational gap played a significant role in the 2002 presidential election. Lee, the GNP candidate, received strong support from those aged fifty and older. He was pro-United States and largely preferred the status quo, although he also

an apology, they were outraged. By the time U.S. military leaders realized this cultural difference between the United States and South Korea, it was too late. See R. Honore, *Survival: How a Culture of Preparedness Can Save You and Your Family from Disasters* (New York: Simon and Schuster, 2009).

called for political reforms to end corruption. By contrast, Roh advocated drastic change and proposed progressive policies. He was popular among low-income groups and the younger generation, especially people in their forties and younger. These clear differences in candidate preferences between generations were unprecedented in South Korean political history.

In addition, the Internet played a key role in this election. *Roh Sa Mo*, the Internet-based group organized by Roh Moo-hyun supporters, introduced a new campaign technique. Because it successfully carried Roh's campaign strategy and raised funds, the *New York Times* wrote after the election, "For years, people will be debating what made this country go from conservative to liberal, from gerontocracy to youth culture and from staunchly pro-American to deeply ambivalent ally – all seemingly overnight. . . . But the most important agent of change has been the Internet."[35]

Another implication of the election of Roh Moo-hyun was the end of the "Three Kims" era – three dominant Korean politicians with the last name of Kim: Kim Young-sam, Kim Dae-jung, and Kim Jong-pil. The three politicians had their own factions and had dominated South Korean politics for decades. Thus, Roh's victory meant the beginning of a new political generation.

The Roh Moo-hyun Administration

One of the most notable differences between the Roh Moo-hyun administration and previous ones was the sources of personnel. Previous administrations filled cabinet and Blue House positions with politicians, career bureaucrats, and major university professors who were generally in their fifties or older. The Roh administration, however, filled these positions with people outside the mainstream and primarily from 386 generation politicians. Despite their young age (late thirties and early forties) and lack of administrative experience, they filled many important positions, particularly in the Blue House, based on their close relationship with President Roh. Former Blue House Press Secretary Yoon Tae-young and former Director of Blue House State Briefing Room Lee Kwang-jae are good examples.

[35] H. French, "Online Newspaper Shakes Up Korean Politics," *New York Times*, March 6, 2003.

Another source was *Minbyun* (Lawyers for a Democratic Society), an organization of progressive lawyers who played an important role in defending democratic activists during the authoritarian governments. Former Minister of Justice Kang Keum-shil and former Director of the National Security Agency (later, National Intelligence Service) Ko Young-koo were members of *Minbyun*. A third source was university professors. Previous administrations recruited professors from top universities (the so-called SKY Universities [Seoul National, Korea, and Yonsei Universities]), but the Roh administration appointed academics from non-major universities who advocated a progressive political ideology. Examples include Kyungpuk University professor Lee Jung-woo, who became Chief of the Blue House National Policy Office, and his successor Kim Byung-joon, a professor at Kookmin University. Finally, some civil society leaders also joined the Roh government; for example, Jeong Chan-yong was appointed chief of Government Administration and Home Affairs. By filling many posts with outsiders, the Roh government named itself *Chamyeo-Jeongboo* (Participatory Government).[36]

From the beginning, the Roh Moo-hyun administration faced problems because of its weak power base. President Roh was not indebted to any elite politician and did not belong to a particular faction. He also lacked the political skill to communicate with the opposition. His political orientation was based on the perception that corrupted elites were only interested in protecting their vested interests by maintaining the status quo, whereas the economically and socially disadvantaged were politically weak. Thus, the Roh administration pursued enhanced welfare policies, but the GNP enjoyed the majority in the National Assembly and was able to block much of President Roh's agenda.

Moreover, many members of his own party, the MDP, were loyal to former President Kim Dae-jung. Because they had wanted to replace Roh with Chung Mong-jun as the MDP's candidate, President Roh and former President Kim and his followers had an awkward relationship. These ties were was further strained when President Roh approved the GNP's request for an independent counselor's special investigation into funding provided to North Korea prior to the historic summit on June 13, 2000. Kim Dae-jung and most MDP

[36] H. Lee, "South Korea in 2003: A Question of Leadership?" *Asian Survey* 44 (2004): 130–8.

members strongly opposed the special investigation. When the independent counselor concluded that the Kim Dae-jung government illegally provided $500 million to North Korea through the Hyundai Corporation, former President Kim Dae-jung felt betrayed.[37] Because of the strained relationship with former President Kim Dae-jung and his followers, President Roh Moo-hyun and his close allies created a new party, *Yeolin Uri Dang* (Open Our Party) in November 2003.[38] This was yet another indication of South Korea's weak and personalized party system.

The creation of the Uri Party had an unexpected ramification for President Roh Moo-hyun because it opened the way for cooperation between the MDP and the GNP, a very unusual occurrence. On March 12, 2004, for the first time in history, the National Assembly, based on the cooperation between the MDP and the GNP, passed an impeachment resolution of President Roh Moo-hyun. According to the ROK Constitution, the measure then moved to the Constitutional Court for a final decision. The reason for the impeachment was President Roh's repeated statements supporting the Uri Party in the upcoming National Assembly election in April 2004 despite warnings from the National Election Commission (NEC) that the president should stay neutral in elections. South Korean law bars its current president from campaigning for a particular party or candidate. President Roh was suspended, and Prime Minister Ko Kun became acting president. The media showed lawmakers of the Uri Party weeping loudly on the floor after the impeachment measure passed, and supporters of President Roh went to the streets protesting the decision.

The impeachment of President Roh produced a serious political backlash for the GNP and the MDP. On April 15, about a month after the impeachment, South Korea held National Assembly elections. President Roh remained out of office while awaiting the final decision of the Constitutional Court. Voter sympathy for President

---

[37] During the investigation, chairman of the Hyundai Corporation, Jung Mong-heon, committed suicide, and Park Ji-won, Kim Dae-jung's Blue House chief of staff and special envoy to North Korea, was sentenced to twelve years in prison for playing a key role in illegally providing $500 million to North Korea and taking $15 million in bribes. In May 2006, however, the Supreme Court ruled that there was not enough evidence to support the bribery allegations, although Park was guilty of wrongdoing in the illegal provision of $500 million to North Korea. See *Donga Ilbo*, May 25, 2006. Park was pardoned in February 2007 and elected as a member of the National Assembly in the 2008 election.

[38] H. Lee, "South Korea in 2003: A Question of Leadership?" 2004.

Table 7. *2004 National Assembly election results*

Party	District seats	Proportional seats	Total seats
Uri Party	129	23	152
Grand National Party	100	21	121
Democratic Labor Party	2	8	10
Millennium Democratic Party	5	4	9
United Liberal Democrats	4	0	4
Independents	3	0	3
			299

Roh and disappointment with MDP and GNP lawmakers regarding the impeachment produced significant support for Uri Party candidates. In the election, voters chose 152 Uri Party candidates, as shown in Table 7, and gave them a majority, which would help President Roh pursue his policy initiatives should he be able to remain in office. On May 14, the Constitutional Court overruled the National Assembly's impeachment decision, allowing President Roh to remain in office. The Court maintained that President Roh's support for the Uri Party did violate campaign laws, but it was not sufficiently serious to impeach him.

Support for the Uri Party and President Roh did not last long, however, as the Roh administration attempted to suppress conservative newspapers. In South Korea three main daily newspapers – *Chosun Ilbo, Donga Ilbo*, and *Joongang Ilbo* – have approximately 70 percent of the South Korean market share. They were all conservative and critical of the Roh administration. To suppress political criticism from these papers, the National Assembly passed a law that capped the market share of these newspapers at 60 percent. These newspaper companies filed a lawsuit, however, and, in June 2006, the Constitutional Court ruled that the law was unconstitutional. The public was upset with this legislation and with the Roh administration in general. As a result, the main opposition GNP won almost all the by-elections until the end of President Roh's term.[39]

The year 2007 saw heavy coverage of the next presidential election scheduled for December 17. In the GNP primary, Lee Myung-bak and

[39] J. Lie and M. Park, "South Korea in 2005: Economic Dynamism, Generational Conflicts, and Social Transformations," *Asian Survey* 46 (2006): 56–62.

Park Geun-hye, daughter of the late President Park Chung-hee, had a neck-and-neck competition. Park Geun-hye repeatedly attacked Lee Myung-bak for corruption, including tax fraud, illicit real estate deals, and alleged involvement in the BBK stock price manipulation case. Among these, the alleged involvement in the BBK case was the most serious issue. BBK was an investment consulting company founded by Kim Kyung-joon in April 1998 based on a partnership with Lee Myung-bak. Later, Kim Kyung-joon took $38 million through stock price manipulation and fled to the United States as 5,200 investors lost approximately $60 million. Because Lee Myung-bak and Kim Kyung-joon had been together for about a year, the key question was whether Lee Myung-bak was involved in the stock price manipulation. Until he was cleared by the Prosecutor's Office, Lee Myung-bak was under heavy attack, but eventually he won the GNP primary and faced four other candidates in the December 2007 election.

There were some unexpected surprises in the 2007 presidential election. Lee Hoi-chang, two-time presidential nominee of the GNP who had retired from politics directly after the previous presidential election, came out of retirement and entered the presidential race as an independent candidate.[40] Considering that his running would split the conservative vote, just like Lee In-je's candidacy did in the 1997 presidential race, conservatives were concerned.

Another surprise was the end of the Uri Party and the creation of a new party for the presidential election. To overcome the unpopularity of the Roh administration, former members of the Uri Party and a few dissidents from the MDP and GNP formed the Unified Democratic Party (UDP) in August 2008.[41] Chung Dong-young, former television news anchor and Minister of Unification in the Roh government, was chosen to be the UDP's presidential nominee. He had a very weak showing, however. The former CEO of Kimberly Clark Korea, Moon Gook-hyun, also joined the race by creating the Renewal of Korea Party. These surprises, however, did not have much impact on the election outcome. Lee Myung-bak, the GNP candidate, won a landslide victory, as shown in Table 8. His win brought the end of a ten-year-long left-wing government and the beginning of a conservative administration.

---

[40] After the election, he created the Liberty Forward Party (LFP) so that he could continue to be an important player in politics.

[41] UDP and MDP merged into the Democratic Party in February 2008.

Table 8. *2007 Presidential election
results*

Lee Myung-bak	48.7%
Grand National Party	
Chung Dong-young	26.1%
Unified Democratic Party	
Lee Hoi-chang	15.1%
Independent	
Moon Gook-hyun	5.8%
Renewal of Korea Party	
Kwon Young-kil	3%
Democratic Labor Party	

The Lee Myung-bak Administration

President Lee was inaugurated as the seventeenth president in February 2008. Just like President Roh Moo-hyun, he came from a poor family and attended a commercial high school. While in college, as president of the student council at Korea University, he participated in protests against the normalization of the Korea–Japan relationship, which led to a brief imprisonment. After college, he joined Hyundai Construction, where he was exceptionally successful and rose to the rank of CEO. While at Hyundai, he developed the image of a bulldozer, which helped him to become elected mayor of Seoul in 2002. He successfully carried out public transportation reform and the Chonggyecheon project[42] against severe opposition, which became high-profile achievements and created an image that he got things achieved. His success as Seoul's mayor and CEO of Hyundai Corporation vaulted him to his win in the presidential election.

In April 2008, the GNP won a significant majority in National Assembly elections, as shown in Table 9. Despite this strong majority in the legislature, however, the Lee administration suffered from a series of crises, and President Lee received heavy criticism for his cabinet appointments.

[42] Chonggyecheon is a brook that ran through downtown Seoul but was covered by an overpass. Because of safety concerns, then–Seoul City Mayor Lee Myung-bak started a project to open up the stream. There was strong opposition from merchants and environmental groups, but Mayor Lee pushed through the project. Now Chonggyecheon is one of the most visited tourist sites in Seoul.

Table 9. *2008 National Assembly election results*

Party	District seats	Proportional seats	Total seats
Grand National Party	131	22	153
Democratic Party	66	15	81
Liberty Forward Party	14	4	18
Pro-Park Alliance	6	8	14
Democratic Labor Party	2	3	5
Creative Korea Party	1	2	3
Independents	25	0	25
			299

Of his fifteen nominees, thirteen were accused of tax evasion or violation of real estate laws, and three of them had to withdraw their nominations prior to confirmation hearings before the National Assembly. These nominees were all wealthy landowners living in the Kangnam area, a wealthy region south of the Han River in Seoul that symbolizes affluence in South Korea. Thus, the media called Lee's first cabinet "Kang Buja cabinet" after a well-known actress named Kang Buja (Buja means "rich people" in Korean). Another satiric name given to the cabinet was "Ko So Young S-line cabinet," also taken from a famous actress's name. It referred to graduates of Korea University, members of Somang Church, those of Youngnam origin, or those who worked in the Seoul city government during Lee Myung-bak's tenure as mayor of Seoul. President Lee Myung-bak is from the Youngnam area, graduated from Korea University, and attended Somang Church. Because he nominated only those he knew well through these connections, his appointments received heavy criticism.

Criticism of President Lee's cabinet appointments was only the beginning. During a visit to the United States, President Lee agreed to the resumption of U.S. beef imports that had been suspended in 2003 because of concerns about mad cow disease. After the visit, *PD Notepad*, an investigative news program on MBC, a progressive TV station, aired a report showing cattle that could not stand or walk and implied there was still a serious danger of U.S. cattle being infected. The program heightened public concerns about the safety of U.S. beef. Thousands of people went to the streets and joined a candlelight vigil that lasted for weeks. After the Lee administration secured extra health safeguards from Washington, such as importing only U.S. cattle fewer than 30 months old because younger cattle have less danger of infection, the protests subsided.[43] The Seoul District Court also ordered MBC to air another report in July 2008 that the danger of mad cow disease was exaggerated and that there were errors in their earlier report.

Despite the heavy criticism of his cabinet appointments and antigovernment protests about U.S. beef imports, President Lee's appointment strategy did not change, and he continued to face condemnation because of this issue. His policy of reducing income tax and corporate tax rates has also been severely criticized by the opposition party and the left. Conflicts between the left and the right continue. Recently, many professors from the left made public declarations concerning the regression of democracy in South Korea, and academics from the right responded with public statements defending the Lee government.

The Lee administration received further criticism in the wake of the suicide of former President Roh Moo-hyun. The so-called Park Youn-cha gate started in November 2008 when the National Tax Service provided an audit of Park Youn-cha, CEO of Taekwang Corporation and a supporter of former President Roh Moo-hyun. After seven months of investigation, the Prosecutor's Office indicted twenty-one people, including two former National Assembly speakers, other lawmakers, and government officials. According to the investigation report, Park gave money to politicians and government officials without being questioned because of his close ties with the Roh family, especially President Roh's brother. In addition, the Prosecutor's Office revealed that Park Youn-cha provided President Roh's family with $6.4 million. Park Youn-cha later confessed that he had provided the money. Was President Roh aware of this bribery? Circumstantial evidence indicated that he knew about this while in office. This was the first time a South Korean president and his wife had ever been called in for interrogation. Because President Roh always touted his clean image and record, it was a shocking blow to his reputation and a public humiliation.[44]

---

[43] S. Choe, "South Korea and U.S. Reach Deal on Beef Imports," *International Herald Tribune*, June 22, 2008.

[44] "The Entity of the Park Gate and the Limit of Investigation." *Chosun Ilbo*, June 12, 2009.

Table 10. *Select indicators of socioeconomic participation of women*

High ranking posts held by women (%)	1990s	2000s
Government (Fifth grade and above)	5.8% (1989)	9.6% (2007)
National Assembly Members	1.0% (1992)	13.0% (2006)
Local Assembly Members	0.9% (1992)	14.5% (2006)
School Principals	2.5% (1990)	9.3% (2007)
University Presidents	8.1% (1990)	10.2% (2007)
University Professors	13.8% (1990)	18.0% (2007)
Physicians	12.7% (1990)	19.7% (2007)
Dentists	10.7% (1990)	23.0% (2007)
Doctors Practicing Oriental Medicine	3.5% (1990)	13.5% (2007)

Source: O. Lee, "More Gender Equality, But Women Still Held Back," in *Social Change in Korea*, ed. K Kim and the *Korea Herald* (Seoul: Jimoondang, 2008), 169.

On May 23, 2009, former President Roh jumped off a cliff behind his residence and killed himself. When the Prosecutor's Office started the investigation of Park Youn-cha, opposition party members distanced themselves from Roh and did not strongly oppose the investigation. After Roh's death, however, they severely criticized the tax investigation and prosecution strategies targeted against Roh Moo-hyun's confidants, alleging it drove him to commit suicide. The prosecutor's office was also under heavy attack for a harsh investigation procedure because Roh was called in to testify instead being asked to answer questions on paper, the typical procedure for questioning a high-ranking government official. Thousands of people stood in line to pay tribute to the late President Roh. The Lee administration received severe criticism, including allegations that the Roh investigation was political revenge. Others, however, argued that President Roh killed himself because he was embarrassed about the tarnishing of the anticorruption image he had worked to develop throughout his political career. The country was severely divided over his death, and the issue remains a sore spot in South Korean politics.

In addition to struggles in the political arena, South Korea also experienced important social change that stemmed from modernization and democratization. One of the most obvious was the increased role of women in society and in the economy. The transition to democracy along with the rise in educational attainment opened the door for women in many areas, as noted in Table 10. For instance, workforce participation of women increased from 36.6 percent in

1980 to 50.3 percent in 2006. In 2005, one of every three couples was a dual-income family.[45] In 1990, only 7.7 percent of women held managerial or administrative jobs, but the number increased to 18.8 percent in 2006. In 1985, only 15.2 percent of women aged eighteen to twenty-one attended college, but, by 2004, 50.7 percent of the same age group were college attendees. Moreover, in 2006, 44.7 percent of people who received master's degrees were women, and 27.3 percent of doctoral recipients were women.[46]

These changes can be attributed to several factors. Economic development provided more opportunities for women to receive higher education, and the transition to democracy allowed women to organize and articulate their interests. Westernization through globalization also introduced western ideas and increased the need for high-quality labor. In addition, the National Assembly passed a series of laws to improve women's rights, including the Equal Employment Law passed in 1987 and the new Family Law in 1989 to improve women's rights in the family. In 1999, the legislature passed the Law to Prohibit and Regulate Gender Discrimination, and, to facilitate greater participation of women in economic and social activities, the government created the Ministry of Gender Equality.[47] Despite the increase in women's participation in the economy and society, however, there is a long way to go. Regardless, these changes are an important step forward.

With greater participation of women in political and economic activities, the traditional values of the paternal society were gradually losing their place. The society started slowly accepting the idea of gender equality in many areas, including education, employment, and career prospects. For instance, according to the 1995 World Values Survey, 37 percent of South Koreans thought college education was only for men, but, in 2006, only 23 percent thought so. The 1995 survey also found that 63 percent of Koreans thought men make better political leaders than women, but the number in 2006 decreased to 48 percent. Although there is some improvement in people's perception toward gender equality, approximately one in four people still think college education is only for men, and approximately half of Koreans still believe that men would make better political leaders.

[45] M. Lee, "Dual Earners Call for Family-Friendly Society," *Social Change in Korea*, ed. K. Kim and the *Korea Herald* (Seoul: Jimoondang, 2008), 175–83.

[46] O. Lee, "More Gender Equality, But Women Still Held Back," in *Social Change in Korea*, ed. K. Kim and the *Korea Herald* (Seoul: Jimoondang, 2008), 167–74.

[47] O. Lee, "More Gender Equality, But Women Still Held Back," 2008.

These numbers are far from ideal, yet it is encouraging that changes are occurring.[48]

The increased role of women in the society, however, introduced a new issue – decreasing childbirth rates.[49] As more women worked, the traditional division of labor based on gender – men are the bread-winners and women care for the household and children – was losing its place. Despite these changes in women's roles, social change, such as sharing family responsibilities, is not keeping pace. According to a survey, the average time spent on domestic duties by working wives is three hours and twenty-eight minutes, compared to only thirty-two minutes for husbands. Consequently, the average age of marriage and childbearing is rising. Moreover, the number of women who do not marry is soaring, and the average number of births per woman is declining significantly. For example, in 1995, only 26.6 percent of women between the ages of twenty-five and thirty-four residing in Seoul, the capital city of South Korea, were unmarried, but the number rose to 50.5 percent in 2005.[50] According to the World Health Organization, South Korea's fertility rate – the average number of births per woman – is the lowest in the world at 1.19.[51] As a result, the average family size, including parents, decreased from 4.5 in the early 1980s to 2.9 in 2007.[52] The Korean Statistics Office estimates population growth between 2005 and 2010 to be 0.30 percent, which is lower than the world average of 1.18 percent. In fact, South Korean population is expected to decline in 2018.[53]

The life expectancy of South Koreans is increasing, however, because of improved medical care and technology. Low birth rates along with longer life expectancy are leading to an aging population. Currently, the population older than sixty-five is 11 percent of total population, yet this number is estimated to increase to 38.2 percent in 2050, which is the highest among the Organisation for Economic

---

[48] K. Kim, "Family Values Changing – But Still Conservative," in *Social Change in Korea*, ed. K. Kim and the *Korea Herald* (Seoul: Jimoondang, 2008), 146–56.

[49] Another significant reason for decreased childbirth per woman is the high cost of child education.

[50] M. Lee, "Dual Earners Call for Family-Friendly Society," 2008.

[51] "Introduction of Childbirth Promotion Policy in Kangnam-Gu," *Chosun Ilbo*, July 23, 2009.

[52] H. Byun, "Homophobia and the Snail Family in Korea," in *Social Change in Korea*, ed. K. Kim and the *Korea Herald* (Seoul: Jimoondang, 2008), 184–93.

[53] "Korea, Pressing Need for Urgent Escape from Low Childbirth and Aging Population," *Chosun Ilbo*, July 10, 2009.

Co-operation and Development (OECD) countries. During the same period, the population younger than fifteen is estimated to decrease from 16.2 percent to 8.9 percent, and the average age of the total population will increase from 37.3 to 56.7. In other words, there will be more people older than sixty-five than younger than fifteen in 2050. This means that the aging population will be a significant economic burden on the younger generation unless birthrates increase significantly.[54] A declining and aging population has important strategic implications for South Korea's economic and political future. As a result, Minister for Health, Welfare and Family Affairs Jeon Jae-hee has made this issue an important priority to address in the years ahead.[55]

Another issue that requires attention is the increasing number of foreign residents in South Korea. For centuries, South Korea has been ethnically homogenous, and therefore social tolerance for diversity has been weak. In May 2009, however, the foreign population in South Korea reached 1.1 million, 2.2 percent of the total population, and approximately 12 percent of the marriages were international. Moreover, because of a sex ratio imbalance, men in rural areas have had a hard time finding spouses. Some of them have met their wives in China or Southeast Asian countries through marriage arrangement agencies. As a result, approximately 40 percent of couples in rural areas are international couples, which resulted in approximately 110,000 mixed-blood children.[56] This number is estimated to increase to 1.7 million by 2020. This raises serious questions about South Korea's national identity. How the country will adjust to becoming a more diverse and multicultural society will be a major challenge in the years ahead.[57]

Another question accompanying the increase in foreign residents and international marriage is racial discrimination. Because South Korea has been ethnically homogenous for centuries, this rather sudden demographic change raised many concerns regarding the treatment of foreign residents and naturalized immigrants, including the protection of foreign labor workers from abuse and military service laws. For instance, mixed-blood children are not required to serve in

---

[54] "Korea, Pressing Need for Urgent Escape from Low Childbirth and Aging Population," *Chosun Ilbo*, July 10, 2009.

[55] J. Lee, "Jeon to Tackle Low Birthrate," *Korea Herald*, July 30, 2009.

[56] D. Lee, "Foreign Residents Exceeds 1 Million," *Donga Ilbo*, August 6, 2009.

[57] O. Lee, "National Identity in the Age of Globalization, "*Social Change in Korea*, ed. K. Kim and the *Korea Herald* (Seoul: Jimoondang, 2008), 320–8.

the military, which will have to be changed. To deal with these issues, some liberal lawmakers supported by the Justice Ministry attempted to pass legislation against racial discrimination without success. Those who oppose the racial discrimination law argue that improving the rights of foreign residents, particularly foreign workers (because most foreign residents are labor workers), may provide privileges to foreigners at the price of Korean workers.[58] As a result, there has been no progress in legislation dealing with these issues.

Conclusion

In 1997, Kim Dae-jung, the opposition party candidate, won the presidential election. This was the first victory in a presidential election by the opposition party, an important step to further democratic consolidation. Yet the usage of old political tactics and ongoing political scandals indicated that South Korea was relatively young in its democratization. In 2008, after a decade of progressive governments, the Lee Myung-bak administration changed the political leadership from the left to the right. During the early period of the Lee administration, the divisions between the left and the right were manifest. At the same time, South Korea has experienced much social change, such as the increasing role of women in the economy and society, low childbirth, an aging population, and increasing diversity with foreign immigrants. How South Korea deals with these issues will be critical for the country to continue its political and economic development in the future.

[58] B. Jung, "Debate Heats Up over Anti-racism Bill," *Korea Herald*, September 10, 2009.

4

Economic Development and Financial Crisis

The story of economic development in South Korea is phenomenal. Shortly after the country was liberated from Japanese colonial rule in 1945, South Korea was demolished during the Korean War, which began in 1950. The three-year war completely devastated the small country and destroyed most of its industries.[1] As a result, South Korea was one of the poorest countries in the world in the 1950s, and its economy was largely dependent on U.S. economic aid. In the 1960s, the economy began to change. With a government-led development strategy begun under Park Chung-hee, South Korea launched an economic development plan that promoted industrialization and increased exports and grew the economy at a rapid pace. For instance, South Korea's per-capita gross national income (GNI) in 1960 was a mere $76 but by 2007 increased to $20,045. Today, South Korea's Gross Domestic Product (GDP) is the thirteenth largest in the world at $970 billion, and it ranks twelfth in the world in total trade at $728 billion. In fewer than five decades, the war-torn economy became a global economic powerhouse.[2]

South Korea's economic success was driven by a government-led development paradigm, which is based on top-down economic directives and regulations from the government rather than a liberal market system. Using depoliticized institutions to intervene in private business under a slogan calling for economic development, authoritarian governments regularly acted to upgrade the country's industrial infrastructure and improve international competitiveness.[3] The

[1] Its GDP was a mere $1.5 billion and per-capita GDP was only $70 in 1954.

[2] See the Korean Government Web site, http://www.korea.net.

[3] R. Wade, *Governing the Market: Economic Theory and the Role of Government in East Asian Industrialization* (Princeton, N.J.: Princeton University Press, 1990).

Korean government also planned and implemented growth-oriented economic policies, such as export-oriented industrialization (EOI) policy, which aims to expedite industrialization by promoting exports of goods so that the country enjoys an international comparative advantage.[4] To this end, the government provided preferential credit allocation and tax breaks to export-oriented industries. Moreover, the government had disciplined accounting without budget deficits and kept inflation in check to stabilize its currency value for export promotion. For the same purpose, the Korean government suppressed the labor movement and co-opted labor with government-sponsored unions to keep wages down.

In addition to the role of government in its economic success, South Korea enjoyed high rates of private savings and investment as well as quality, highly educated human capital with relatively low labor costs. High rates of domestic savings allowed the country to be less dependent on foreign capital, and heavy investment in education produced a quality labor force.[5] The South Korean people were also willing to work long, hard hours for national pride and a better life for their children. All of these factors made a significant contribution to economic development in South Korea.

Since launching its first economic development plan in 1962, South Korea enjoyed average annual growth rates close to 10 percent until it faced the first threat of crisis in the 1970s from the two oil shocks. The first oil shock in 1973, caused by the Arab oil embargo that was part of the Arab–Israeli conflict, raised inflation rates from 3.2 percent to 20 percent in 1974, yet South Korea still managed economic growth of 4 to 6 percent during 1972 and 1975.[6] The second oil crisis, caused by the Iranian revolution in 1979, hit South Korea in conjunction with a poor harvest and political instability following the assassination of Park Chung-hee. South Korea experienced inflation rates greater than 20 percent, an export slowdown, and increased unemployment. As a result, the economy generated negative growth for the first time since

[4] A contrasting policy is import substitution industrialization (ISI) policy, which aims to reduce foreign dependency by promoting local production and consumption to reduce imports of industrial goods. This policy was widely used in Latin America, whereas EOI was commonly used in East Asia.

[5] A. Amsden, *Asia's New Giant: South Korea and Late Industrialization* (Oxford: Oxford University Press, 1989).

[6] S. Collins and W. Park, "External Debt and Macroeconomic Performance in South Korea," in *Developing Country Debt and Economic Performance*, ed. J. Sachs and S. Collins (Chicago, Ill.: The University of Chicago Press, 1989), 153–69.

the country started its economic rise in 1962.[7] To cope with these problems, the authoritarian Chun Doo-whan government restructured the economy, reduced inflation, and minimized the economic impact of the oil shock.

In the late 1980s, South Korea experienced the transition to democracy. Democratization had a significant impact on South Korea's political development, but it also had important side effects on the economy. Democracy allowed organized labor to grow, resulting in hikes in labor costs and a decline in international competitiveness. Legalization of labor unions aggravated labor-management conflict, and strikes were frequent, resulting in a drastic increase in lost workdays. The strikes and wage increases led to a dramatic decline in exports. At the same time, the government opened financial markets, allowing for a significant increase in international capital inflows. Short-term debt with less than a one-year maturity also increased during a short time period. These factors created a perfect storm for the Korean economy and led to a financial crisis in 1997. South Korea received a bailout from the International Monetary Fund (IMF) worth $56 billion, the largest in IMF history to that point. In this chapter, we discuss factors that contributed to South Korea's economic success, the second oil shock and economic adjustment, the effects of the transition to democracy on economic performance, and the 1997 financial crisis.

Economic Development

One of the dominant theoretical frameworks that explains South Korea's economic success is the government-led development paradigm, or the so-called statist approach. According to this approach, the state designs and implements economic policies, and the private sector follows the government's lead. Business enterprises are privately owned, but the government plays a significant role in managing the economy. Therefore, state autonomy and cooperation between government and dominant social, economic forces, such as *chaebol*, were crucial. With the government-led development approach, the South Korean government provided preferential credit allocation and tax

---

[7] J. Lee, "Economic Growth and Human Development in the Republic of Korea, 1945–1992," United Nations Development Program Occasional Paper 24, http://hdr.undp.org/docs/publications/ocational_papers/oc24aa.htm.

breaks to promote exports. Because of this favoritism, some family-owned business companies grew to become large enterprises owning divisions in a variety of sectors such as electronics, construction, automobiles, and chemicals.[8]

Because the authoritarian governments in the 1960s through the 1980s lacked political legitimacy, they focused on economic growth and political stability. To benefit from the preferable terms offered by the government, the *chaebol* worked with the government under its plan. Describing this relationship, sociologist Peter Evans writes that "government was embedded in a concrete set of social ties that binds the state to society and provides institutionalized channels for the continual negotiation and re-negotiation of goals and policies."[9]

Because President Park Chung-hee had come to power via military coup, he focused on economic development to compensate for his lack of political legitimacy. He also believed that economic growth was necessary to protect South Korea's security and reduce its dependence on U.S. economic aid. As long as South Korea relied on U.S. aid, Washington would have too much leverage over South Korean decision making. Because of poor natural resources, a large population, and the need to develop quickly, the Park Chung-hee administration adopted the government-led development approach and an EOI policy. As a first step, the South Korean government focused on transforming the economy from one dependent on foreign aid (particularly U.S. aid) to one that was more self-reliant and independent. Government expenditures focused on improving social and economic infrastructure to improve the foundation of the economy. Throughout the 1960s and 1970s, about one-third of gross domestic investment (GDI) concentrated on infrastructure improvement.[10] In addition, under the slogan of *suchul ipguk* (nation building through exports), the government determined credit allocation based on export orientation, set and monitored export targets, adopted preferential tax and credit allocation policy for export businesses, maintained an export-friendly trade regime, and supported international marketing efforts through

[8] Y. Lee, *The State, Society and Big Business in South Korea* (London: Routledge, 1997), 18–28.

[9] P. Evans, *Embedded Autonomy* (Princeton, N.J.: Princeton University Press, 1995), 12.

[10] H. Kim, *Han-gook-jung-chi I-ron* (The Theory of Korean Politics) (Seoul: Park-Young Sa, 1990), 135. See also B. Koo, *Han-gook-gyung-je-ui Yeok-sa-jeok Jo-Myung* (The Historical Approach on Korean Economy) (Seoul: Korea Development Institute, 1991), 188.

the Korean Trade Promotion Corporation (KOTRA) established in 1962.[11]

Because South Korea possessed limited capital and lacked advanced technology, the government initiated export promotion with labor-intensive light industrial goods, such as textiles, toys, and shoes. To facilitate technological improvement, the government increased its support to the Korean Institute for Science and Technology (KIST) established in 1961. To provide preferential credit allocation to export-oriented industries, the government purchased bank stocks to acquire the main banks. There were three reasons for this policy move. First, the government needed to maintain a favorable value of the Korean currency, the *won*, to stabilize exports. Exchange rates affect the price of export items, which in turn influences competitiveness in the international market. For South Korean goods to have a price advantage in international markets, the value of Korean currency was kept low. Second, the government moved capital from the private money market to banks by raising the interest rates of savings accounts, which became an important source of domestic investment. High interest rates on bank accounts attract people to deposit their money at the bank instead of using the private money market. Because banks gave loans to business companies, high rates of savings at the bank meant that more capital was available for domestic investment for new business or business expansion. Finally, these policies buttressed the government's autonomy by controlling credit allocation and limiting the boundary of interest rates. Because private firms received loans from banks, becoming a primary holder of bank stocks gave the government control of banks in terms of credit allocation and interest rates.[12]

With the South Korean government's efforts to maintain exchange rate stability, the *won* remained stable without significant hikes in its value. Furthermore, the government consistently devalued its currency to maintain a favorable exchange rate for exports. For instance, in 1964 the government devalued the *won* by 100 percent, then by another 20 percent in 1974, and by another 20 percent in 1980. Repeated devaluation increased inflation, however. To control inflationary pressure, the South Korean government kept its budget deficit under

[11] Y. Rhee, B. Ross-Larson, and G. Pursell, *Korea's Competitive Edge: Managing the Entry into World Markets* (Baltimore, Md.: Johns Hopkins University Press, 1984).
[12] S. Haggard, B. Kim, and C. Moon, "The Transition to Export-led Growth in South Korea: 1954–1966" *Journal of Asian Studies* 50 (1991): 850–73.

control and prohibited real wage increases from exceeding productivity growth. The government also employed various forms of price controls to combat inflation, including the Price Stabilization Act of 1973, which regulated prices on a wide range of items. When inflationary pressure became high again because of the construction boom in the Middle East and the second oil shock in the late 1970s and early 1980s, the government adopted tight fiscal and monetary policies. Throughout this development period, the South Korean government kept inflation under control to maintain its currency value to keep export items competitive in the international market and to promote domestic savings.[13]

The adoption of an EOI policy had four implications for the South Korean economy. First, South Korea became self-sufficient in light industrial goods and no longer needed to import these items. Second, there was a significant change in South Korea's industrial structure. Prior to the launch of an EOI policy, South Korea's industrial structure was based on primary industry, such as agriculture, fishing, and mining, which accounted for approximately 40 to 50 percent of its production. By the late 1960s, however, the primary and secondary industries, such as manufacturing and construction, were balanced at approximately 30 percent each of the industrial structure. Third, in the early 1970s, the South Korean government adopted the Heavy Chemical Industrialization (HCI) policy and started promoting capital-intensive exports instead of labor-intensive light industrial goods. As a result of these changes, the dependency of business on government credit allocation significantly increased, and government–business ties deepened further.[14] Finally, these measures were designed to eventually lead the economy to be competitive in international markets through gradual liberalization.[15]

Another notable role of government in South Korea's economic success was fiscal management and policy flexibility. For example, the HCI policy launched in the early 1970s required an expansionist fiscal

---

[13] K. Kim and D. Leipziger, "Korea: A Case of Government-Led Development," in *Lessons from East Asia*, ed. D. Leipzeiger (Ann Arbor: University of Michigan Press, 1997), 155–212.

[14] K. Kim and D. Leipziger, "Korea: A Case of Government-Led Development," ibid.

[15] G. White and R. Wade, "Development; States and Markets in East Asia: An Introduction," in *Developmental States in East Asia*, ed. Gorden White (New York: St. Martin's Press, 1988), 182.

policy. The government provided the necessary funds for the policy while maintaining a budget deficit of less than 3 percent of GDP during 1971 and 1979. Moreover, despite the first oil shock in 1973, the government continued export-oriented growth policies and enjoyed an average annual growth rate of 9 percent in the 1970s. As inflationary pressure increased, however, because of the second oil shock in 1979, the government quickly reduced its investment in the HCI policy and realigned the approach by forcing each business conglomerate to choose only one of the heavy industries for specialization. By doing so, the government reduced unnecessary competition between domestic firms and dealt with overproduction capacity. The authoritarian government had no fear of making quick policy shifts, and it implemented these changes effectively.[16]

Domestic Savings and Private Investment

Domestic savings and private investment are critical for economic growth because they provide crucial capital resources. Economists argue that it is necessary to maintain domestic savings of at least 12 to 15 percent of GDP to have proper investment levels for meaningful growth.[17] South Korea's domestic savings averaged approximately 10 percent of GDP in the 1960s but increased to 35 to 38 percent in the 1980s. Savings prior to the 1960s were modest because the government maintained low interest rates to promote export financing. In 1965, however, the government increased the deposit ceiling rate – maximum interest rates that can be paid on savings at federally insured commercial banks – from 15 percent to 30 percent to encourage higher interest rates. Because of the change, banks raised their rates and savings rose significantly. Since then, the domestic savings rate has been consistently above 30 percent of GDP.[18]

In addition to high interest rates, what led South Korea to enjoy high levels of domestic savings and investment? First, the South Korean government provided investment-friendly environments by maintaining macroeconomic stability. For instance, inflation was under control,

---

[16] Kim and Leipziger, "Korea: A Case of Government-Led Development."
[17] E. Hagen, *The Economics of Development*, 4th ed. (Homewood, Ill.: Irwin, 1986).
[18] In 2008, its domestic savings rate was 30.7 percent. Bank of Korea Web site, http://www.bok.or.kr/contents/total/ko/boardView.action?menuNaviId=551... boardBean.brdid=61029...boardBean.menuid=551.

the budget deficit was in check, exports were increasing because of EOI policy, and the economy was continuously growing. Second, as the economy grew, individuals and businesses enjoyed higher incomes, which significantly increased tax revenues.[19] In other words, there was a virtuous cycle occurring within the South Korean economy. With control of the financial sector, the government induced high rates of domestic savings through macroeconomic stability and business-friendly policies. Successful exports led to increased profits that were reinvested, leading to further economic growth. Third, because of the lack of a house mortgage system, South Koreans had to save enough money to buy houses in cash. Fourth, Koreans focused heavily on their children's education and were willing to devote a large percentage of family income to this goal. To finance higher education, South Koreans did not borrow funds and had to be careful savers. Thus, the mortgage and education systems enforced high savings rates.

Education

Although it has a population of 50 million, South Korea has a small land area. The country is about the same size as Indiana, but one-third of the land is mountainous and uninhabitable. Despite its mountainous terrain, South Korea has few natural resources. With a large population in a small area with few natural resources, job opportunities in South Korea are limited and competition is intense. As a result, the country has traditionally focused on education, and enrollments in secondary and higher education have grown significantly over time. Table 11 shows the pattern of higher education in South Korea since 1945, which demonstrates exponential growth in higher education enrollment.

As a result of heavy investment in education, South Korea enjoyed high-quality student performance in international rankings. According to a 2003 assessment, South Korea ranked third internationally in mathematics, second in reading literacy, fourth in science, and first in problem solving. In 2006, South Korea was ranked fourth in mathematics, first in reading literacy, and eleventh in science.[20] Because

---

[19] U. Heo and S. Kim, "Financial Crisis in South Korea: Failure of the Government-led Development Paradigm," *Asian Survey* 40 (2001): 492–507.

[20] Programme for International Student Assessment, http://www.pisa.oecd.org.

Table 11. *Growth of higher education in South Korea*

Year	Number of schools	Number of students	Number of instructors
1945	19	7,819	1,490
1955	74	84,996	2,626
1960	80	81,519	4,027
1970	168	201,436	10,270
1980	237	647,505	20,662
1990	265	1,691,681	42,911
2000	372	3,363,549	57,632
2005	419	3,548,728	66,862
2008	405	3,562,844	73,072

Source: Y. Kim. "Universalization of Tertiary Education," Research Report (2009). Korean Education Development Institute, 5. This is a short version of the table that appears there.

of South Korea's heavy investment in education and miraculous economic development, the World Bank describes South Korea as follows: "Korea's successful knowledge-based development experience offers many valuable lessons for developing economies. The country has invested heavily in education and training, boosting innovation through intensive research and development, and developing modern and accessible infrastructure."[21]

Although South Korea focused heavily on education, its education spending patterns are different from those of other developed countries. Whereas most OECD countries rely primarily on public spending on education, South Korea has a much higher level of private spending. For instance, in 2007, South Korea's public expenditure on education was 4.3 percent of GDP, which was similar to the OECD average of 5 percent.[22] In 2008, however, South Korean families' private spending on education reached 7.3 percent of their total family consumption. This is significantly higher than the average private spending on education by families in other OECD countries. For example, the average private spending on education by families

[21] World Bank Web site, http://web.worldbank.org/WBSITE/EXTERNAL/
COUNTRIES/EASTASIAPACIFICEXT/KOREAEXTN/0,,menuPK:324651
~pagePK:141159~piPK:141110~theSitePK:324645,00.html.
[22] H. Lee, "Education Spending Hits Record High," *Korea Times*, February 28, 2008; J. Na, "Korea to Hike Spending on Public Education," *Korea Times*, May 15, 2009.

in the United States and Japan in 2008 was 2.6 percent and 2.2 percent, respectively. In the same year, the average private spending on education by families in the United Kingdom, France, and Germany was 1.4 percent, 0.8 percent, and 0.8 percent, respectively. In other words, the average spending on education by South Korean families is nine times more than that of families in France and Germany.[23]

Economists Robert Barro and Jong-wha Lee describe the value of education concerning economic growth: "A greater amount of educational attainment implies more skilled and productive workers, who in turn increase an economy's output of goods and services. An abundance of well-educated human resources also helps to facilitate the absorption of advanced technologies from developed countries."[24] Consequently, education has played an important role in South Korea's economic success.

The Second Oil Shock and Economic Adjustment

South Korea enjoyed high rates of growth and economic stability until it was hit by the second oil shock in 1979. The shock followed in the wake of the Iranian revolution that deposed the Shah and brought the Ayatollah Khomeini to power. The unrest disrupted Tehran's oil production, which stayed low even after the new government was established. As a result, the global petroleum price skyrocketed, and South Korean inflation increased to almost 20 percent. Initial government efforts to lower inflation were not very successful.[25] As a result of the international recession caused by the oil shock, the demand for South Korean exports also declined. To stabilize the economy, the Chun Doo-whan administration employed aggressive economic policies. First, to control inflation, the government froze its expenditures in 1984, raised interest rates, and reduced available credit. To this end, the administration froze government salaries and the price it paid farmers for rice to subsidize their production. Moreover, the Chun government adopted a tight fiscal policy and reduced the budget

---

[23] "The Average Spending on Education by Korean Families is Three to Nine Times More than That of Advanced Countries," *Chosun Ilbo*, October 19, 2009.

[24] R. Barro and J. Lee, "International Data on Educational Attainment: Updates and Implications," *Oxford Economic Papers* 3 (2001): 541.

[25] Kim and Leipziger, "Korea: A Case of Government-Led Development," 1997.

deficit by 39 percent by 1985. Because of these policies, the inflation rate remained less than 3 percent from 1983 to 1987.[26]

Second, the South Korean government attempted to overhaul the country's economic structure. South Korea's growth relied heavily on the success of the *chaebol*. In an effort to reduce this dependency and create a more stable overall economy, the government implemented the Policies for Restraining Economic Centralization in 1980. This policy introduced a cap on credit allocation to the *chaebol* and required the government's approval before a *chaebol* could launch a new business. The Chun government also introduced the Monopoly Regulation and Fair Trade Act in 1981 to reduce the role of government in the economy and promote competition in the market. There were two implications of this policy move. First, it was an attempt to change the political-business ties by increasing government influence on the *chaebol* through limiting *chaebol* expansion. Second, the government changed its credit policy by redirecting some of the credit allocation from the *chaebol* to medium and small-sized enterprises, although it still largely concentrated on supporting the export-oriented *chaebol*.[27]

Third, to improve the effectiveness of the national economy, the Chun administration "restructured" businesses by pressuring the companies to improve their performance or closing them down. As a result, fifty unprofitable companies were liquidated through acquisition, seventeen companies were merged, and one company was put under legal management. By 1988, approximately seventy companies had been reorganized in some form. Moreover, the government changed its approach to promoting economic growth. Rather than maintaining direct involvement in the economy through preferential tax policies and credit allocation to export-oriented businesses, the government abolished these strategies and put greater effort toward improving the business environment and economic infrastructure.[28]

These policy changes successfully controlled inflation, and the South Korean economy avoided the impact of the second oil shock,

---

[26] S. Haggard and C. Moon, "Institutions and Economic Policy: Theory and A Korean Case," *World Politics* 42 (1990): 210–37.

[27] U. Heo, H. Jeon, H. Kim, and O. Kim, "The Political Economy of South Korea: Economic Growth; Democratization, and Financial Crisis," *Maryland Series in Contemporary Asian Studies (Monograph Series)*, University of Maryland School of Law, 2008.

[28] Heo et al., "The Political Economy of South Korea: Economic Growth; Democratization, and Financial Crisis."

resuming its strong economic performance. For instance, in 1980, its economic growth rate was −1.5 percent, but the average growth rate in the 1980s was approximately 8 percent. There are two important points that should be noted here. First, most economic policy measures employed by the Chun Doo-whan administration were possible because it was an authoritarian government. As a result, a strong, autonomous state could aggressively pursue its policy goals, employing nondemocratic policy measures with few obstacles, and do so quickly. Second, this period was a turning point at which the South Korean government reduced its direct role in the economy and gave way to a more liberalized economy, although the government still played a leading role in guiding the country's economic development.[29]

Democratization, the Roh Tae-woo Administration, and the Economy

When President Roh Tae-woo came to office, the South Korean economy still enjoyed high rates of growth, with 12.1 percent in 1988. Exports remained the engine of economic development by growing 27 percent from the previous year.[30] The transition to democracy, however, ushered in many changes. First, democratization introduced new values, such as better distribution of public wealth, freedom of speech and press, and political participation, which led to fundamental changes in the government's economic development approach. The formerly suppressed labor sector started to organize, demanding higher wages and better working conditions, which led to frequent strikes and increased labor costs. For example, the number of unionized labor workers in 1980 was 948,000, but this increased to 1,267,000 in 1987. The authoritarian governments had harshly suppressed the labor movement to keep wages down so that South Korean exports remained competitive in global markets, but the transition to democracy opened the door for a robust labor movement. The average annual wage increase in the first half of the 1980s was 5.5 percent, but wages went up by 15.3 percent from 1986 to 1995 and 45 percent from 1987

[29] P. Evans, D. Rueschemeyer, and T. Skocpol, *Bringing the State Back In* (Cambridge: Cambridge University Press, 1985).
[30] Economic Planning Board, *Korea Statistical Yearbook* (Seoul, 1990).

to 1989.[31] Wage hikes in manufacturing were particularly high, with an annual average increase of 26 percent during the same period.[32] In addition, farmers joined the labor movement, demanding a significant increase in the price the government paid to purchase their rice and the amount of money in the government loan program for farmers. To address these demands, the Roh government invested $6 billion during the next ten years for the farmers' loan program. Politicians, particularly opposition party leaders, supported the labor movement and initiated other populist policies for their own political gain. Thus, political advantage instead of economic vision dominated many of these economic policy decisions.[33]

Labor strikes and lost workdays also increased significantly. In 1985, prior to democratization, the number of lost workdays due to strikes was only 64,000. After the transition to democracy, however, it increased to 4,487,000 in 1990.[34] These changes significantly decreased South Korea's productivity and international competitiveness. Entrepreneurs lost their will and ability to stay in manufacturing, which led businesses to look abroad for cheaper labor and fewer strikes. As a result, South Korea's foreign investments, particularly in the United States, China, and Southeast Asia, sharply increased[35] and moved from manufacturing to real estate and stock markets.

Another noticeable change was increased freedom of speech and press that focused on the abysmal wealth gap between the rich and the poor (binbu kyokcha in Korean). By reporting on conspicuous overconsumption of the nouveau riche, the media highlighted unequal wealth distribution, which heightened public dissatisfaction with the rich. To make matters worse, the wealthy tried to defend their vested interests (kidukkwon in Korean), which further stirred public anger. The Roh Tae-woo government did not directly intervene in the economy or adopt specific policies to deal with the issue, however. As a result, the public, regardless of their wealth, were disappointed with the Roh administration and mocked the Roh government by calling

---

[31] C. Kang, "Segyehwa Reform of the South Korean Developmental State," in Korea's Globalization, ed. S. Kim (New York: Cambridge University Press, 2000), 76–101. See also R. Bedeski, The Transformation of South Korea: Reform and Reconstruction in the Sixth Republic under Roh Tae Woo 1987–1992 (London: Routledge, 1994).

[32] Oh, Korean Politics, 113.

[33] C. Kim, The Korean Presidents, 230–5.

[34] See ILO, Task Force on Industrial Relations, World Labour Report 1997–98: Industrial Relations, Democracy, and Social Stability (Geneva: ILO, 1997), Table 4.3.

[35] Oh, Korean Politics, 114.

it the "no" government (anarchy) and the president "mool (water) Tae-woo," meaning incapable government or president.[36]

These sudden changes resulted in poor economic performance. Inflation during 1990 and 1992 increased to 13 to 19 percent. The value of real estate skyrocketed by 27.5 percent in 1988 and another 32 percent in 1989. The trade surplus became a deficit of $5 billion in 1990 and grew to $10 billion in the following year.[37] These alarming economic indicators raised fears within all sectors of South Korean society of the potential of a crumbling economy. As a result, labor-management relations temporarily improved, which reduced the number of strikes. This change was a short-term fix rather than a permanent solution for labor-management conflict and the wealth gap between the rich and the poor, however. These issues reemerge later, leading to further divisions in South Korean society.

The Kim Young-sam Administration and the 1997 Financial Crisis

When President Kim Young-sam came to office, he emphasized two policy goals: cleaning up corruption and *segwehwa* (globalization). Citing an old Korean saying, "Upstream must be clean to keep the downstream clean," he announced that he would not take any political contributions from business entrepreneurs. This declaration was believable; because South Korea had transitioned to a democracy, a president could serve only a single, nonrenewable term of five years, meaning that President Kim could not run for another term. President Kim's declaration also meant the end of the long-lasting, vicious cycle of political-business ties that gave the *chaebol* preferential credit allocation without going through the proper lending process of business analysis and securing collateral. In return, these corporations provided slush funds to the president called a "ruling fund" or, to politicians and statesmen, a "political fund." These political-business ties led to

---

[36] Oh, *Korean Politics*. Because of the lack of policy visions and implementation, a South Korean economist argued that the Roh Tae-woo administration provided the weakest economic leadership since the 1960s. J. Chung, "Daetongruyung ui kyongje Leadership (Presidents' Economic Leadership) (Seoul: Hanguk Kyungje Sinmunsa, 1994), 250–4. See also C. Kim, *The Korean Presidents*, 234.

[37] K. Schoenberger, "Speculators Fuel Real Estate Fever in South Korea," *Los Angeles Times*, March 18, 1990.

corruption and public demands for accountability, as had occurred in the trials of Chun Doo-hwan and Roh Tae-woo discussed in Chapter 2.

To further advance his anticorruption initiative, President Kim adopted two measures: a requirement for politicians to disclose their assets and the real-name financial transaction system. For the first measure, President Kim Young-sam voluntarily disclosed his assets, and cabinet members, ranking bureaucrats, and National Assembly members followed suit. In the wake of these disclosures, the media had a field day scrutinizing the numbers. Subsequent investigations discovered countless discrepancies between actual market values and the reported amounts. Approximately fifteen hundred government officials resigned from their positions following allegations that they abused their government positions to increase their wealth. To institutionalize this policy, the government crafted the Ethics Law for Public Officials, and the National Assembly passed this into law on May 20, 1993.[38]

The second policy measure to clean up corruption was the real-name financial transaction system, designed to promote transparent financial dealings. This measure required that all individuals and businesses have the same name on their resident registration, bank accounts, and tax identification information. Under the old system, individuals could use multiple aliases or the names of friends, relatives, and acquaintances to hide information. The new system required all financial transactions, including regular banking, stock trading, and security deals, to use real names. This policy was expected to reduce tax dodging and illegal monetary transactions. Soon after adopting this policy, stock trading and financial transactions slowed. As a result, a number of small and medium-sized enterprises became insolvent, but the economy gradually adjusted to this system and improved the transparency of financial transactions.

The second goal of President Kim Young-sam was to change the South Korean economy to cope with the challenges of globalization under the slogan of *segwehwa*. To this end, the administration opened South Korean financial markets by easing or removing government regulations on international financial transactions, including foreigners' possession of stocks and real estate. Another reason for this policy

---

[38] Y. Na, Asset Disclosures by Public Officials (Seoul: Pullbit Publishers, 1993). See also Oh, *Korean Politics*.

move was South Korea's pursuit of membership in the OECD, which required greater economic liberalization. Moreover, the government abolished the law that banned collective protests and legalized labor unions.[39] President Kim also reduced the power of the central government and transferred this authority to local governments. As a result, each province started electing its own governors and mayors, who had been appointed by the central government in previous administrations.

The impact of the Kim government's reform efforts was limited for two reasons. First, to reduce government intervention in the economy and allow the market to play a greater role, the government needed a fundamental overhaul of its economic structures, such as the elimination of the multitude of government agencies and departments that supervised economic activities. The administration, however, increased its role by creating the Fair Trade Commission (FTC).[40] As a result, the Kim government's reform efforts were largely confined to areas outside of government. Second, although it was necessary to have a change in corporate governance structure, especially in the family-owned *chaebol*, no reform efforts were made because the *chaebol* lobbied the government hard to oppose them. Instead of reforming the *chaebol*, the Kim administration actually adopted pro-*chaebol* policies that allowed them to expand without government interference. This is why Nicholas Eberstadt noted, "The Kim Young-sam government does not have a way to restructure the economy in any way that the *chaebol* do not have an enormous role."[41]

The 1997 Asian Financial Crisis

Although the Asian Financial Crisis began in 1997, the South Korean economy had already started showing signs of decline in 1996. Industrial output growth cooled from 14 percent in 1995 to 10 percent in 1996, and manufacturing sales growth also declined to 10 percent

[39] J. Cotton, *Politics and Policy in the New Korean State* (New York: St. Martin's Press, 1995).

[40] The head of the FTC was given full ministerial status, and it was required that other ministries consult with the FTC to make economic policies. This policy change increased the role of the FTC and sent a positive signal to the market that the government was supporting the market system. I. Pirie, *The Korean Developmental State: From Dirigisme to Neo-Liberalism* (London: Routledge, 2008), 96.

[41] Cited in D. Kirk, *Korean Crisis: Unraveling of the Miracle in the IMF Era* (New York: St. Martin's Press, 2000), 74.

in the same year from 20 percent in the previous year. Two-thirds of the *chaebol* reported low profits, and the South Korean stock market (KOSPI) fell by 35 percent in 1996. The trade deficit reached $23.1 billion in 1996, which was 4.8 percent of the GDP.[42] In February 1997, the *New York Times* reported the economic decline in South Korea, and, in the following month, the Korean Financial Research Institute and the Samsung Economic Research Institute issued separate public warnings of a potential crisis.[43]

To deal with the economic problems, the Kim Young-sam administration attempted to reform the economy with two bills. Based on the perception that the main cause of economic decline came from high labor costs due to rigid labor markets, the Kim administration submitted a labor reform bill to the National Assembly to allow businesses to lay off workers. The logic behind this bill was that, since the creation of the Korean Confederation of Trade Unions (*Minjunochong* – KCTU), organized labor had become more influential and powerful, resulting in more lost workdays due to strikes, which damaged international competitiveness and worsened the economic decline. Thus, the labor reform bill was designed to make labor markets more flexible and reduce the power of the KCTU. Although the bill was an outcome of negotiations within the Tripartite Commission of Labor, Business, and Government (*Nosajong wiwonhoe*), which was formed to deal with labor-management issues, the proposal faced strong opposition from labor unions. When the bill came to a vote in the National Assembly, opposition parties stalled the measure, largely to curry favor with labor. Instead of continuing negotiations, the ruling party passed the bill during a late-night session without the presence of opposition lawmakers. Citizens were outraged by this move and enormous protests followed, forcing President Kim to rescind the bill in the face of this strong public backlash.

In January 1997, the Hanbo Steel Company, one of the thirty largest *chaebol*, collapsed because of a $6 billion debt. This bankruptcy revealed a political scandal involving large-scale bribery and kickbacks, which had a significant impact on the Korean economy and politics.

---

[42] U. Heo, "South Korea: Democratization, Financial Crisis, and the Decline of the Developmental State," in *The Political Economy of International Financial Crisis*, ed. S. Horowitz and U. Heo (Lanham, Md.: Rowman & Littlefield Publishers, 2001), 151–64.

[43] A. Pollack, "South Korea: Despite World-Class Economy, Sense of Decline," *New York Times*, February 4, 1997.

Shortly thereafter, another *chaebol*, Sami Steel Corporation, collapsed, and Kia Motors requested bankruptcy protection. The bankruptcies of these corporations left toxic assets to financial institutions, which created serious financial trouble for lenders. A review of existing lending practices and better supervision of financial transactions were imperative.

To this end, the Kim Young-sam administration submitted a financial reform bill in August 1997. The bill was designed to enhance the supervision of lending practices by creating a new government agency that would oversee all financial institutions. A turf battle occurred, however, between the Bank of Korea and the Ministry of Finance regarding which of them this new agency would report to, as the Bank of Korea oversaw commercial banks whereas the Ministry of Finance guided other financial institutions. In addition, the financial bill included the government's efforts to grant more autonomy to the Bank of Korea so that monetary policy decisions would be independent of politics. Unfortunately, partisan politics dominated the National Assembly, and the bill did not pass until the crisis broke out at the end of the year. To make matters worse, it was revealed that President Kim's son was involved in corrupt lending. This scandal significantly weakened President Kim's political and moral authority, leading to his early lame-duck status. As a result, the Kim government was never able to raise or address fundamental issues in the financial sector, such as deregulation, transparent lending practices, effective monitoring of financial transactions, and reforming the corporate governance structure.[44]

In 1997, signs of financial trouble were not limited to the South Korean economy. In July, the Bank of Thailand abandoned the fixed exchange rate system and adopted the managed float system because of its inability to support the pegged exchange rate.[45] For a smooth transition, the Thai government requested "technical assistance" from the IMF. The financial trouble in Thailand and the change in Thai

---

[44] U. Heo and S. Kim, "Financial Crisis in South Korea: Failure of the Government-led Development Paradigm" *Asian Survey* 40 (2000): 492–507.

[45] Thailand had a fixed change rate system, which pegs the value of Thai *baht* to the U.S. dollar. Because of the lack of foreign exchange reserves, however, the Thai government halted the fixed exchange rate system and adopted the managed float system, which allowed fluctuation of exchange rates according to market conditions, while the government (or the central bank) occasionally intervened to change the direction of its currency value.

currency had significant implications for South Korean financial organizations because they had $173 million in loans invested in Thailand. The economies of Malaysia and Indonesia started showing signs of collapse as well. Because approximately one-third of South Korean exports went to Southeast Asian countries, financial trouble in Thailand and others in the region had serious repercussions for the South Korean economy.

As a result, worry among foreign investors about the potential fallout from the struggling economies in Southeast Asia on other parts of Asia spread rapidly, and foreign capital started leaving Asian markets at a rapid pace. In October 1997, the Hong Kong stock market crashed, raising concerns that another Asian economy was about to collapse. Credit rating organizations, such as Moody's Investors Service and Standard & Poor's, rushed to downgrade financial institutions in South Korea, which led foreign investment to dry up in the KOSPI. Exchange rates skyrocketed from 890.5 Korean *won* for $1 in July 1997 to almost 2,000 *won* for $1 in early 1998. The South Korean government, however, did not have enough foreign exchange reserves to defend the value of the Korean *won*. In November 1997, the South Korean government requested that the IMF provide a rescue fund to bail out the economy.

On December 4, the IMF announced a $56 billion bailout for South Korea and facilitated the conversion of short-term loans of $15 billion to long-term debts through negotiations with the South Korean government. The IMF also required the South Korean government to adopt tight fiscal policies and high interest rates, which led to a flood of bankruptcies and high unemployment rates. This economic trouble was rather sudden and surprising, considering the long period during which the South Korean economy had enjoyed high rates of growth. What caused the financial crisis in South Korea?

One of the most immediate causes was the significant increase of dollar-denominated short-term loans in a short time period and the shortage of foreign currency reserves to defend the value of the Korean *won*. Multiple factors were part of this growing problem. According to a report by the Ministry of Finance and Economy for the National Assembly, dollar-denominated short-term loans increased by $3.2 billion between December 1996 and March 1997 and totaled $64.2 billion.[46] What caused this unusual increase in short-term loans?

---

[46] "Total National Debt Exceeds $110 Billion," *Chosun Ilbo*, October 1, 1997.

Beginning in the 1980s, the government gradually reduced its direct role in the economy but still played a significant role in financial markets until the early 1990s by providing preferential credit allocation to export-oriented industries and by regulating foreign exchange transfers. International lending by South Korean financial institutions and the ownership of domestic property by foreign residents was also strictly limited. Because of these heavy regulations, a large but unregulated curb market[47] developed that played a significant role in financial markets. Because of its unofficial nature, this curb market had high interest rates and was very risky, but individual households, along with small and medium-sized enterprises, relied heavily on curb markets because of difficulties in obtaining credit from the formal credit market.

When President Kim Young-sam came to office, his administration started deregulating financial markets as part of an effort to join the OECD. To this end, the Kim government opened the KOSPI to foreign investors in 1992. To facilitate stock transactions, the cap on foreign ownership of company shares was increased to 15 percent. As a result of these changes, foreign ownership of South Korean stocks in 1993 was a mere 5.8 percent, but in 1997 it almost tripled, reaching 14.6 percent.[48] To further ease international capital flow, the government lifted the ban that prevented businesses from obtaining loans from foreign financial institutions to purchase capital goods and eased constraints on foreign currency banking.

In addition, the Kim government attempted to include the operations of the curb market in formal financial dealings through quasi-financial institutions called merchant banks (in Korean, *chong-hap-kum-yung-sa* or simply *chong-kum-sa*, meaning comprehensive financial company). Merchant banks were not allowed to conduct regular banking activities, such as accepting deposits, but they were permitted to provide credit to firms based on loans from commercial banks or other mercantile banks. Because these merchant banks dealt with non-banking financial transactions, such as leases and installment loans, they previously were virtually unregulated by the government, although they continued high-risk lending to small and medium-sized firms. Because of the lack of regulation and the ban on *chaebol* ownership

---

[47] A market for non-bank lending or the sales of stocks not listed on a stock exchange.
[48] H. Smith, "Korea," in *East Asia in Crisis: From Being a Miracle to Needing One?* ed. R. McLeod and R. Garnaut (London: Routledge, 1998).

of commercial banks, many *chaebol* and insurance companies established merchant banks or quasi-financial institutions. Although the
risks were high, the merchant banking business became an important
cash supplier to the *chaebol* because of high rates of profit resulting from
high interest rates during the good economic period. For the same
reason, many commercial banks also entered into merchant banking
and quasi-financial businesses.

In addition, the South Korean government stopped its formal
appointment of bank presidents as part of financial liberalization.
Further deregulation followed, which included fewer restrictions on
financial product innovation and the interest rates on various forms
of borrowing, a relaxed cap on the amount banks could lend, and
greater autonomy for bank management.[49] As a result, the number of
merchant banks and similar types of quasi-financial institutions sharply
increased. Because of the lack of supervision, however, these institutions operated in a lax regulatory environment, investing in foreign
assets and directly borrowing from foreign financial institutions with
lower interest rates than domestic commercial banks.

These changes in the financial sector introduced a drastic increase
in foreign debt. In December 1996 the amount of long-term foreign
debt was $2.4 billion, but it increased to $46.1 billion by March 1997.
Particularly alarming was the significant increase in short-term debt,
from $3.2 billion to $64.2 billion during the same period. Driving
the sudden hikes in short-term loans were the interest rate differences
between South Korea and the rest of the world. The South Korean
government had maintained high rates of interest to promote domestic
savings. Taking advantage of the interest rate differences, South Korean
commercial banks and other financial institutions, such as merchant
banks, took short-term loans in the international market and lent
them to domestic firms. Although international loans were often short
term, most credit allocations to domestic firms were made for long-
term investments, as firms were seeking fixed assets (e.g., real estate,
factories, and machinery) for business expansion. During the booming
economic period, this lending practice worked well, as short-term
loans were often rolled over. All lenders, financial intermediaries, and
borrowers enjoyed the benefits of these transactions.

As the economy started slowing down, however, the return on
investments declined. Because of unusual corporate governance of

[49] OECD, *Economic Survey of Korea* (Paris: OECD, 1996).

financial institutions in South Korea, poor business performance of borrowers became a serious problem for lenders. Much of the problem was caused by a lack of transparent lending practices, including business analysis and securing collateral. Because the South Korean government was the largest shareholder of most commercial banks prior to the crisis and appointed the chief executives of these banks, excessive lending based on political-business ties was common. Thus, the sluggish economy left domestic intermediary lenders vulnerable because foreign creditors called in their short-term loans based on economic concerns. This created a chain reaction of business collapses, leading to the bankruptcy of countless financial institutions during the 1997 financial crisis.

Another related issue was the lack of accounting transparency. South Korean foreign currency reserves were deposited in foreign branches of domestic banks. They gave loans to foreign subsidiaries of domestic companies based on the foreign exchange reserves. When the economy was booming, these transactions were not problematic. Moreover, the amount of foreign currency reserves seemed to be sufficient. Then IMF managing director Michel Camdessus announced after an IMF investigation in mid-1997 that South Korea was unlikely to experience a financial crisis. When foreign capital started drying up and exchange rates began to rise, however, reserves disappeared quickly, and the Bank of Korea could not defend the value of Korean *won* because most of the foreign currency reserves were tied up in loans to domestic companies. In other words, there was a significant difference in the available amount of foreign currency on the accounting books and the actual amount available because a large portion of the foreign currency reserves became part of the nonperforming loans – loans in default – which was one of the causes of the crisis.

The Government's Response

Despite a number of warnings about the potential crisis, the government's response was limited. Some problems could have been fixed easily with minor adjustments. For instance, the increased debt was largely due to interest rate differences between South Korea and other advanced countries. By raising interest rates, this problem could have been fixed. When the Samsung Economic Research Institute issued a report noting the rapid increase of debt, particularly short-term debt, in March 1997, the government could have changed the interest rates to control short-term loans. No adjustment was made, however. When the LG Economic Research Institute warned of a possible foreign capital exodus and South Korea's weak crisis-coping capabilities in July 1997, appropriate measures should have been taken to prepare for the worst-case scenario, but the South Korean government did not take any measures to address the impending disaster.

The reasons for this may be found in both the lack of the political and economic institutions required to have a well-performing democratic market system that can respond to warning signs and President Kim Young-sam's lame-duck status. There are a number of explanations why there were no appropriate political and economic institutions in place. First, although South Korea had experienced the transition to democracy, conversion to a market-oriented system from a government-led economic development paradigm was a different matter. Economic reforms occurred slowly because government bureaucrats and economic technocrats resisted change, labor unions strongly opposed labor reform, and opposition parties refused cooperation for political gains.

The government-led development approach employed by Presidents Park Chung-hee and Chun Doo-whan from the early 1960s through the late 1980s allowed economic technocrats to drive economic growth to the highest levels possible. As long as the economy was growing, corruption stemming from the close relationship between political (politicians and bureaucrats) and economic (*chaebol* owners and bank presidents) elites was tolerated. With the transition to democracy, however, the public demand for economic freedom, less regulation, and transparent economic policy implementation rose significantly. Despite the heightened public demand, government bureaucrats and economic technocrats resisted liberalization because they did not want to give up their power over private business despite the market system's requirement of more freedom and less government intervention. This resistance delayed economic liberalization and the development of political and economic institutions for a democratic market system. For instance, when the Kim Young-sam administration submitted a finance reform bill to improve the supervision of lending practices, the Bank of Korea and the Ministry of Finance engaged in a turf battle instead of analyzing the merits of the bill. Considering that an economic crisis was looming, they should have focused on making policy adjustments to deal with the economic issues. The bill would have helped the Bank of Korea to operate independently from party politics. Because of the turf battle, however, the bill was delayed. Moreover, a study reported no improvements in the myriad of bureaucratic red tape across various government agencies for foreign direct investment between the Kim Young-sam administration and the Chun-Doo-whan government in the 1980s.[50] Thus, a delay in government structural adjustment led to the inadequate government response prior to the crisis.[51]

Another reason for the failure of timely economic liberalization was political gridlock and opposition to economic reform. Typically, newly democratized countries face reform in both political and economic arenas. In the implementation of reforms, the ruling party tries to provide equity so that groups share the benefits and costs of the reforms. Thus, the ability of the government to carry out reforms depends largely on the power of existing political and economic institutions as well as on the resistance of interest groups.[52] Prior to the crisis, the South Korean government had an opportunity to reform the economy. The *chaebol*, labor unions, the ruling party, and opposition parties, however, all acted against economic reform to protect their vested interests.[53] For instance, prior to the crisis, the Kim Young-sam administration attempted to reform the labor market with the labor reform bill. The bill would have allowed management to lay off workers according to business conditions, which would have made the labor market more flexible, but the government's efforts were defeated by strong opposition from labor unions and opposition parties.

The opposition parties and labor unions had a close relationship for mutual benefit. Although the unions opposed labor reform, they pressured the opposition parties to demand corporate governance reform, as corporate governance was largely based on family ownership and

---

[50] G. Corsetti, P. Pesenti, and N. Roubini, "What Caused the Asian Currency and Financial Crisis?" *Japan and the World Economy* 11 (October 1999): 305–73.

[51] H. Root, *The New Korea: Crisis Brings Opportunity* (Santa Monica, Calif.: Milken Institute, 1999).

[52] S. Haggard and R. Kaufman, *The Political Economy of Democratic Transitions* (Princeton, N.J.: Princeton University Press, 1995); N. Jesse, U. Heo, and K. DeRouen Jr., "A Nested Game Approach to Political and Economic Liberalization in Democratizing States: The Case of South Korea," *International Studies Quarterly* 46 (2002): 401–22.

[53] J. Mo, "Political Culture and Legislative Gridlock: Politics of Economic Reform in Pre-crisis Korea," *Comparative Political Studies* 34 (1999): 467–92.

lacked professional management. The opposition parties responded positively to the request because labor unions were strong supporters of the opposition parties, and the demand for reforming corporate governance undermined the current government while giving political advantage to the opposition. The *chaebol*, however, opposed allowing foreigners to gain a significant stake in *chaebol* governance by becoming major shareholders. Because responding to labor's demands for liberalization of corporate governance would likely have led to severe political costs for the ruling party and reduced contributions from the *chaebol*, the ruling party opposed corporate governance reform.

In summary, the *chaebol*, labor unions, the ruling party, and opposition parties all pursued their own interests, making it difficult for the government to develop a comprehensive and coherent liberalization policy that would satisfy all actors while still reforming the economy to avoid the severe downturn.[54] The Kia Motors case is a good example. When Kia Motors requested protection from bankruptcy, investors watched the response of the Kim administration. Following the economic logic of a market system, Kia Motors should have been allowed to go bankrupt. Opposition parties and labor unions, however, strongly demanded that the government accept Kia's request. Thus, the Kim government made a concession and protected Kia from bankruptcy. These moves made it difficult for the government to earn market confidence and eventually led investors to question whether the South Korean government had the capability and the will to deal with the crisis.[55]

In addition, President Kim Young Sam's lame-duck status also made an effective government response difficult. President Kim became a lame duck not only because he had only a short time left in office, but also because his son was indicted for involvement in the Hanbo corruption scandal. President Kim had come to office determined to clean up corruption. He introduced strong anticorruption measures and indicted two of his immediate predecessors, Chun Doo-hwan and Roh Tae-woo. Many high-ranking government officials implicated in these scandals lost their jobs because of the anticorruption campaign, yet President Kim's anticorruption reputation was severely damaged

[54] N. Jesse, U. Heo, and K. DeRouen Jr., "A Nested Game Approach to Political and Economic Liberalization in Democratizing States: The Case of South Korea," *International Studies Quarterly* 46 (2002): 401–22.

[55] Heo and Kim, "Financial Crisis in South Korea: Failure of the Government-led Development Paradigm."

when it was revealed that Kim Hyun-chul, one of his sons, was implicated in the Hanbo bribery scandal. As a result, the Kim Yong-sam government had little moral standing to push the reform policies prior to the crisis.

Conclusion

Direct intervention of the government in the economy played a key role in South Korea's economic success, but it also led to corruption and unusual lending practices. The transition to democracy brought in political liberalization, such as the legalization of labor unions, greater freedom of speech and press, direct popular election of the president, and the adoption of local autonomy. Economic reform did not follow because of resistance from social and economic actors, however. Instead, labor activism, rapid wage hikes, political and economic actors' efforts to protect their vested interests, and the lack of consistent macroeconomic policy resulted in an economic slowdown and eventually a financial crisis. There were no formal and informal rules or economic institutions in place commensurate with the effective functioning of democracy. Thus, the 1997 financial crisis in South Korea was a classic example of an immature democracy undermining the government's ability to manage the economy.

5

Economic Reform and the Korea–U.S. Free Trade Agreement

President Kim Dae-jung came to office in February 1998, only a few months after South Korea received its International Monetary Fund (IMF) bailout. Although President Kim won the 1997 presidential election by 1.6 percent, the slimmest margin of any previous South Korean presidential election, the Kim administration was in a much better position to implement reforms than was the previous Kim Young-sam administration. The political and economic environment had changed drastically in favor of reforms because of the financial crisis and the bailout. The IMF required the Kim government to implement reform policies to meet the conditions of the IMF bailout program. In addition, the new government under Kim Dae-jung's Millennium Democratic Party (MDP) had a close relationship with organized labor, making the labor sector more cooperative with the reform policies of the Kim Dae-jung government.

The first reform efforts by the Kim Dae-jung administration changed the government structure with a reorganization bill. The administration pointed to the Kim Young-sam administration's inadequate response to the warning signs of the 1997 crisis and attempted to improve the effectiveness and efficiency of the government in creating economic policy. With this bill, the Kim administration downsized the government and established the Planning and Budget Commission under the president's direct supervision for closer oversight of the economy.

The Kim government continued the reform drive with institutional and procedural reform to transform economic governance and meet the expectations of the IMF. With pressure from the IMF and the public, the long-stalled Bank of Korea (BOK) Act, part of the financial reform bill providing more autonomy from political control for the central bank, finally passed in the National Assembly on December 31, 1997. This law was designed to transform the BOK into a highly autonomous organization with the ability to make politically independent monetary policy decisions, such as controlling interest rates. This change was important because the role of the BOK formerly was limited to implementing credit allocation based on the government's guidance instead of making independent policy decisions.[1] This bill led to a number of important changes. First, the governor of the BOK instead of the minister of the Ministry of Finance and Economy (MOFE) became the head of the Monetary Policy Committee (MPC). To enhance autonomy of individual MPC members, the BOK Act made it nearly impossible for politicians to remove MPC members. Moreover, the act required that three of the seven MPC members be nominated by private business institutions, including the Korean Securities Dealers' Association and the Federation of Banks.[2] These private institutions represent the sector of the financial community that does not support active government intervention in the economy through industrial policies. The Act removed the power of the MOFE to overturn MPC decisions, and all requests by the MOFE to the MPC would need to be made public. As a result, the MPC became independent from political influence and equipped with almost complete control of monetary policies.[3]

In addition, the Act created the Financial Supervisory Commission (FSC, *Kumyoong Wiwonhoe* in Korean) to provide independent but unified financial supervision of the government. Prior to the crisis, four government agencies monitored banks, securities companies, insurance firms, and merchant banks, respectively. They were neither effective nor free from political control. Political elites manipulated financial regulations for their personal political and economic gain. Thus, it was necessary to have an independent regulatory agency to supervise financial institutions with consistent standards. To this end and upon an IMF request, the government created the FSC. The FSC has a wide range of authority, such as promulgating and amending

[1] S. Maxfield, "Financial Incentives and Central Bank Authority in Industrializing Nations," *World Politics* 46 (1994): 333–61.

[2] The other four members are nominated by the economic bureaucracy, including the MOFE.

[3] I. Pirie, *The Korean Developmental State: From Dirigisme to Neo-Liberalism* (London: Routledge, 2008). See also R. Emery, *Korean Economic Reform: Before and Since the 1997 Crisis* (Aldershot, United Kingdom: Ashgate, 2001).

rules of financial oversight, authorizing start-up business activities and financial institutions, and inspecting, auditing, and sanctioning financial institutions.[4]

The FSC's role in financial regulation has been criticized for two reasons. First, although the FSC was created to be autonomous, it was not completely free from political control. Because of the vagueness of the law, the MOFE provided the FSC with limited freedom in financial oversight and retained influence over the FSC. Second, despite the fact that the FSC was not totally independent from political influence, it intervened extensively in the economy to discipline financial institutions. Although the FSC was created to deregulate and supervise financial institutions without political influence, its members were appointed by the government, thereby increasing indirect government intervention.[5]

The Kim Dae-jung government also emphasized enhancing economic openness to attract foreign investment. To this end, the government adopted a number of policy measures: 1) elimination of most regulations on foreign investment; 2) liberalization of financial transactions and foreign land ownership; 3) increasing ceilings on foreign equity ownership from 26 to 55 percent; 4) loosening restrictions on foreign investment; 5) establishing the Korean Investment Service Center (KISC) to simplify the process of opening foreign businesses; 6) providing tax incentives to foreign investors; and 7) allowing autonomy for local governments to pursue foreign direct investment (FDI) through foreign investment zones. With these changes, average annual inward FDI increased from $1.2 billion between 1991 and 1996 to $2.9 billion in 1998, $5.2 billion in 1999, and $9.3 billion in 2000.[6] Foreign portfolio investment and foreign purchases of South Korean stocks also significantly increased. As of December 2005, foreign shares of South Korean stocks reached 40 percent of total stocks and 46.5 percent of the top-ten *chaebol*.[7]

The South Korean government adopted these policy changes to attract more foreign investment for two reasons. First, because of

---

[4] Y. Shim, *Korean Bank Regulation and Supervision: Crisis and Reform* (The Hague: Kluwer Law International, 2000).

[5] J. Shin and H. Chang, *Restructuring Korea Inc.* (London: Routledge, 2003).

[6] Influx of inward FDI has fluctuated since 2001. It plummeted to $3 billion in 2002 but increased to $9.25 billion in 2004. See United Nations Conference on Trade and Development, *World Investment Report 2006: FDI from Developing and Transition Economies: Implications for Development* (New York: United Nations, 2006), 301.

[7] Pirie, *The Korean Developmental State*.

foreign debts, South Korea was in dire need, and the government had to open up the market to attract foreign capital. Second, the South Korean government had learned from the 1997 financial crisis that industrial policies oriented toward domestic firms slow down the improvement of international competitiveness.[8] Because the government employed protection measures, domestic firms did not make the necessary adjustments to globalization to remain competitive. Reform efforts continued in the corporate, labor, and financial sectors, and we discuss these reform policies next.

Corporate Reforms

Economic reform generally deals with deregulation and liberalization because government intervention in the market via regulation distorts and disrupts the market. Economic reform in the corporate sector after the financial crisis, however, included government intervention to improve the profitability of some industries by the artificial downsizing of production capacity and the enhancing of some regulations, in addition to liberalization. Prior to the crisis, because of the lack of transparent accounting practices and regulation, corporations could only provide select information to investors. Thus, it was necessary to reform the corporate sector with respect to the accountability of management through corporate governance structure reform and enhancement of economic openness of firms through transparent accounting practices and financial transactions among the *chaebol* and their subsidiaries.[9]

To this end, as recommended by the IMF, President Kim Dae-jung met with the *chaebol* owners and business leaders to discuss corporate reforms as soon as he assumed office.[10] After a series of discussions with business leaders, the government announced the "five plus three" principles for corporate reform. The five principles were "enhancing transparency in accounting and management, resolving mutual debt guarantees among *chaebol* affiliates, improving a firm's financial structure, streamlining business activities, and strengthening managers'

[8] Ibid., 141–2.

[9] U. Heo and J. Woo, "South Korea's Experience with Structural Reform: Lessons for Other Countries," *Korean Social Science Journal* 33 (2006): 1–24.

[10] C. Kim, *The Korean Presidents*, 317. See also T. Park, "South Korea in 1997: Clearing the Last Hurdle to Political-Economic Maturation," *Asian Survey* 38 (1997): 1–10.

Table 12. *An overview of five plus three principles*

	Principles	Institutions and policy
Five Principles (Jan. 13, 1998)	Enhanced Transparency	Consolidated Financial Statements
		Outside Directors (50 Percent)
		Protection of Small Shareholders
		Collective Litigation
	Control Intra-Group Transactions	Ban on Intersubsidiary Debt Payment Guarantees
	Improved Financial Structure	Reduction of Debt–Equity Ratio to 200 Percent
	Streamlining Business Lines	Separation and Sale of Nonspecialized Affiliates
	Stronger Accountability	Accountability Provisions for CEOs
Three Principles	Improve Management Structure of Secondary Financial Institutions	Limits on Cross-Equity Holding at 7 Percent
	Limit on *Chaebol* Equity Investment	Cap on Total Amount of Equity Investment of 25 Percent of Net Assets
	Prevention of Irregular Inheritance and Gift Giving	Amendment of Related Laws

Source: J. Mo and C. Moon, "Business-Government Relations under Kim Dae-jung," In *Economic Crisis and Corporate Restructuring in Korea*, ed. S. Haggard, W. Lim, and E. Kim (New York: Cambridge University Press, 2003), 132.

accountability." The three supplementary principles were regulation of *chaebol*'s control of non-bank financial institutions, restriction on circular equity investment by *chaebol* affiliates, and prevention of irregular inheritance and gift giving among family members of *chaebol* owners.[11] An overview of these principles is provided in Table 12.

---

[11] J. Mo and C. Moon, "Business-Government Relations under Kim Dae-jung," in *Economic Crisis and Corporate Restructuring in Korea*, ed. S. Haggard, W. Lim, and E. Kim (New York: Cambridge University Press, 2003), 127–49.

The main five principles were designed to reform the top *chaebol*, including Hyundai, Samsung, and LG, and the three supplementary principles were for restructuring other *chaebol* as well as medium and small-sized firms. One of the problems of the top five *chaebol* was that they had expanded far beyond their original size, buying up subsidiary companies that often had no relationship to the company's main business. In many cases, these purchases were simply for the sake of making the *chaebol* larger rather than making the business more profitable. For the top five *chaebol*, the principles encouraged business swaps (the so-called Big Deals) to shed some of the subsidiaries and focus on the main business to decrease overcapacity and improve profitability. To this end, the Kim administration offered tax incentives and signaled a possible tax probe for the *chaebol* that did not comply. At the same time, the Kim government pressured these *chaebol* to sell marginal businesses and grant more autonomy to their subsidiaries. The government also employed "workout" programs under court receivership or composition proceedings. Court receivership involves an appointment of a receiver who manages the troubled company, allowing it to "work out" of its economic problems. By contrast, under composition proceedings, creditors and debtors have a settlement that is a lesser amount than the actual debt, and the current management of the financially distressed company retains control of the firm, although all of the company's assets could be lost to bankruptcy if it does not become profitable.

Restructuring strategies were tailored based on the size of the corporation, because "medium-sized *chaebol*s would not have too much shock to the economy even if they defaulted during the restructuring process. On the other hand, the five largest *chaebol*s were judged to be too large to be restructured by the commercial banks and thus were excluded from bank-led restructuring programs," relying instead on a government-directed effort at reform.[12]

Initially, the government planned business swaps in nine key industries to improve their international competitiveness by reducing excessive production capacity. Six business swaps among the *chaebol* followed, which substantially reduced production costs and eliminated excess capacity.[13] Under the Big Deal program Hyundai Motors

---

[12] K. Park, "Bank-led Corporate Restructuring," in ibid., 185.

[13] Scholars disagree on the success/failure of the Big Deal program. Weiss (2003) and Mo and Moon (2003) argue that this program was effective and significantly improved the international competitiveness of these industries. By contrast, Pirie (2008) asserts that this program was largely a failure because the scale of the

annexed Kia Motors; Samsung sold its auto business to Renault;[14] Daewoo Motors was sold to General Motors; Korea Aerospace Industries was created from a merger of the aerospace divisions of Hyundai, Samsung, and Daewoo; Hyundai purchased the semiconductor portion of LG; and Korea Heavy Industries and Construction (Hanjung) took over the power components of Samsung Heavy Industries and Hyundai Industries.[15] In addition, large *chaebol* pursued joint ventures with multinational corporations (MNCs) to improve their competitiveness and profitability. By doing so, these firms attempted to learn and improve their technological, marketing, and managerial expertise. LG Philips is a great example of a successful joint venture.[16]

In addition, many criticized the governance structure of most *chaebol* because *chaebol* owners dominated decision making through the group chairmanship, where these owners played the role of a control tower. These chairmen controlled group subsidiaries and made the ultimate decisions but were not responsible for any mismanagement. Thus, it was necessary to limit the power of *chaebol* owners so that management accountability became transparent. To rectify the situation, the Kim government pressured the *chaebol* to eliminate the group control tower system. By doing so, the corporate governance structure changed to a system in which each group subsidiary made its own business decisions and was responsible for these moves. In addition, the *chaebol* were required to employ outside directors as a check on their decision making. Although the mismanagement occurred before the reforms were enacted, the government pressured owners and managers to contribute their private assets to pay off debts and cover the loss of their management failures.[17]

Big Deal program was reduced and two of the top five *chaebol*, Daewoo and Hyundai, collapsed. L. Weiss, "Guiding Globalization in East Asia: New Roles for Old Developmental States," in *States in the Global Economy: Bringing Domestic Institutions Back In*, ed. L. Weiss (Cambridge: Cambridge University Press, 2003), 245–70; J. Mo and C. Moon, *Business-Government Relations under Kim Dae-jung*, 127–49.

[14] Technically, Samsung's sale of its auto industry to Renault is not a business swap between the *chaebol*. It is considered a business swap, however, because the South Korean government pressured Samsung to sell the auto business to downsize the country's auto production capacity and improve the profitability of the auto industry.

[15] S. Yoo, *Are the Chaebol the Real Culprits of the Economic Crisis?* (Seoul: Korea Development Institute, Bibong Press, 2000).

[16] "LG, Philips to Discuss Closer Cooperation," *Korea Herald*, June 8, 2002,

[17] Mo and Moon, "Business-Government Relations under Kim Dae-jung."

To enhance the transparency and reliability of accounting practices, the Kim Dae-jung government submitted two bills to the National Assembly: the Act on External Audit of Stock Companies and the Monopoly Regulation and Fair Trade Act. With the Act on External Audit of Stock Companies, the government forced the *chaebol* to submit financial statements containing accurate information about their firm's overall financial condition, including intersubsidiary shareholdings and debt payment guarantees, to ensure accurate information about the *chaebol's* financial management and condition. With the Monopoly Regulation and Fair Trade Act, the government dealt with the issue of debt payment guarantees among *chaebol* subsidiaries. These subsidiaries had taken on excessive loans through an arrangement in which they guaranteed each other's loans. This assured they could borrow more than a bank would normally allow based on the size of the company. To remove these existing debt guarantees, the legislation required *chaebol* to reveal their debt guarantees and banned them from making any future debt guarantees among subsidiaries of the same *chaebol*.[18]

To deal with the existing debts, the Kim government pressured the top five *chaebol* to reduce their debt/asset ratios to below 200 percent. To this end, the government abolished tax deductions for interest payments on "excessive" loans beginning in 2000. In response, the *chaebol* started selling some subsidiary companies, closing down inefficient businesses, and laying off workers to improve productivity. The government also developed the Capital Structure Improvement Plan (CSIP) to direct banks to negotiate with their debtor companies about the financial restructuring agreement.[19]

For firms smaller than the top five *chaebol*, the Kim government employed three supplementary principles. Among them, the government adopted workout programs to allow them to recover from their financial trouble, often with court receivership and composition. The FSC directed the restructuring process and made decisions with the intent of using public money to save these financial institutions. The FSC also made a decision regarding if, how, and to whom these institutions should be sold. In addition, the FSC made an arrangement

[18] H. Root, *The New Korea: Crisis Brings Opportunity* (Santa Monica, Calif.: Milken Institute, 1999).
[19] Mo and Moon, "Business-Government Relations under Kim Dae-jung." See also M. Cho, "Reform of Corporate Governance," in *Economic Crisis and Corporate Restructuring in Korea*, 286–306.

between banks and troubled small and medium-sized firms to restructure them. In the process, the FSC determined which firms would receive financial support.[20]

In terms of actual implementation of workout programs, credit banks took the lead by proposing restructuring procedures and the time needed for rehabilitation. In the process, creditors and subject firms negotiated remedy measures. If negotiations deadlocked, outside arbitrators intervened in the process to conclude an agreement. The South Korean government preferred this measure for small and medium-sized firms for two reasons. First, the South Korean government did not intend to allow these firms to pursue "self-directed restructuring," such as a business swap, because of their lack of financial resources. Second, the workout program allowed firms to continue to do business so that credit banks could increase the retrieval rate of their loans.[21]

The workout program began by establishing the Committee for Corporate Insolvency Evaluation (CCIE) in May 1998. Prior to the implementation of the workout program, the CCIE conducted an evaluation of 313 troubled firms. Among them, the CCIE selected 104 firms for the workout program. Despite the preevaluation of firms, only thirty-six successfully completed the program and recovered from financial trouble. Part of the problem was that the workout programs were not implemented based on economic logic. If some firms did not perform and had no hope for recovery, they should have been removed from the program, but a firm's regional base and political connections often kept it in the program. In other words, political considerations affected the implementation of the workout programs and delayed the dissolution of failing firms. Moreover, management was allowed to stay in control during the workout program. Instead of trying to get through the program, management pursued their own interests instead of the companies', raising serious ethical questions.[22]

Along with the workout programs, the government also reformed the corporate bankruptcy system. Prior to the crisis, the corporate reform system was rarely used because the Korean Asset Management Corporation (KAMCO) sold the assets of bankrupt firms through auctions before the bankruptcy process began under court oversight. The

[20] Pirie, *The Korean Developmental State*, 148.
[21] Park, "Bank-led Corporate Restructuring."
[22] Ibid.

corporate bankruptcy system was revised with the Rule on Corporate Reorganization Procedure (RCRP), which included two major changes. First, the new bankruptcy procedure based on the RCRP required consideration of economic efficiency as a criterion to qualify for judicial bankruptcy.[23] Second, the new system adopted an automatic freeze of the insolvent firm's assets from creditors filing to secure their claims. Moreover, the struggling firm was guaranteed the right to go through a settlement process, such as corporate reorganization, composition, or a workout program after the official bankruptcy.[24]

Labor Reforms

Prior to the crisis, labor reform failed because of strong opposition from labor unions and opposition parties. The Kim Dae-jung government had to make the labor market more flexible, however, to deal with the rapid decline in labor demand because of soaring interest rates and reduced product demand that forced South Korean businesses out of the market. Thus, based on the consent of the Tripartite Commission of Labor, Business, and Government, the government adopted major revisions in labor laws, including, when necessary, the legalization of worker layoffs by management.[25] With the new law, companies were able to lay off excess workers as well as outsource workers through a temporary work agency. Moreover, the new law allowed firms to replace workers on strike to continue production. This change was significant because labor unions used strikes as a tool to fight for better compensation. Worker replacement was rarely used, however.[26]

Many firms downsized their production capacity by laying off workers to improve their profitability. Insolvent firms also generated a significant number of jobless people. In addition, privatization of

---

[23] If a firm has two or more debtors and cannot pay off at least one of them, a court can declare bankruptcy based on the firm's or creditor's request.

[24] Y. Lim, "The Corporate Bankruptcy System and the Economic Crisis," in *Economic Crisis and Corporate Restructuring in Korea*, 207–32.

[25] Although the new law allowed management to lay off workers, firms were required to exhaust all possible measures, such as wage reduction, work sharing, avoiding new hires, and not replacing vacancies, to avoid it. Management also had to consult with labor union leaders about the details of layoffs.

[26] D. Kim, "The Korean Labor Market: The Crisis and After," in *Korean Crisis and Recovery*, ed. D. Coe and S. Kim (Washington, D.C.: International Monetary Fund and Korea Institute for International Economic Policy, 2002), 261–92.

Table 13. *Unemployment rate*

Year	Unemployment	Year	Unemployment
1995	2.07	1996	2.06
1997	2.62	1998	6.95
1999	6.58	2000	4.43
2001	4.02	2002	3.28
2003	3.57	2004	3.68
2005	3.73	2006	3.47
2007	3.25			

Source: http://www.indexmundi.com/south_korea/unemployment_rate.html. Compiled from various issues of *World Economic Outlook* by the International Monetary Fund.

publicly owned companies led to massive layoffs, with 18 percent of the labor workforce in these publicly owned companies losing their jobs from 1998 through 2000. Those who survived the layoffs faced reduced wages for longer hours. This change lowered labor costs, but unemployment rose from 3 to 4 percent prior to the crisis to 7 percent after these changes.[27]

To fight unemployment, the government spent approximately $19 billion during 1998 and 1999 on wage subsidies for job sharing and reemployment, unemployment insurance, public programs for the poor, a loan program for new businesses targeting venture opportunities, and training and placement services for the unemployed. These programs provided more than three hundred thousand jobs for workers and forty five thousand internships for new college graduates.[28] As a result, unemployment decreased (see Table 13).

Despite reduced labor costs and decreases in unemployment, the profitability of most firms did not improve because of fringe benefit costs for regular workers. To deal with this issue, companies hired more part-time, temporary workers, called "irregular" workers because the cost of these employees was less than half that of regular workers. As a result, the number of "irregular" workers soared, with 32.8 percent of the 14.1 million employed in 2003 hired as "irregular" workers. This change reduced production costs but cut overall income and

[27] See Korean Democratic Labor Party. *Kim Dae Jung Chongbu 3 nyon Pyonggawa Taean* (Evaluation of the Kim Dae Jung Government's First Three Years and Provision of Alternatives) (Seoul: Ihu, 2001), 267.

[28] D. Kim, "The Korean Labor Market," 265–7.

lowered private consumption, resulting in lower aggregate demand.[29] More "irregular" workers also meant a decrease in the rate of labor unionization because management–labor negotiations excluded part-time workers. The rate of labor unionization was 23.3 percent in 1989, but it decreased to 11.5 percent in 2000. Despite this decline after the 1997 crisis, labor–management relations remained a serious issue. Labor unions continued to be militant and confrontational while resisting reforms and restructuring. Frequent strikes for better compensation and working conditions significantly affected productivity and drove capital investment away.[30] For instance, Korea 3M cancelled its plan to expand its production facility. Carrier, an American company, closed its refrigerator production facility, and approximately one hundred workers lost their jobs. Officials from both companies pointed to labor–management conflict as the primary reason for their moves. During the period from January to June 2009, foreign corporations pulled approximately $1 billion dollars from South Korea.[31]

Financial Reforms

Before the financial crisis, loans were the primary source for corporate investment and business expansion, but there was no systematic check on lending practices by financial institutions. Risk control by screening projects based on business analysis, monitoring corporate performance, and securing collateral did not exist prior to the crisis.[32] Although there was no transparency in lending practices, the South Korean government implicitly guaranteed the loans of the *chaebol* without monitoring their activities and financial conditions.

---

[29] F. Lowe-Lee, "Economic Trends: IMF Report on Korea," *Korea Insight* (Washington, D.C: Korea Economic Institute, March 2004).

[30] According to the Ministry of Commerce, Industry, and Energy, South Korea lost approximately $1.7 billion of production and $608 million exports as a result of labor strikes in 2002. F. Lowe-Lee, "Improving Labor Market Flexibility: A Key to Economic Success," *Korea Insight* (Washington, D.C.: Korea Economic Institute, August 2003).

[31] During the same period, incoming FDI was $2.6 billion. Incoming FDI is still larger than outflow FDI, but the incoming FDI of $2.6 billion was a significant drop from $4 billion during the same period a year ago. Hostile and militant labor unions are pointed out as the main reason for declining FDI inflow and increasing FDI outflow. Y. Kim and J. Kim, "Foreign Corporations Tired of Militant Labor Unions and Leave Korea," *Chosun Ilbo*, October 28, 2009.

[32] T. Park, "South Korea in 1998: Swallowing the Bitter Pills of Restructuring," *Asian Survey* 39 (1999): 133–44.

According to economist Morris Goldstein, there was too much connected lending without proper control and oversight, something he
called "crony capitalism." South Korea was enmeshed in a serious
moral problem after the financial crisis broke. For instance, to improve
the liquidity of foreign currency, the Kim administration submitted
a bill to the National Assembly to provide a guarantee for foreign
debt incurred by domestic banks, and the National Assembly passed
it. These debts originated from the loans of private firms; if the firms
went bankrupt, the government paid the debt using public funds
despite the fact that they were private loans.[33]

To reform the financial sector, the government employed three different strategies. The first was privatization of publicly owned banks.
The government sold a large portion of its shares in banks to the private sector to end its involvement in management. Foreign investors
purchased many of the government shares because they were significantly devalued. As a result, foreign ownership of commercial
bank stocks soared. For instance, Newbridge Capital became the primary shareholder of Korea First Bank, one of the largest banks in
South Korea prior to the crisis. Lonestar took over Korea Exchange
Bank, and Citigroup purchased KorAm Bank. In addition, Goldman
Sachs, ING Group, Bank of New York, Commertz Bank, and Allianz
Group bought substantial shares of South Korean commercial banks,
which reached 59 percent of total equity in the South Korean banking
sector.[34]

The second strategy was supporting some of the major commercial
banks with public money for rehabilitation. To this end, the government poured huge sums into a handful of commercial banks to save
them from collapse. The Kim administration intended to strengthen
the commercial banks as the heart of its economic recovery strategy.
As a result, five major banks were placed under complete government control. For instance, the government purchased the majority
of equity in Woori Bank, the second largest in South Korea.[35] In
addition, the government spent approximately $80 billion between

---

[33] M. Goldstein, *The Asian Financial Crisis: Causes, Cures, and Systemic Implications*
(Washington, D.C.: Institute for International Economics, 1998).

[34] Pirie, *The Korean Developmental State*, 151–2.

[35] The government changed its approach later to promote the development of domestic banks to large, internationally competitive banks. To this end, the government
sold nationalized commercial banks to healthy domestic financial institutions. For
instance, Hana Bank purchased Seoul Bank in 2002.

1997 and 2004 to purchase all toxic assets from insolvent banks and to promote bank mergers by providing capital to raise their capital adequacy ratios (CAR).[36] CAR is a measure based on the ratio between capital and risk that indicates the stability and efficiency of financial systems around the world. In addition, the government improved its monitoring of the financial sector and heightened capital adequacy requirements on banks to 8 percent Bank for International Settlements (BIS)[37] ratio – capital/asset ratio – through the rules of the FSC and the Financial Supervisory Service.[38] Banks that failed to meet the criteria were forced to reduce their loan amounts to the corporate sector. With these changes, profits of commercial banks significantly improved starting in 2001.[39]

The third strategy was allowing non-bank financial institutions, such as merchant banks, to fail with virtually no support. As discussed in Chapter 4, prior to the crisis, the merchant banking sector grew because of lax control and the disparities in interest rates between South Korea and foreign countries. As a result, aggressive lending practices by the merchant banks without proper control and monitoring resulted in 20 percent of their loans becoming nonperforming, and the majority of them had no secured collateral. The government did not offer public money to save these struggling institutions. Instead, they were allowed to collapse, which led to twenty-eight of the thirty merchant banks closing their doors or merging with other financial institutions by 2004.[40]

In addition, the government made it easier to obtain consumer credit to boost domestic consumption and stimulate the economy. With a particular effort to promote credit card usage, the government provided tax incentives to merchants accepting credit cards, and

---

[36] Pirie, *The Korean Developmental State*, 152–3.

[37] BIS is an international organization of central banks that "fosters cooperation among central banks and other agencies in pursuit of monetary and financial stability. Its banking services are provided exclusively to central banks and international organizations." See http://www.bis.org.

[38] The BIS ratio indicates the solvency of a bank – the ratio between the risk-bearing capital and the risk-weighted assets.

[39] Despite the improvement, some scholars argue that the banking sector in South Korea has a serious problem in internal management structures because these banks still lack the ability to adequately assess business proposals, which may have serious ramifications for profitability in the long run. See C. Ahn, "Financial and Corporate Restructuring in Korea: Accomplishments and Unfinished Agenda," *The Japanese Economic Review* 54 (2001): 252–70.

[40] Pirie, *The Korean Developmental State*, 156–7.

individuals were allowed to have a tax deduction linked to credit card purchases. The government also removed the administrative cap on monthly cash advances from credit cards. As a result of these measures and the overall lack of capital in South Korea, credit card usage sky-rocketed, increasing from 39 million credit cards in 1999 to 105 million in 2002. During the same period, the number of credit card trans-actions increased more than sixfold. Additional factors that increased credit card use included low corporate loan demand, leading banks to increase the amount available for consumer lending; intensified com-petition in the credit card market by lowering lending standards; and lack of credit reporting.[41]

Increased domestic consumption spurred by credit-based purchases and the government's reform policies sparked South Korea's economic recovery and graduation from the IMF bailout program sooner than expected. Lingering effects of the crisis, such as high unemployment and low investment, continued, however. Moreover, the credit card bubble became a serious problem shortly after President Roh Moo-hyun came to office as credit-based consumption resulted in a signif-icant increase in household debt. Juggling these debts led to increases in borrower credit lines or the use of multiple credit cards to avoid payment delinquency. Credit card companies sensed trouble and tight-ened credit control, but tighter credit control resulted in more payment defaults, which soared by 41 percent to 3.7 million in 2003. Some credit card users committed suicide because of the distress. Increased credit card payment delinquency also hurt the credit card companies. Thus the Roh government stepped in and paid the debt for approx-imately one million people. The government also provided a rescue package of $4 billion to troubled credit card companies such as LG Card through the Korean Development Bank. The 2003 credit card crisis showed the importance of detecting early warning signs and proper government control of the credit card market.[42]

The Roh Moo-hyun Administration and the KORUS FTA

President Roh Moo-hyun was elected president in 2002 on a cam-paign platform that focused on wealth redistribution and income

---

[41] T. Kang and G. Ma, "Credit Card Lending Distress in Korea in 2003," in *Household Debt: Implications for Monetary Policy and Financial Stability*, Bank for International Settlements papers (Basel: 2009), 95–106.

[42] Kang and Ma, "Credit Card Lending Distress in Korea in 2003."

equality. To this end, the government adopted a number of economic policies, such as tax increases and enhanced welfare programs. The government instituted various types of taxes, such as an income tax for high-income brackets, a property tax, a capital gains tax on housing sales, and a comprehensive property tax. The comprehensive property tax was created in 2005 to impose a tax on large real estate holders whose property value of land and housing exceeded 600 million *won* (approximately $600,000). These tax increases for the wealthy were aimed at creating resources for enhanced welfare programs and curbing rising real estate values.[43]

The Roh government also promoted balanced development across the country. Almost half of the South Korean population lives in the Seoul metro area. This concentration of population drove housing prices sky high, and the local economy outside Seoul experienced economic decline. Thus, the Roh government attempted the relocation of the capital by creating a new administrative city south of Seoul. The government also pushed publicly owned companies to move their headquarters outside Seoul. This balanced development policy was designed to scatter the Seoul population and boost local economies outside the capital. The Constitutional Court ruled, however, that the relocation of the capital city would be unconstitutional. Moreover, people have been reluctant to leave Seoul, and instead, property values have simply increased in other parts of the country.

The Roh government was also friendly toward labor unions, which resulted in intensified strife between unions and management in various industries. Hostile labor–management relations, along with high wages and land prices, tight business regulation in the Seoul metro area, and slow economic growth, drove foreign capital away. For instance, FDI inflow was $8.997 billion in 2004, yet it steadily decreased to $7.055 billion in 2005, $4.881 billion in 2006, and, finally, $2.628 billion in 2007.[44]

In contrast to these left-oriented policies, the Roh government pursued a free trade agreement (FTA) with the United States. The initial reason for starting the negotiations was trade friction between the two countries. South Korea enjoyed a perennial trade surplus,

---

[43] C. Kim, *The Korean Presidents*, 2007.

[44] United Nations Conference on Trade and Development, *World Investment Report 2008: Transnational Corporations and the Infrastructure Challenge* (www.unctad.org/wir). See also M. Jung, *Korea's Sluggish Inward Foreign Direct Investment and Its Causes* (Seoul: Samsung Economic Research Institute, 2008); J. Kim, "Foreign Investors Turn Away from Korea," *Korea Times*, May 5, 2008.

whereas the United States complained about the deficit and unfair trade practices. Considering the alliance between the two countries, Seoul and Washington looked for a solution to deal with the issue. The two governments explored the possibility of an FTA by having think tanks and government agencies in both countries independently study the economic implications. After a long investigation of the economic effects of a bilateral FTA, numerous studies in both countries concluded that the arrangement would be beneficial to both, and negotiations for an FTA began in February 2006.

Despite the positive effects on the economy reported by multiple studies in both countries, an FTA between the two countries generated much intense debate from the beginning. As soon as the negotiations began, South Korean opponents launched an anti-FTA campaign by organizing the Korean Alliance against the Korea–U.S. (KORUS) FTA. According to the opponents, the FTA would allow South Korean markets to be dominated by comparatively cheap American agricultural products, while South Korean farmers would lose market share and suffer from decreased profits. Many farmers would eventually abandon their land, which would seriously hurt the rural environment as well as the economy.[45]

In general, the South Korean argument against the FTA can be summarized as follows: The FTA will open markets, and uncompetitive sectors of the South Korean economy will collapse, leading to increased unemployment. For instance, South Korea's screen quota, a critical shield for South Korea's film industry, will have to be abolished or at least reduced when the FTA is fully implemented. U.S. pharmaceutical companies and gas, electricity, and water firms will introduce new competition in South Korean markets, which will likely lead to price hikes and privatization of publicly owned companies. As a result, winners will enjoy the benefits of the FTA at the expense of losers, worsening income inequality in South Korean society. In summary, opponents of the FTA contend that the deal would give preferential treatment to foreign investors at the expense of the public interest. As a result, small business will lose opportunities and job losses will soar.[46]

Proponents of the FTA argue that these opponents made similar arguments in the past regarding the FTA with Chile and the Uruguay

[45] Korean Alliance against the Korea-U.S. FTA, http://nofta.or.kr/en/category/Statements.
[46] Ibid.

Round of the General Agreement on Tariffs and Trade (GATT), and the negative effects were not as significant as predicted. Accordingly, when South Korea signed the Uruguay Round of the GATT in 1993, the Korea Rural Economic Institute (KREI) predicted a significant decline in the number of farmers in South Korea because of the economic effects of opening the agricultural market. They forecasted that the number of farmers would drop to 2.4 million in 2001 from 5.7 million in 1992 and that the agricultural trade deficit would increase from $4.2 billion to $13 billion by 2001. These forecasts were exaggerated, however. For instance, according to a report by KREI, the number of farmers in 2003 was 3.979 million and decreased only slightly to 3.697 million in 2005.[47] In other words, although the number of farmers has declined since the FTA with Chile and the Uruguay Round went into effect, the magnitude of the reduction has not been nearly as large as KREI's forecast. The agricultural trade deficit was $3.5 billion in 2003, $7.2 billion in 2006, and $8.5 billion in 2007, still much lower than KREI's forecast.[48] Moreover, according to the United Nations Conference on Trade and Development (UNCTAD), FDI brought in from the FTA provides a valuable financial resource for private investment to generate jobs from new businesses or the expansion of existing business.[49]

The Expected Effects of the KORUS FTA

The U.S. International Trade Commission predicts that the KORUS FTA would increase annual U.S. GDP by $10 to $12 billion as a result of the benefits generated from reductions and elimination of South Korean tariffs. When the FTA is approved, 95 percent of consumer and industrial products traded between the two countries will be duty-free, and most remaining tariffs will also be removed within the following

---

[47] C. Kim, M. Lee, and Y. Kim, *Gross Domestic Product of Agriculture Related Industries and Estimation of Workers* (Nongeop kwanryeon saneopeui GDPwa jongsaja choojeong), (Seoul: KREI, 2007).

[48] See *Joongang Ilbo*, April 4, 2007, and Kyungnam Development Institute, "Ag-flation and Response of Agriculture and Dairy Industries," *Issue Analysis* (2008): 5.

[49] *World Investment Report* 1999 (Geneva, Switzerland: UNCTAD, 1999). See also S. Hahm and U. Heo, "The Economic Effects of US and Japanese Foreign Direct Investment in East Asia: A Comparative Analysis," *Policy Studies Journal* 36 (2008): 385–402.

ten years. According to the U.S. Trade Representative (USTR), the
KORUS FTA is expected to provide the following benefits to the
United States: First, the KORUS FTA will open up new markets
to U.S. industrial producers. Given the size of the South Korean
economy, approximately $1 trillion, this added market will provide
opportunities for new businesses. Second, the FTA will remove the
8 percent tariff on U.S. passenger cars. Tires and pick-up trucks will
also enjoy the elimination of tariffs within five and ten years, respectively. South Korea has agreed to end the engine displacement tax
and address non-tariff barriers on automobile trade. These changes
will make American automobiles and tires more competitive in the
South Korean market. Third, South Korea is currently the sixth-largest
market for U.S. agricultural exports at approximately $1.6 billion per
year. The FTA will eliminate tariffs on more than half of all agricultural items immediately and remove the remaining tariffs gradually
over time. This benefit is significant to U.S. farmers, considering that
South Korea's average tariff on agricultural products is 52 percent.[50]
Fourth, the KORUS FTA will open up financial and media markets.
As a result, U.S. financial institutions will be able to establish or acquire
financial businesses, which means that U.S. firms can open branches
of banks and insurance companies and place asset managers in South
Korea.

Overall, the USTR argues that the KORUS FTA will further promote trade between the two countries, as 95 percent of products
traded between the two countries will become duty-free. It is expected
that almost all tariffs will be removed within ten years of the FTA's
approval.[51] Thus, the USTR states on its Web site, "If [the United
States–Korea Free Trade Agreement (KORUS FTA) is] approved, the
Agreement would be the United States' most commercially significant
free trade agreement in more than 16 years."[52]

In addition, a report by The Heritage Foundation contends that the
FTA will facilitate the full economic potential of cooperation, such as

---

[50] Office of the USTR, "FTA: United States and Republic of Korea Economic and
Strategic Benefits," *Trade Facts*, February 2006.
[51] Office of the USTR, "Free Trade with Korea: Summary of the KORUS FTA,"
Trade Facts, April 2007.
[52] The text of the agreement is available at http://www.ustr.gov/trade-agreements/
free-trade-agreements/korus-fta. The KORUS FTA will be the largest FTA for
the United States since the North American FTA (NAFTA) with Canada and
Mexico in 1994.

"giving U.S. businesses an important bridgehead into the Asian market, counterbalancing South Korea's growing trade ties with China, potentially allowing the U.S. to regain its position as Seoul's preeminent trade partner; serving as a powerful statement of Washington's commitment to Asia and broaden the U.S.–South Korea relationship beyond the military alliance, and establishing formal channels through which ongoing trade concerns can be addressed."[53] The report concludes that failing to approve the FTA will be a costly mistake.

In terms of the effects of the KORUS FTA on the South Korean economy in the next ten years, a study by the Korean Development Institute and the Korean Institute for International Economic Policy predicts that South Korean exports to the United States will increase by $13.3 billion in the next ten years, while the increase in U.S. imports will be limited to $8.6 billion during the same period. Thus, the study concludes that South Korea will enjoy an annual rise in its trade surplus of $4.6 billion.[54] All top-fifteen export items to the United States will enjoy the benefit of the FTA.[55] Among the beneficiaries, the automobile, electronics, and textile sectors are likely to enjoy the most benefits, whereas farmers are likely to pay the highest price. The Korea Institute for Industrial Economics and Trade (KIET) predicts that automobile exports to the United States will increase by $764 million per year in the next fifteen years as a result of the elimination of the 2.5 percent tariff on Korean automobiles. Automobile production is estimated to increase annually by $2.9 billion for the first fifteen years after the FTA becomes effective.[56] The cost to the agricultural sector from opening the market is estimated to be $670 million per year in the first ten years.[57] Fishery products are also expected to decrease by $281 million annually for the first fifteen years.[58] In addition, South Korea

[53] B. Klingner and D. Markheim, *KORUS FTA Strengthens the U.S. Economy and Alliance with Korea*, June 15, 2009, http://www.heritage.org/research/tradeandeconomicfreedom/wm2485.cfm.

[54] "Korea–US FTA: Cost and Expected Benefits Decreased Prior to the Signing of the FTA," *Joongang Ilbo*, April 30, 2007.

[55] "Top Fifteen Export Items Are All Benefitted from the KORUS FTA," *Joongang Ilbo*, April 4, 2007.

[56] "Korea–US FTA: Auto Industry, the Largest Beneficiary, Steel and Chemical Industries are OK," *Joongang Ilbo*, April 30, 2007.

[57] "Korea–US FTA: Agricultural Products Decrease by $670 Million," *Joongang Ilbo*, April 30, 2007.

[58] "Korea–US FTA: Fishery Products Decrease by $281 Million Per Year," *Joongang Ilbo*, April 30, 2007.

is expected to pay $7 million a year for twenty years for intellectual property rights, and South Korean consumers are expected to spend $136 million a year more for ten years for increased prescription drugs.[59]

The benefits generated from increased trade will lead to growth in manufacturing of $5.5 billion a year and create an average of 33,600 new jobs in South Korea annually. Moreover, South Korean consumers will enjoy greater choices and lower prices because of enhanced competition in the market and the elimination of tariffs. The annual benefit is estimated at $688 million.[60] The total estimated benefit to the South Korean economy is $2.1 billion a year. FDI by U.S. firms and other foreign transnational companies is also likely to increase. U.S. FDI in South Korea in 2005 was $18.8 billion, which is expected to rise by between $2.3 and $3.2 billion.[61] According to a survey conducted in March 2007 by Korea Invest, a suborganization of the Korea Trade-Investment Promotion Agency, 29 percent (73 of 250) of foreign companies doing business in South Korea responded that they would increase their investment if the KORUS FTA is approved.[62] In addition to direct investment, the KORUS FTA is likely to lead to a rise in foreign portfolio investment. For instance, the signing of the KORUS FTA brought about a significant rise in the KOSPI, the South Korean stock exchange. Prior to negotiations on the FTA, the KOSPI was at 1,367.07 on February 1, 2007, but rose to more than 1,500 after the conclusion of the negotiations, and the total amount

---

[59] "Korea–US FTA: Additional Cost of Prescription Drugs Estimated $136 Million," *Joongang Ilbo*, April 30, 2007; "Korea–US FTA: Increased Intellectual Property Right Cost of $7 Million per Year for 20 Years," *Joongang Ilbo*, April 30, 2007.

[60] "Korea–US FTA: Consumer Benefits in Industrial Goods and Agricultural and Fishery Products $688 Million," *Joonang Ilbo*, April 30, 2007. American consumers will enjoy the same benefits on the grounds that this is a benefit of trade. The price of this benefit is conversion cost. The reason is that some domestic industries may lose business because of newly introduced competition in the market. Those who work in the industries may have to be retrained to get a different job, and the facility will have to be converted for other uses. According to classical liberal economics, this cost is limited, whereas the benefits of trade are widely enjoyed by all consumers.

[61] U.S. direct investment is largely concentrated in the manufacturing, banking, and wholesale trade sectors; see Office of the USTR, "Free Trade with Korea: Summary of the KORUS FTA," *Trade Facts*, April 2007.

[62] "The Third Liberation of the Nation: 29 Percent," *Joongang Ilbo*, April 9, 2007.

of capital in the South Korean stock market exceeded \$800 billion.[63] Since then, the KOSPI continued to rise until the 2008 financial crisis began on Wall Street.

Ratification of the KORUS FTA in South Korea

Washington and Seoul concluded bilateral negotiations and signed the agreement in 2007. Despite the accord, legislatures in both countries have yet to ratify the agreement. In the United States, the Obama administration perceives the agreement as unfair. For instance, USTR Ron Kirk told the Senate Finance Committee in his confirmation hearing in spring 2009 that "the KORUS FTA was not fair and simply isn't acceptable." He asserted that the agreement will have to be changed before going forward.[64] While campaigning, Obama wrote a letter to President George W. Bush and said that the agreement "would give Korean exports essentially unfettered access to the U.S. market and would eliminate our best opportunity for obtaining genuinely reciprocal market access in one of the world's largest economies." He was especially concerned about auto trade based on a perception that the current FTA agreement is unfair to the U.S. auto industry because it would not eliminate all of the barriers on U.S. automobile exports to South Korea.[65]

Moreover, the Obama administration is facing domestic pressures for protectionism to restrict competition from foreign firms. Labor unions oppose all FTAs and argue that these agreements bring about a long-term decline in employment and stagnate real wages.[66] Thus, President Obama made it clear that the agreement would have to change before it is sent to Congress for a vote. He said at a press

[63] "KOSPI Index Score Highest Ever, Total Amount Reach \$800 Billion," *Joongang Ilbo*, April 4, 2007; and "New Record in the Korean Stock Market, Where Is the End?" *Joongang Ilbo*, April 11, 2007.

[64] "USTR Nominee Calls for FTA Renegotiation," *Korea Times*, March 10, 2009.

[65] Despite the Obama administration's concerns about auto trade, the Office of the USTR initially predicted that the U.S. automobile industry will be one of the prime winners of the KORUS FTA. See also Klingner and Markheim, *KORUS FTA Strengthens the US Economy and Alliance with Korea*.

[66] J. Schott, "The Korea-US Free Trade Agreement: A Summary Assessment," Policy Brief, PBO 7–7 (Washington, D.C.: Peterson Institute for International Economics, August 2007).

conference with President Lee Myung-bak after a summit meeting, "We want to make sure that we have . . . an agreement that I feel confident is good for the American people, that President Lee feels confident is good for the South Korean people, before we start trying to time when we would present it."[67] As a result, President Obama has yet to ask the U.S. Congress to vote on the agreement.

Ratification of the KORUS FTA is also stalled in South Korea despite strong public support for the agreement. According to a recent poll by the *Hankook Ilbo* and the *Korea Times*, 31.6 percent support the immediate ratification of KORUS FTA and another 35.1 percent responded that the National Assembly should pass the motion as long as the U.S. Congress does the same.[68] The Lee Myung-bak administration and the ruling GNP would also like to pass the agreement, yet the Democratic Party, the main opposition party, wants to delay the vote. They argue that it is necessary to have further study on the overall economic effects of the FTA and to craft compensation plans for the industries that will be hurt by the agreement. On February 25, 2009, a judicial subcommittee of the National Assembly, despite a boycott by the opposition Democratic Party, endorsed a bill to ratify the KORUS FTA. Although this bill requires approval by the subcommittees for foreign affairs, trade, and unification before it is submitted to a plenary session of the National Assembly, it is an important step forward. It appears unlikely, however, that the FTA will become a reality anytime soon in its current form.

The Lee Myung-bak Administration

On February 25, 2008, Lee Myung-bak was inaugurated as President of South Korea, bringing a conservative to office for the first time in ten years. The Lee administration's economic vision is based on a campaign promise called the 747 platform, which proposed 7 percent annual growth, reaching $40,000 per capita income, and becoming the seventh-largest economy in the world. To this end, the government pushed the implementation of the KORUS FTA and employed economic reform policies. To break out of the stalled agreement in

---

[67] "News Conference with Obama and Lee," *New York Times*, June 16, 2009.
[68] S. Kim, "Two-Thirds of Koreans Back FTA with US," *Korea Times*, June 8, 2008.

both the Korean National Assembly and the U.S. Congress,[69] the Lee administration agreed to readmit U.S. beef imports with a slightly lower standard of supervision than from some other countries. This rather quick decision to do so right before the April 2008 summit meeting with President Bush, along with the media's concern for the safety of U.S. beef, particularly old beef, led to an explosion of public discontent. Thousands of people joined candlelight protests. Surprised by the scale of the demonstrations, the Lee administration asked Washington to allow South Korea to import beef only from cattle younger than 30 months. Because of past outbreaks of anti-Americanism, especially when two teenage girls were killed during a U.S. military training exercise, the Bush administration quickly accepted President Lee's request. Shortly after Washington's decision, protests ended, but the Lee administration was politically damaged.[70] In addition, the Seoul government pushed an FTA with the European Union (EU) and concluded the negotiations on July 13, 2009. The agreement is expected to expand trade between South Korea and the EU to the tune of $106 billion.

Because the South Korean economy was struggling because of domestic (increased tax burden, rise in labor cost, the labor–management conflict) and international (the world financial crisis, reduced demand for imports) reasons, the Lee administration also employed tax reform to boost private consumption and business investment. To this end, the government proposed a 2 percent cut in personal income tax by 2010 lowering the tax range from 8 to 35 to 6 to 33 percent. The corporate tax was cut from 25 percent to 22 percent in 2009 and to 20 percent in 2010. The capital gains tax on housing will also be reduced by raising the threshold that is not subject to the tax, and the Comprehensive Property Tax will be cut by increasing the cap on

---

[69] Frustrated with the U.S. Congress, former Korean Ambassador Lee Tae-sik said, "US products used to have the highest market share in the Korean market, but in the recent past, its market share has been the third or fourth. If US Congress delays the ratification of the KORUS FTA, South Korea and European Union may pass their FTA before the ratification of the KORUS FTA. In that case, the United States should not blame South Korea even if European products dominate the Korean market." "Ambassador Lee Tae-sik Upset at the US Due to the Delay of the KORUS-FTA Ratification," *Chosun Ilbo*, September 11, 2008.

[70] R. Jones, "Tax Reform in Korea," *Korea's Economy 2009* (Washington, D.C.: Korea Economic Institute, 2009).

property value exceeding 900 million Korean *won* from 600 million
won.[71]

Furthermore, the Lee government pushed privatization of publicly
owned companies, with the government strongly encouraging mergers or privatization to improve productivity. According to announced
plans, twenty-eight publicly owned companies will be privatized,
thirty-one companies will be merged into fourteen, and three companies will be closed.

Conclusion

Since the 1997 financial crisis, the South Korean government has continuously adopted reform policies to avoid another economic catas-
trophe. Initially, resistance to Kim Dae-jung's reform efforts was limited, in part because of anxiety about the financial crisis. As a result,
early reform policies dealt with many existing problems and greatly
helped the South Korean economy recover quickly from the crisis,
although some policy measures, such as the promotion of credit cards,
led to later economic trouble. After South Korea graduated from the
IMF bailout program, however, labor–management conflict continued to be a serious problem. Labor strikes were frequent, and the
lack of mature institutions in the political and economic systems often
resulted in street protests and violence.

The KORUS FTA put forth by the Roh administration is expected
to be beneficial to both countries, although political pressures from
interest groups continue to affect the ratification process. The Korea-
EU FTA is also likely to help the Korean economy to grow and
become internationally more competitive, but there will be many
obstacles to overcome before these agreements are implemented.

[71] Ibid.

6

Inter-Korean Relations and the North Korean Nuclear Crisis

The relationship between the two Koreas shows two distinctively different characteristics during two different time periods: 1) Cold War confrontation during South Korea's military regimes, and 2) greater exchanges and increased dialogue during the civilian governments after the transition to democracy. After South Korea's transition to democracy in 1987, democratization and the end of the Cold War had a significant impact on inter-Korean relations. During the Cold War, tension in the region remained high because of infiltrations and terrorist attacks by the North. South Korea's government's policies focused on national security and considered inter-Korean relations a zero-sum game. In general, both Koreas confronted each other without much dialogue.

The transition to democracy and the end of the Cold War, however, gave way to fundamental change in South Korea's approach to the North. The end of the Cold War allowed South Korea to normalize its relationship with China and the Soviet Union. Because of high levels of public support, South Korea's civilian presidents aggressively pursued engagement with the North and, along with the rest of the world, provided a lot of economic aid and investment for North Korea. As a result, trade between the two Koreas has increased significantly, but these efforts have been largely fruitless in promoting economic reform in North Korea and have failed to halt Democratic People's Republic of Korea (DPRK) efforts to develop nuclear weapons and long-range missiles. To describe the changes in inter-Korean relations, we start with a brief history of this relationship under the military regimes and then address how democratization, particularly the emergence of civilian presidents, changed the nature of South Korea's policy toward the North. By doing so, we show how the transition to democracy initiated an approach grounded more in engagement and dialogue than in confrontation in inter-Korean relations.

Inter-Korean Relations under the Former Military Generals

South Korea's policy toward North Korea in the 1960s through the 1970s under the Park Chung-hee administration was largely based on national security and anti-communism. South Korea was technically at war (and still is) with North Korea, as the armistice that ended the Korean War was only a ceasefire, and South Korea never signed the document. The world was divided into two blocks – communist and capitalist – under the Cold War system, and the two Koreas were firmly entrenched on opposite sides. North Korea regularly sent agents to South Korea to collect intelligence, and commando raids to attack specific targets in the South or the Republic of Korea (ROK) military in the demilitarized zone were frequent. The North Korean armed raids peaked from 1967 through 1969 with more than 750 infiltrations, including an unsuccessful attempt by thirty-one commandos to assassinate President Park Chung-hee at the Blue House in 1968. In 1967 alone, 224 North Korean infiltrators were killed.[1]

With U.S.–Soviet détente in the early 1970s, however, North Korea's insurgency campaign ended, and South Korea's anti-communist stance also mellowed. Moreover, the U.S.-China rapprochement brought changes in the world political environment. To ease tensions on the Korean Peninsula, President Park Chung-hee announced a plan for peaceful unification on August 15, 1970, and urged North Korea to recognize United Nations (UN) efforts to achieve a unified, democratic Korea. A series of talks commenced between Seoul and Pyongyang, the first since the end of the Korean War. On July 4, 1972, Seoul and Pyongyang signed the North-South Joint Communiqué, which introduced significant changes in the relationship. The two Koreas agreed to pursue reunification without external influence, install direct telephone lines, and cooperate to facilitate Red Cross talks for families separated by the Korean War. Seoul and Pyongyang also consented to have various nonpolitical exchanges, such as cultural

---

[1] U.S. Department of State, *American Foreign Policy: Current Documents, 1967* (Washington, D.C.: Government Printing Office, 1967), 788–90. See also Armed Conflict Events Database, http://www.onwar.com/aced/data/kilo/korea1966.htm.

exchanges and sports events, in an effort to promote a better understanding of each other.[2]

Because of the lack of trust, however, the nature of the relationship between the North and South did not change, and little in the agreement was ever implemented. Both Koreas perceived the inter-Korean relationship as a zero-sum game, and confrontation rather than cooperation determined the relationship between the two sides. In 1974, North Korea sent an agent to assassinate President Park, and inter-Korean relations returned to harsh confrontation.[3]

In 1979, President Park Chung-hee was assassinated by Kim Jae-kyu, the director of the Korean Central Intelligence Agency. With his death, the South Korean people expected a democratic government to follow, but Major General Chun Doo-hwan came to power through a bloodless coup, destroying hopes for democracy. Because Chun lacked political legitimacy, he faced strong political opposition. To divert public attention from domestic politics, he made a drastic change to North Korean policy by proposing a summit meeting in 1981. His proposal included an official invitation to Kim Il-sung to visit Seoul with no preconditions and a suggestion that they hold a conference to draft a constitution for a unified Korea.

North Korea's response, however, was cold. Pyongyang rejected all the proposals and showed no interest in a dialogue with Seoul. Instead, North Korea demonstrated greater hostility toward the South by launching a series of terrorist attacks. For instance, in October 1983, North Korean agents made an unsuccessful attempt to assassinate President Chun Doo-hwan by setting off a bomb in Rangoon, Myanmar, where he was visiting with some cabinet members. President Chun survived, but seventeen South Korean officials and journalists along with four Burmese nationals were killed in the incident. In November 1987, another terrorist attack followed. Two North Korean agents blew up Korean Air Flight 858 over the Andaman Sea, killing all 115 people on board. It was believed that the bombing was intended to disrupt the South Korean presidential election scheduled

[2] U. Heo and C. Hyun, "The 'Sunshine Policy' Revisited: An Analysis of South Korea's Policy Toward North Korea," in U. Heo and S. Horowitz, eds., *Conflict in Asia: Korea, China-Taiwan, and India-Pakistan* (Westport, Conn.: Greenwood, 2003).

[3] V. Cha, "Korea Unification: The Zero-Sum Past and Precarious Future," in *Two Koreas in Transition: Implications for US Policy*, ed. I. Kim (St. Paul, Minn.: Paragon House, 1998).

for December and dampen international attendance at the 1988 Summer Olympic Games in Seoul.[4] This deadly attack led the U.S. State Department to include North Korea on the list of State Sponsors of Terrorism.[5] Because of the repeated terrorist attacks by North Korea, there was no dialogue between Seoul and Pyongyang during the Chun Doo-hwan administration, and Korean relations were hostile.

In December 1987, South Korea held a direct presidential election for the first time since 1971 and chose Roh Tae-woo. As mentioned in Chapter 3, this election was significant in South Korean politics because it began the transition to democracy after decades of military dictatorship. This transition to democracy in South Korea occurred at the same time that the Cold War was coming to an end. The East-West relationship began to thaw, and the United States and the Soviet Union concluded important arms control agreements, including the Intermediate Range Nuclear Forces Treaty signed on December 8, 1987.

To take advantage of the changing global environment, the Roh Tae-woo administration pursued an important change in foreign policy by adopting *Nordpolitik* (Northern Policy) to develop a relationship with former communist countries.[6] Prior to the Roh administration, South Korea's foreign policy relied heavily on the United States and was grounded in anti-communism. With the end of the Cold War, however, the Roh government sought to expand its foreign relations. To this end, South Korea normalized relations with China in August 1992 and established diplomatic ties with Russia in November 1992. Earlier, South Korea also established full diplomatic ties with Hungary, Poland, and Yugoslavia in 1989 and Czechoslovakia, Bulgaria, and Romania in 1990.

North Korea was aware of the changes in the region and proposed high-level talks with the South to discuss political and military issues. Seoul responded positively but suggested that the talks cover a

---

[4] T. Roehrig, "Assessing North Korean Behavior: The June 2000 Summit, the Bush Administration, and Beyond," in *Conflict in Asia: Korea, China, and India-Pakistan*, ed. U. Heo and S. Horowitz (Westport, Conn.: Praeger, 2003), 70.

[5] See T. Roehrig, "North Korea and the US State Sponsors of Terrorism List," *Pacific Focus* 24, no. 1 (April 2009): 85–106.

[6] The Roh Tae-woo administration's *Nordpolitik* was named after West Germany's *Ostpolitik* (Eastern Policy), which aimed to normalize the relationship with the then-communist East Germany.

comprehensive list of issues concerning the two Koreas. After several rounds of meetings, the first since those in the early 1970s, North and South Korea signed the "Agreement on Reconciliation, Nonaggression and Exchanges and Cooperation between the South and the North" in December 1991. With this agreement, the two Koreas recognized each other's political system and pledged not to intervene in each other's domestic affairs. Further talks in February 1992 generated the "Joint Declaration of South and North Korea on the Denuclearization of the Korean Peninsula," designed to stop North Korea's nuclear weapons ambitions, although the North has not fulfilled its obligations under the agreement. In addition, the Roh government sought nonpolitical exchanges with North Korea through the "balanced development" policy, which included open trade of goods and services, exchange visits, and developing a joint community between the two Koreas.[7]

In September 1991, another significant political change occurred. After repeated failures, both South and North Korea finally joined the UN. South Korea had repeatedly attempted to join the UN, but the Soviet Union and China had vetoed Seoul's bid because of North Korean opposition. Because China and Russia were moving toward normal relations with Seoul, they no longer opposed South Korea's entry. If South Korea alone became a member of the UN, North Korea would have been diplomatically isolated and weakened in the international arena. Therefore, North Korea agreed to join the UN together with the South.

Despite all the positive developments surrounding the two Koreas, the essence of the relationship remained largely hostile. There was no trust between Seoul and Pyongyang; both suspected each other's intentions and focused on national security. As a result, the Roh Taewoo administration was not willing to abandon its hard-line assessment of North Korea.[8] The Roh administration's only interest in improving North–South relations was to increase domestic support for the government by enhancing peace and stability on the Korean Peninsula and establishing closer relations with the former Soviet bloc countries and China.[9]

[7] N. Levin and Y. Han, *Sunshine in Korea: The South Korean Debate over Policies toward North Korea* (Santa Monica, Calif.: RAND, 2002).

[8] M. Hart-Landsberg, *Korea: Division, Reunification and US Foreign Policy* (New York: Monthly Review Press, 1998).

[9] Heo and Hyun, "The 'Sunshine Policy' Revisited."

The Kim Young-sam Administration and the First North Korean Nuclear Crisis

In 1992, President Kim Young-sam was elected the first civilian president since 1960. Because he had no military background and enjoyed high rates of public support (83.4 percent), he attempted to distinguish himself from previous leaders by making a fundamental change in North-South relations. In his inaugural address, he stated, "No foreign ally is better than our compatriots. No ideology can bring greater happiness than our compatriots." To persuade North Korea to begin a dialogue, the Kim government proposed four-party talks that would include the United States and China. The Kim government also used economic aid as an inducement to improve inter-Korean relations by providing 150,000 tons of rice in 1995.[10] His plan faced a serious hurdle, however, because of the first North Korean nuclear crisis, which significantly increased tensions on the Korean Peninsula.

North Korean efforts to develop nuclear weapons date back to the 1950s. After nearly losing in the Korean War, North Korean leader Kim Il-sung decided to pursue nuclear weapons.[11] To this end, North Korea signed nuclear cooperation agreements with the Soviet Union and China and received a small nuclear research reactor from the Soviet Union in 1965. The reactor was installed in Yongbyon and became operational in 1967. Because the nuclear reactor was so small, it was not a concern to other countries.

In 1982, however, U.S. satellite photographs detected construction at the Yongbyon nuclear site of new reactor facilities and a reprocessing plant. It was later discovered that North Korea constructed a five-megawatt, gas-cooled, graphite-moderated nuclear reactor, which became operational in 1986. The possibility of North Korea becoming a member of the nuclear club raised serious security concerns for four reasons. First, North Korea already had a conventional force of more than a million personnel along with chemical and biological weapons.

---

[10] U. Heo and J. Woo, South Korea's Response: Democracy, Identity, and Strategy," in *Identity and Change in East Asian Conflicts: The Case of China, Taiwan and the Koreas*, ed. S. Horowitz, U. Heo, and A. Tan (New York: Palgrave Macmillan, 2007).

[11] U. Heo, "North Korea's Nuclear Test: Cause, Implications and Prospects," Praeger Security International, 2006, http://psi.praeger.com/commentary/commentary.aspx.

The addition of nuclear weapons to the DPRK arsenal only made matters worse. Second, North Korea's possession of nuclear weapons could lead South Korea, Japan, and possibly Taiwan to pursue nuclear weapons, which might spur a regional nuclear arms race. Third, North Korea already had a ballistic missile program, which could provide a delivery system for nuclear warheads if it developed the necessary technology for intercontinental ballistic missiles (ICBM). Fourth and perhaps of greatest concern, given the dilapidated economy, North Korea might be tempted to sell nuclear material or technology, which would hurt U.S. nonproliferation efforts.[12]

Because of these concerns, the United States pressured the Soviet Union to urge North Korea to join the Nuclear Non-Proliferation Treaty (NPT), and Pyongyang joined in 1985. NPT membership requires that a member state meet the safeguards requirements within eighteen months of joining, which includes filing forms reporting all plants using fissile materials and permitting inspections of all the sites by the International Atomic Energy Agency (IAEA). North Korea did not complete the required inspections in a timely manner, however, and neither the IAEA nor the United States pressured North Korea to arrange IAEA inspections because of Chinese and Soviet pressure.[13]

In 1989, North Korea shut down the 5-megawatt reactor in Yongbyon for three months without IAEA inspectors present, raising suspicion that North Korea had removed the spent nuclear fuel rods that contained plutonium. These rods would be sufficient to make one or two bombs and was a clear violation of the NPT. To ease security concerns and to make a political gesture, North Korea signed the Treaty of Reconciliation and Nonaggression with South Korea on December 13, 1991, and later agreed not to develop nuclear weapons. Pyongyang also concluded an NPT safeguards arrangement with the IAEA in 1992, although the following conditions were attached to the agreement: withdrawal of U.S. nuclear weapons from South Korea and cancellation of the annual U.S.-South Korean military exercise, Team Spirit. To meet these demands, the United States removed all

[12] T. Roehrig, *From Deterrence to Engagement: The US Defense Commitment to South Korea*, 142–3.

[13] P. Leventhal and S. Dolley, "The North Korean Nuclear Crisis," Nuclear Control Institute, 1994, http://www.nci.org/n/nkib1.htm.

tactical nuclear weapons from South Korea by December 1991[14] and suspended the 1992 Team Spirit military exercise.[15]

In May 1992, North Korea finally allowed IAEA inspections, but it prevented inspectors from visiting two key facilities at the Yongbyon site. Moreover, North Korea announced that a number of damaged nuclear fuel rods had been removed from the 5-megawatt nuclear reactor when it was shut down for three months in 1989 and had been reprocessed once in 1990. Upon the IAEA's request, North Korea provided samples of plutonium obtained from reprocessing the spent nuclear fuel rods. Based on the analysis of the plutonium samples, the IAEA concluded that North Korea had reprocessed the spent nuclear fuel at least three different times, then they requested further inspections of the two sites at the Yongbyon facility. North Korea strongly denied the IAEA's charge of multiple reprocessing and refused to allow any further inspection of the site. On February 25, 1993, the IAEA Board of Governors demanded special inspections, but North Korea responded the next month with an announcement of its intention to withdraw from the NPT.[16]

Because the NPT requires a three-month notice for a member to withdraw, the IAEA and the United States attempted to persuade North Korea to maintain its NPT membership. These efforts failed, and the IAEA sent the case to the UN Security Council (UNSC), which is responsible for handling IAEA safeguards violations. The UNSC passed a resolution demanding that North Korea stay in the NPT and comply with the IAEA. As the resolution contained no specific penalties for noncompliance, North Korea rejected the UNSC resolution and declared its right to withdraw from the NPT before the three-month period expired. In June 1993, however, North Korea suspended its decision to leave the NPT after it began talks with the United States.

In March 1994, North Korea permitted partial inspections of the Yongbyon site without allowing complete access to IAEA inspectors. The IAEA had repeatedly requested complete access to all of the facilities at the site, but the North Korean government refused to comply. Instead, North Korea unloaded the nuclear reactor, producing eight thousand spent fuel rods that could be reprocessed to make

---

[14] H. Kristensen, "A History of US Nuclear Weapons in South Korea," September 28, 2005, http://www.nukestrat.com/korea/koreahistory.htm.

[15] Leventhal and Dolley, "The North Korean Nuclear Crisis."

[16] Ibid.

weapons-grade material. Moreover, Pyongyang ejected IAEA inspectors from the country on March 15 and started preparing to reprocess the unloaded eight thousand fuel rods. On March 21, 1994, the IAEA reported to the UNSC that inspectors were unable to validate that North Korea had not produced nuclear materials to develop nuclear weapons. To pressure North Korea to allow IAEA inspections, the United States offered a draft resolution to the Security Council that called for sanctions on North Korea unless Pyongyang granted further inspections.[17] Others, such as Senator John McCain, suggested even stronger measures if diplomacy failed.[18] North Korea announced that sanctions would be considered an act of war and that "Seoul will turn into a sea of fire."[19] Tension levels in the region skyrocketed, and the nuclear crisis seemed headed to conflict. The Clinton administration started developing contingency plans, including surgical air strikes on the Yongbyon nuclear site.[20] The U.S. military also deployed Patriot missiles to defend South Korea from a North Korean missile attack in case the crisis escalated.

As a last resort to resolve the crisis, former U.S. President Jimmy Carter visited Pyongyang in June 1994. Because both the United States and North Korea did not want to escalate the crisis to a military conflict, North Korean leader Kim Il-sung agreed to freeze its nuclear program and allow IAEA inspectors to examine the Yongbyon site. The United States and North Korea also agreed to hold high-level talks to further discuss the North Korean nuclear program.[21]

When Carter returned from Pyongyang, he delivered an important message from North Korean leader Kim Il-sung to South Korean President Kim Young-sam. According to Carter, Kim Il-sung said, "I don't know why the top leaders of the North and South have

---

[17] L. Niksch, "U.N. Security Council Consideration of North Korea's Violations of its Nuclear Treaty Obligations," Congressional Research Service: Report for Congress, No. 94–299 F, April 6, 1994, http://www.fas.org/spp/starwars/crs/94-299f.htm.

[18] Congressional Record. United States Policy and The Crisis in Korea (Senate – May 24, 1994), S6245, http://www.fas.org/spp/starwars/congress/1994/s940524-dprk.htm.

[19] M. Gordon, "U.S. Will Urge U.N. to Plan Sanctions for North Korea," New York Times, March 20, 1994, A1.

[20] The operational plan for an air strike is called OPLAN 5026, and more detailed information about OPLAN 5026 can be found at http://www.globalsecurity.org/military/ops/oplan-5026.htm.

[21] M. Creekmore, Jr., A Moment of Crisis: Jimmy Carter, the Power of a Peacemaker, and North Korea's Nuclear Ambitions (New York: Public Affairs, 2006).

never met. They should have met much earlier. If there had been summits, the situation on the peninsula would not come to such a critical state. I want to meet President Kim Young-sam anywhere, anytime without conditions and at an early date."[22] Hwang Jang-yeop, a high-level North Korean official who defected in 1997, believed Kim Il-sung was not only interested in easing the tension on the Korean peninsula but also wanted a summit meeting to promote a potentially lucrative project. Kim hoped to resume railroad connections through North Korea for the South's railroad shipments to China and Russia, expecting to make approximately $1.5 billion from the arrangement.[23] After two preliminary meetings, Seoul and Pyongyang agreed to hold a summit in Pyongyang on July 25–27, 1994. Unfortunately, however, North Korean leader Kim Il-sung died on July 8, 1994. The scheduled summit meeting was cancelled, and all contacts between the two Koreas halted.

Nevertheless, talks between the United States and North Korea continued on the nuclear issue and generated the Agreed Framework that was signed in Geneva on October 21, 1994.[24] The Agreed Framework sought to resolve the nuclear issue with four main provisions. First, the United States agreed to replace North Korea's graphite-moderated reactors by 2003 with modern light-water reactors (LWRs) capable of generating approximately 2,000 megawatts of electricity. To implement the agreement, the United States agreed to organize the Korean Energy Development Organization (KEDO). While construction of the LWRs was taking place, the eight thousand fuel rods would be stored and monitored for eventual removal to another country. Second, while the LWRs were under construction and to offset the foregone energy when North Korea froze its nuclear program, the United States would provide an annual delivery of 500,000 tons of heavy fuel oil for heating and electricity production. Third, upon receipt of the heavy fuel oil and the U.S. commitment for the LWR,

---

[22] C. Chung, "If the 1994 South-North Summit Were Realized," in *There is No End in the Career of an Official*, ed. S. Horowitz, U. Heo, and A. Tan (Seoul: Myungsol, 2001), 50.

[23] Hwang Jang-Yeop reportedly said this in a lecture for Program in North Korea Democratization. *The Daily NK*. June 1, 2007, http://www.dailynk.com/korean/read.php?cataId=nk02200...num=41902.

[24] For an assessment of the Agreed Framework, see T. Roehrig, "'One Rogue State Crisis at a Time!': The United States and North Korea's Nuclear Weapons Program," *World Affairs* 165, no. 4 (Spring 2003): 155–78.

North Korea would freeze and eventually dismantle its nuclear program. Fourth, the United States and North Korea also agreed to pursue normalization of political and economic relations between the two countries, starting with opening a liaison office in the other's capital, which would be upgraded to the ambassadorial level as progress was made. Both countries agreed to lift economic sanctions, and Washington consented to providing formal assurances that it would not threaten or use nuclear weapons against the North. Pyongyang also agreed to implement the 1992 North-South Joint Denuclearization Agreement and to restart a dialogue with the South.[25] For the time being, this appeared to settle the nuclear crisis.

On April 16, 1996, the Kim Young-sam administration proposed four-party talks with North Korea to include the United States and China. To entice a positive response from the North, the Kim government announced that it would not oppose direct talks between Washington and Pyongyang as well. Bilateral talks between the United States and North Korea had two important political implications. First, South Korea had been opposed to direct contact between Washington and Pyongyang in the past, as this would have excluded South Korea from the dialogue on Korean security issues. Thus, the Seoul government had insisted that the relationship between Washington and Pyongyang should be contingent on improved inter-Korean relations. With the proposal for the four-party talks, the Kim administration abandoned this position. Second, the proposal of four-party talks affirmed Washington's implicit recognition of Pyongyang, making it possible for the United States to provide economic aid to North Korea. This change in South Korea's policy toward the North was clearly different from the previous governments' policies.[26] Another difference between the Kim Young-sam administration and previous governments was President Kim's willingness to use economic aid as an inducement to bring North Korea to negotiations. When North Korea asked for food aid in 1995, the Kim government provided 150,000 tons of rice, the first direct assistance to the North since the country was divided. In return, Seoul demanded official talks between the two Koreas.

[25] The Korean Peninsula Energy Development Organization. Agreed Framework between the United States of America and the Democratic People's Republic of Korea, Geneva, October 21, 1994, http://www.kedo.org/pdfs/Agreed Framework.pdf.
[26] B. Koo, "Challenges and Prospects for Inter-Korean Relations under the New Leadership," *Korean Journal of Defense Analysis* 10, no. 1 (1998): 79.

Pyongyang did not agree to do so, but South Korea provided the aid nonetheless.[27]

What made these changes possible? The answer may be found in changes in the global political environment resulting from the end of the Cold War and public support for the first civilian president after the transition to democracy in South Korea. With the end of the Cold War, the Soviet Union and China normalized relations with South Korea, which made North Korea uneasy and isolated. Furthermore, North Korea feared it may have become less important to the Soviet Union and China, and economic aid from these allies remained a necessity.[28] Many experts in Korean affairs also predicted an imminent North Korean collapse because of economic difficulties caused by food shortages.[29] Thus, South Korea was willing to give up its previous concerns.

Second, the first president after the transition to democracy was Roh Tae-woo, a former military general hand-picked by the previous military dictator, Chun Doo-hwan. As a result, public support for President Roh was rather limited, which constrained his ability to alter South Korean policy. In contrast, Kim Young-sam was the first civilian president in thirty-two years and thereby enjoyed high levels of public support, especially compared with his predecessor, Roh Tae-woo. For instance, President Kim Young-sam's job approval rating was 87.6 percent in his first year. It declined over time, but he still enjoyed 44.9 percent in his third year.[30] President Roh Tae-woo had only 28.4 percent approval in his first year in the office, a number that continued to drop throughout his term.[31] In summary, the transition to democracy had a significant impact on South Korea's policy toward North Korea. Further changes followed when power shifted to the opposition progressive party, with Kim Dae-jung as the next president.

[27] Heo and Hyun, "The 'Sunshine Policy' Revisited."

[28] Oberdorfer, The Two Koreas, 260–1.

[29] On December 30, 1996, the Los Angeles Times reported that former CIA director John Deutch predicted the collapse of North Korea. See also K. Kim, "No Way Out: North Korea's Impending Collapse," Harvard International Review 18, no. 2 (March 22, 1996), and C. Kim, "The Uncertain Future of North Korea: Soft Landing or Crash Landing," Korea and World Affairs 21, no. 4 (1996): 623–36.

[30] S. Park, "Reasons for the Failure of Democratic Consolidation and the Experience of the Kim Young-sam administration in Korea," Trend and Prospects 34 (1997): 8–27.

[31] H. Joo, "A Year After Inauguration of President Lee Myung-bak: Job Approval Rating in Economics Is the Lowest," Seoul Daily, February 24, 2009.

The Kim Dae-jung Administration and the "Sunshine Policy"

On February 25, 1998, Kim Dae-jung assumed the presidency, ushering in a new direction in ROK politics and foreign policy, particularly concerning perceptions of and approaches to North Korea. Kim Dae-jung, the former dissident leader, developed a policy approach for reunification, which he named the "three principles and three stages unification formula." The three principles included "peaceful coexistence, peaceful exchange, and peaceful unification." The three stages were essentially a roadmap for reunification, starting with the union of the republic (or the state), union by federalism, and complete unification. In other words, the two Koreas would start with acknowledging each other's existence as separate nations, move on to have exchanges under the same government as in a federal system, and finally work together to achieve reunification. Public support for Kim Dae-jung's unification policy plan, however, was generally lukewarm.[32]

Nevertheless, once in office, President Kim Dae-jung implemented his unification policy, named the "sunshine policy," as the plan for dealing with North Korea. In his inaugural address, Kim made it clear that the sunshine policy would be a top priority of his administration. The sunshine policy had four main principles. First, South Korea sought a peaceful relationship with North Korea, although no military provocation would be tolerated. Second, instead of attempting to unify with North Korea by absorption, South Korea pursued peaceful coexistence with North Korea to facilitate reunification. These two principles were designed to convey the message that South Korea was not trying to undermine the North Korean government for regime change or unification. Instead, Seoul was only interested in peaceful coexistence, although reunification was desirable in the long run. Third, South Korea separated economics from politics to promote economic, social, and cultural exchanges between the two Koreas. With this move, Seoul signaled that the United States and Japan could also improve their relationship with the North in the hope that normalized relations with these countries would enhance North Korea's engagement with the rest of the world. This move was also

[32] K. Quinones, "South Korea's Approaches to North Korea: A Glacial Process," in *Korean Security Dynamics in Transition*, ed. K. Park and D. Kim (New York: Palgrave, 2001), 43.

designed to induce the private sector to provide more economic aid to North Korea to compensate for limited government resources.[33] Finally, South Korea applied the principle of reciprocity to the implementation of the sunshine policy, hoping that both countries would make concessions.[34] This principle, however, was changed to "provide first and expect later," because the Kim government believed that the policy would benefit the nation regardless of North Korea's concurrent uncooperative response.[35]

As a first step to implementing the sunshine policy, on April 30, 1998, President Kim Dae-jung announced policy measures that made it easier to conduct business activities in the North.[36] The new measures included simplified legal procedures to obtain permission for business activities in North Korea, elimination of the private investment cap, removal of item restrictions for private investment, and reduced travel restrictions for businessmen. President Kim hoped to promote inter-Korean economic cooperation on the grounds that increased interactions between the two Koreas would ease tensions and improve trust between them. In summary, the sunshine policy aimed to establish peaceful coexistence between the two Koreas by increasing economic aid to help develop the North Korean economy and to encourage North Korea to engage with the rest of the world. The Kim Dae-jung government viewed all of these efforts as an investment in the eventual goal of reunification.

Easing these restrictions on travel to North Korea allowed Chung Ju-yung, honorary chairman of the Hyundai Corporation, to visit North Korea on June 16, 1998. On his trip, he took five hundred heads of cattle on one hundred trucks as a gesture to ease the North's food shortages. He also discussed possible tourism ventures with North Korean officials and received permission to start the Kumkang Mountain cruise/tourism project. The first cruise went to Kumkang Mountain in November 1998 and allowed South Koreans to visit the North

---

[33] Young Whan Kihl, "Seoul's Engagement Policy and US-DPRK Relations," *Korean Journal of Defense Analysis* 10, no. 1 (1998): 21.

[34] Chung-in Moon, "Understanding the DJ Doctrine: The Sunshine Policy and the Korean Peninsula," in *Kim Dae-jung Government and Sunshine Policy: Promises and Challenges*, ed. Chung-in Moon and David I. Steinberg (Washington, D.C.: Georgetown University Press, 1999).

[35] Heo and Hyun, "The 'Sunshine Policy' Revisited."

[36] M. Lee, "Elimination of Political and Legal Huddle in Inter-Korean Economic Cooperation," *Munhwa Ilbo*, May 1, 1998.

for the first time since the end of the Korean War. These tours were expected to make a significant contribution to improving inter-Korean relations.

In addition, the sunshine policy led to the creation of the industrial complex in Kaesong in 2002. The Kaesong industrial region, located just across the border in North Korea, opened up an opportunity for many private-sector companies, particularly small and medium-sized enterprises, to start businesses and take advantage of cheap labor in the North. The Kaesong industrial complex, along with the Kumkang Mountain tourist project, has generated significant revenue for North Korea. The project began with Hyundai's commitment to provide $12 million per month – $1 billion over six years – to the North Korean government. Because the tourism project would provide hard currency to North Korea, previous administrations did not allow it. The Kim Dae-jung administration, however, strongly supported these types of efforts to buttress the sunshine policy.[37]

The most symbolic event of the sunshine policy was the summit meeting between South Korean President Kim Dae-jung and North Korean leader Kim Jong-il held in Pyongyang on June 13–15, 2000. The meeting led many people to hope that this would be the first step toward the eventual reunification of the two Koreas. The meeting resulted in an agreement with five provisions.

(1) The South and North, as masters of national unification, will join hands in efforts to resolve the issue of national unification independently.

(2) Acknowledging that the different formulas that the North and South favor for reunification have common factors, they will strive to work together to achieve this goal.

(3) The South and North will exchange groups of dispersed family members and their relatives around Aug. 15 and resolve as soon as possible humanitarian issues, including the repatriation of Communist prisoners who have completed their terms in jail.

(4) The South and North will pursue a balanced development of their national economies and build mutual trust by accelerating exchange in the social, cultural, sports, health and environmental sectors.

[37] See C. Kim, *The Korean Presidents*, 332.

(5) In order to put these agreements into practice, the South and
North will hold a dialogue between government authorities at
an early date. President Kim Dae Jung cordially invited National
Defense Commission chairman Kim Jong Il to visit Seoul, and
he agreed to do that at an appropriate time.[38]

After the historic summit, Korean defense ministers met for the first
time since the Korean War to discuss easing tensions on the Korean
Peninsula.[39] In this meeting, the two Koreas agreed to reconnect the
Kyongui (Seoul-Shinuiju) railroad, cut off since the division of the
country. South Korea was interested in discussing a broad range of
inter-Korean issues but only ended up agreeing to establish a hotline
between the two military commands and to continue holding regular
working-level meetings. Follow-up meetings, however, did not lead
to further progress. Nevertheless, on August 15, 2000, families that
had been separated as a result of the division of Korea held a reunion,
and Hyundai launched the overland Kumkang Mountain tour.

U.S.-North Korean relations also improved as a result of the summit.
In October 2001, North Korean General Jo Myung-rok visited Washington and met with President Bill Clinton to discuss North Korea's
nuclear and ballistic missile programs. He also delivered Kim Jong-il's
invitation to President Clinton to visit North Korea. Shortly after,
U.S. Secretary of State Madeleine Albright traveled to Pyongyang to
further discuss the missile and nuclear issues. President Clinton considered a visit to Pyongyang to finalize a missile deal, but decided not
to do so because his term was nearing its end and the incoming Bush
administration had already expressed lukewarm support for the deal.[40]

Despite the Kim Dae-jung administration's aggressive efforts to
engage North Korea, Pyongyang just enjoyed the economic benefits
from the South without meeting Seoul's expectation to reciprocate.
Instead, North Korea indicated it did not trust South Korea and criticized the sunshine policy as a "sunburn" policy, suspecting it was a
disguised approach to undermine the regime.[41] Instead, the Kim Jong-
il government adopted a new constitution that upgraded the National
Defense Commission (NDC) to the highest government organization,

[38] "In Words of the Pact: 'To Work Together,'" *New York Times*, June 15, 2000.
[39] H. French, "Defense Chiefs of Two Koreas Meet on Reducing Tensions," *New York Times*, September 26, 2000, A10.
[40] T. Roehrig, *From Deterrence to Engagement*, 213.
[41] S. Kim, "North Korea in 2000," *Asian Survey* 41, no. 1 (2001): 14.

and Kim Jong-il became the chairman of the NDC, in charge of political, economic, and military affairs. He adopted "the military first" policy with a motto, *Kangsong Taeguk*, meaning a "strong and prosperous great power."[42]

Furthermore, a number of military provocations occurred. For instance, on August 31, 1998, North Korea fired a long-range missile (*Taepodong* 1) over Japan, which shocked the world.[43] Because many feared that the long-range missile could one day deliver nuclear warheads, it intensified the security concerns in the region. In June 1999, North Korean ships crossed the Northern Limit Line (NLL), the maritime boundary designated by the United Nations Command (UNC) after the Korean War, starting the first Yeonpyeong naval conflict.[44] Both Koreas had respected the NLL since the end of the Korean War, but North Korea challenged the line by sailing in and out of the NLL, which significantly raised the tension level. After South Korean boats challenged the incursion, a North Korean patrol boat opened fire on the South Korean ships. ROK vessels returned fire, sinking one of the North Korean boats and damaging five others. The conflict over the NLL did not end there. On June 29, 2002, North Korean patrol boats again crossed the NLL. South Korean patrol boats were sent to protect fishing boats in the area, and when they attempted to stop the North Korean ships, they opened fire. The South Korean ships responded, badly damaging one DPRK ship that was burning as it was towed back to its base. The South Korean ship that was hit in the opening salvo eventually sank, and six sailors on board the vessel were killed and nineteen were injured. Approximately thirty North Korean sailors were reported killed or injured. In April 2008, the conflict was officially named The Second Yeonpyonghaejeon (The Second Yeonpyong Engagement).[45]

To make matters worse, the second North Korean nuclear crisis broke out in October 2002. Unlike the Clinton administration, the Bush administration was not enthusiastic about South Korea's engagement policy, because President Bush did not trust North Korea and

---

[42] C. Kim, *The Korean Presidents*.

[43] Ibid., 332.

[44] For a detailed discussion of the NLL, see T. Roehrig, *Korean Dispute over the Northern Limit Line: Security, Economics, or International Law?* (Baltimore: University of Maryland School of Law, 2008).

[45] Department of Navy, ROK, Article 2 Yeonpyeonghaejeon, http://www.navy.mil.kr/info/memorial/memorial_3.jsp.

largely perceived the policy as a failure. President Kim Dae-jung tried
to persuade President Bush at a summit meeting early in the Bush
presidency in March 2001, without much success. On October 3,
2002, a U.S. delegation led by U.S. special envoy James Kelly visited North Korea to discuss a wide range of pending issues, such as
Pyongyang's nuclear weapons programs, the development and export
of missiles, and human right issues.[46] At the meeting, Kelly mentioned
to North Korean delegates that the United States had evidence of a
North Korean nuclear program based on highly enriched uranium
(HEU).[47] After first denying the accusation, North Korean officials
later acknowledged its truth. A North Korean HEU program was a
clear violation of the spirit and letter of the Agreed Framework. The
Opposition Grand National Party in South Korea requested that the
Kim Dae-jung government halt economic aid to North Korea until
Pyongyang stopped the HEU program.[48]

In an effort to diffuse tension over the nuclear issue, on October 23, 2002, the two Koreas announced an agreement to cooperate
on all issues, including the nuclear dispute, in a joint statement following ministerial talks, the eighth round since the June 2000 summit
meeting, and the North Korean Foreign Ministry proposed a non-
aggression pact with the United States. On November 15, the executive board of KEDO decided to suspend the delivery of crude oil
to North Korea because of its violation of the Agreed Framework.
Pyongyang responded by announcing it would restart its nuclear facilities at Yongbyon with the removal of surveillance cameras and disabling seals on the nuclear facilities. To avoid escalating the crisis, on
December 31, 2002, President George W. Bush declared that Washington would use diplomacy to resolve the dispute peacefully. On

---

[46] Ministry of Foreign Affairs of Japan, Visit of Assistant Secretary of the United
States James Kelly to North Korea (Explanation to Japanese Side), http://www
.mofa.go.jp/region/asia-paci/n_korea/us0210.html.

[47] North Korea's HEU-based nuclear program was first revealed when Hwang Jang-
yeop, a North Korean defector, mentioned the trade between North Korea's long-
range missile technology and Pakistan's HEU technology. On June 9, 2000, the
Japanese newspaper *Sankei Shimbun* reported that North Korea has an HEU facility
in Mountain Chonma based on Chinese government sources. In late 2001, the
U.S. CIA reported to Congress that North Korea attempted to acquire centrifuge-
related materials, which are critical for the HEU program. See L. Niksch, "North
Korea's Nuclear Weapons Program," *CRS Report for Congress*, October 5, 2006.

[48] D. Kirk, "Nuclear Issue in North Korea Colors a Race in the South," *New York
Times*, October 19, 2002.

January 6, 2003, the IAEA passed a resolution calling for North Korea to again freeze its nuclear program; however, Pyongyang responded by declaring its intention to withdraw from the NPT. Thus, the second North Korean nuclear crisis began as the term of President Kim Dae-jung came to a close in February 2003.

In summary, despite North Korea's disappointing response to the Kim Dae-jung administration's sunshine policy, the Kim government continued to provide economic aid almost unconditionally. Under the sunshine policy, the Kim administration (March 1998–February 2003) provided $855.7 million in economic aid to North Korea, quadrupling the $188 million provided to North Korea during the Kim Young-sam administration. Furthermore, the Kim Dae-jung administration provided $500 million to North Korea to hold the June 2000 summit meeting. When North Korea showed no signs of changing its ways, despite the massive economic aid, the Kim Dae-jung administration abandoned the reciprocity principle of the sunshine policy and replaced it with "provide first and expect later." The sunshine policy sparked a strong public backlash for providing aid to a seemingly ungrateful North Korea, and consequently public support for the policy declined over time. Nevertheless, the engagement policy initiated by President Kim Dae-jung continued during the Roh Moo-hyun administration, but it was renamed the Peace and Prosperity Policy.

The Roh Moo-hyun Administration

The Second North Korean Nuclear Crisis

When President Roh Moo-hyun came to office in 2003, the second North Korean nuclear crisis was escalating. The Bush administration had adopted a hard-line policy and demanded the complete, verifiable, irreversible dismantlement of North Korea's nuclear program before the initiation of any discussion about compensation. North Korea refused to meet U.S. demands and complained about delays in the construction of the LWRs. Pyongyang also suggested that the solution to the nuclear crisis was a comprehensive deal that required simultaneous moves by both Washington and Pyongyang. Both sides hurled harsh rhetoric at each other, and no progress was made to resolve the crisis.

In April 2003, the United States, North Korea, and China met in Beijing in separate rooms, with China acting as a mediator in an effort to hold talks while accommodating Washington's demands to refrain from bilateral negotiations with North Korea. Little was accomplished in this meeting, but China continued to push for dialogue, leading to the creation of the six-party talks in August that included South Korea, North Korea, the United States, China, Japan, and Russia. The first round of six-party talks failed to conclude an agreement, and, by October, North Korea completed reprocessing its spent fuel rods to develop nuclear weapons. North Korea claimed that the purpose of the move was to strengthen their deterrent force and that they had no choice but to do so to defend themselves from the hostile U.S. policy. On October 20, 2003, the Bush administration responded by offering North Korea a five-state security guarantee. On November 21, KEDO decided to suspend construction of the LWRs for a year, starting on December 1, 2003. North Korea proposed simultaneous steps to resolve the nuclear issue with economic compensation provided at the same time that Pyongyang abandoned its nuclear program.

At the end of February 2004, members held the second round of six-party talks in Beijing. The meeting only confirmed the differences between North Korea and the United States, and little progress occurred. After the meeting, South Korea, the United States, and Japan met and officially demanded North Korea's complete, verifiable, irreversible nuclear dismantlement (CVID), but North Korea again refused to comply with the demand. The North Korea-Japan summit meeting in May 2004 and the third round of the six-party talks in June 2004 followed, yet no progress was made. On July 24, North Korea announced that it was not interested in further discussions because the United States had set unacceptable preconditions on the abandonment of its nuclear program in return for economic compensation. Pyongyang reiterated its demand that the provision of economic aid and the abandonment of its nuclear program be simultaneous and part of a package deal.

On February 10, 2005, North Korea declared that it possessed nuclear weapons and that future dialogue concerning its nuclear program, including the six-party talks, should address North Korea as a formal nuclear weapons state. In response, South Korean and U.S. officials announced that, if North Korea abandoned its nuclear program, Washington would discuss improving its relations with Pyongyang, including the provision of a security guarantee. To consider this offer, the fourth round of six-party talks began in July 2005. The meeting deadlocked but resumed on September 13, this time reaching a breakthrough. On September 19, the six members adopted a joint statement in which North Korea agreed to give up all its nuclear weapons and programs and rejoin the NPT. Washington reaffirmed that it had no intention to attack North Korea and that it was willing to provide a security guarantee. Regarding North Korea's long-desired LWRs, the agreement noted only that it would be discussed "at an appropriate time." A day later, however, Pyongyang announced that it would not scrap its nuclear programs until the LWRs were received, raising serious doubts about the joint statement. On September 15, 2005, while the fourth round of six-party talks was occurring in Beijing, the U.S. Treasury Department designated Banco Delta Asia (BDA) in Macau a "financial institution of primary money laundering concern" and restricted transactions of U.S. financial institutions with BDA. In response, the Bank of Macau froze and audited all North Korean accounts at BDA, which led other financial institutions to follow suit.[49] North Korea responded strongly and suspended its participation in the six-party talks, completely nullifying the September 19 joint statement. Furthermore, North Korea announced that it would resume its nuclear program. Efforts to bring North Korea back to the six-party talks failed, and, in July 2006, North Korea test-fired missiles, including a long-range *Taepodong* 2, in a demonstration of defiance and an effort to gain leverage.[50]

The nuclear crisis further escalated when North Korea tested its first nuclear weapon on October 9, 2006, despite warnings from the United States, China, and the UNSC.[51] The UNSC condemned the test and passed UN Resolution 1718, which demanded that North Korea stop further nuclear or ballistic missile tests and return to the six-party talks immediately. It also included a provision that cargo ships traveling to and from North Korea might be inspected for materials related to weapons of mass destruction (WMDs). The resolution imposed economic sanctions on North

---

[49] D. Rennack, "North Korea: Economic Sanctions," Report for Congress by Congressional Research Service (Washington, D.C.: The Library of Congress: October 17, 2006).

[50] B. Demick, "With Few N. Korea Facts, a Rumor Got Launched," *Los Angeles Times*, July 7, 2006, A-1.

[51] A. Faiola and M. Fan, "North Korea's Political, Economic Gamble," *Washington Post*, October 10, 2006, A12.

Korea, including bans on weapons-related items and luxury goods. Finally, the resolution banned international travel of North Korea's weapons program personnel and froze all overseas assets related to the program.[52]

In December 2006, the fifth round of six-party talks began and, on February 13, 2007, reached another apparent breakthrough. After several meetings, North Korea agreed to shut down the Yongbyon nuclear reactor and related facilities within sixty days. In return, North Korea received approximately $400 million in fuel oil, and IAEA inspectors were allowed to return to monitor and verify the disabling process.[53] In response, the United States released the $25 million in BDA that belonged to North Korea. In July 2007, an IAEA inspection team confirmed that North Korea had shut down the Yongbyon reactor. The accord, however, did not address three important issues: allegations of North Korea's HEU program, its existing nuclear weapons stockpile, and assistance it may have given to other countries.

In November 2007, North Korea issued a nuclear inventory report and demanded continuing aid because it had fulfilled its end of the bargain. The United States, however, claimed that the inventory report needed to be verified and therefore it would suspend aid until a complete report was provided. Christopher Hill, the U.S. chief envoy to the six-party talks, demanded explanations for "uranium traces found in tube parts, detailed disclosure of nuclear weapons and weapons programs, and equal disclosure of its proliferation activities, especially regarding Syria."[54] North Korea refused to submit another report, claiming that the earlier disclosure was sufficient. There was no further communication, and the six-party talks stalled.

The Peace and Prosperity Policy

The Roh Moo-hyun government's North Korean policy, labeled the Peace and Prosperity policy, made it clear that he intended to continue the sunshine policy. In an interview with *Time* magazine, President Roh maintained, "I don't think there is a particular reason to promote

[52] UNSC Resolution, http://www.un.org/Docs/sc/unsc_resolutions06.htm.

[53] J. Yardley and D. Sanger, "In Shift, Accord on North Korea Seems to Be Set," *New York Times*, February 13, 2007.

[54] K. Lee, "Delay in North Korea's Denuclearization." *Vantage Point* 31, no. 1 (January 2008): 14–15.

a different policy from the former President's policy. I will try to improve the methodology by consulting with the opposition party, winning more approval of the people and increasing transparency of the process."[55] In other words, President Roh Moo-hyun did not perceive the sunshine policy as a failure. Instead, he seemed to think the policy was a good approach that only needed improvement in implementation.

To this end, the Roh administration proposed two goals and four principles for the implementation of the Peace and Prosperity policy. The two goals included promoting peace and prosperity on the Korean peninsula.[56] With respect to the four principles, the first emphasized problem solving through dialogue between the two Koreas. This principle was based on the logic that, through dialogue, inter-Korean relations can improve and the engagement policy can be better implemented. The second principle emphasized enhancing mutual trust based on reciprocity. The rationale behind this principle was that an equal relationship based on reciprocity will provide mutual benefits that augment mutual trust. The third principle stressed international cooperation, because inter-Korean relations are unlikely to improve without international support. Thus, the Peace and Prosperity policy called on other nations to engage North Korea. The fourth and final principle involved citizen participation.[57] The Sunshine policy faced public criticism because of the North's lack of response, and the Roh government intended to reflect public opinion better in the implementation of its North Korean policy. This move was particularly needed given the lack of public support for the policy in the wake of the second North Korean nuclear crisis.[58]

With the Peace and Prosperity policy, the Roh government expanded its aid to North Korea. According to statistics from the Ministry of Unification, total trade between the two Koreas increased to $1.8 billion in 2007 from $724 million in 2003 at the beginning of the Roh administration. In addition, economic aid and travel to

---

[55] *Time*, March 3, 2003, 41.

[56] The Ministry of Unification, *The Participatory Government's Peace and Prosperity Policy* (Seoul: Ministry of Unification, 2003).

[57] M. Cho, "Roh Moo-hyun Government's Peace and Prosperity Policy: Prospects and Tasks," *Unification Policy Studies* 12, no. 1 (2003): 1–27.

[58] H. Yoon, "The Peace and Prosperity Policy and the South–North Relationship: Evaluation and Future Tasks," in *Peace and Prosperity Policy and Peace Regime on the Korean Peninsula: The Limits of Coercive Diplomacy in Korean Peninsula*, ed. I. Kang (Seoul: Institute for East Asian Studies, 2005).

North Korea also increased. In 2002, the last year of the Kim Dae-jung administration, South Korea provided $322.6 million in economic aid, an amount that increased to $439.7 million by 2007, the last year of the Roh administration. In addition, the number of workers at the Kaesong Industrial Park increased to 22,538 at the end of 2007 from a mere 2,000 in March 2005.

Furthermore, President Roh Moo-hyun had a summit meeting with North Korean leader Kim Jong-il in Pyongyang on October 2, 2007. On October 4, the two leaders signed a peace declaration that focused on building a peace mechanism and enhancing economic cooperation between the two Koreas. To this end, the declaration called for international talks to replace the current armistice with a permanent peace treaty. To improve economic ties, the two leaders agreed to set up a special economic zone in Haeju and create a joint fishing area close to the NLL in the disputed waters of the Yellow Sea. Moreover, South Korea offered to reopen a railroad between Kaesong and Sinuiju and build an expressway between Kaesong and Pyongyang in addition to constructing a shipbuilding complex in Nampo.[59] Conservatives in South Korea were highly critical of the outcome of this second inter-Korean summit meeting because nuclear issues were not discussed, although the meeting occurred in the midst of the nuclear crisis. Critics were also upset with the high cost of these proposed projects.

The Lee Myung-bak Administration

Continuation of the Second Nuclear Crisis

In February 2008, President Lee Myung-bak, a conservative who often disagreed with the approach of the previous two administrations, came to office as the second North Korean nuclear crisis continued. North Korea failed to meet a December 31, 2007, deadline to provide a complete report of its nuclear programs. Washington urged North Korea to fulfill its commitments, but Pyongyang responded that the U.S. government should stop its hostile policies. According to many analysts, North Korea did not want to admit its HEU program and was

---

[59] N. Onishi, "Korea Summit Results Exceed Low Expectations," *New York Times*, October 5, 2007.

reluctant to discuss its transfer of nuclear technology to Syria.[60] In the face of North Korean resistance, the Bush administration backed away from its demands, including a North Korean admission of involvement in Syria's nuclear program. Washington also did not press its demand that North Korea provide a complete report on its uranium-based nuclear program.[61]

The North did submit 18,000 pages of documents containing information about the plutonium-based nuclear program dating back to 1990, but the documents did not address the HEU program, the size of North Korea's current stockpile, or the nuclear proliferation issue. All of these issues were important steps toward implementing the February 13, 2007, deal. As a symbol of a North Korean commitment to end its nuclear program, however, Pyongyang destroyed the cooling tower at Yongbyon on June 27, 2008. Thus, for the moment, it appeared possible that North Korea might be willing to give up its nuclear weapons ambitions.

With this progress, the United States provided one million tons of heavy fuel oil to North Korea, and the North Korean government allowed international aid workers to monitor distribution. Six-party talks resumed, and negotiators agreed that North Korea would disable the main nuclear complex in Yongbyon by the end of October 2008 in exchange for 1 million tons of heavy fuel oil and economic aid. Because there was no timetable set for full dismantlement of the North Korean nuclear program and there were no specifics set for a verification process, difficulties lay ahead. It was an important step forward, however, considering that the talks had stalled for some time.[62]

Based on previous discussions, the United States had pledged to remove North Korea from the U.S. State Department's State Sponsors of Terrorism list when North Korea provided a full accounting of its nuclear materials and activities.[63] The report was due on December 31, 2007, but was delayed. Finally, in June 2008, North Korea

[60] S. Choe, "North Korea Says War Games Could Set Back Nuclear Talks," *New York Times*, March 4, 2008.

[61] H. Cooper, "Past Deals by North Korea May Face Less Study," *New York Times*, April 18, 2008.

[62] J. Yardley and J. Hooker, "Deal on Verifying North Korean Disarmament," *New York Times*, July 13, 2008.

[63] For a more detailed discussion of this issue, see T. Roehrig, "North Korea and the US State Sponsors of Terrorism List, 82–106, and L. Niksch and R. Perl, "North Korea: Terrorism List Removal?" *CRS Report for Congress*, RL 30613, January 14, 2008.

provided the report, and Pyongyang believed it had fulfilled its obligations. According to U.S. law, removing a state from the list required a forty-five-day waiting period, meaning that North Korea's removal would happen sometime in August 2008. By mid-August, however, it was becoming clear that the United States was not moving on the process for removal, and Pyongyang decided to act. On August 26, North Korea announced that it was stopping the disabling process at Yongbyon and restoring the nuclear facility, declaring that it did not care if it remained on the list or not. On October 1, Christopher Hill, the Bush administration's top envoy, visited Pyongyang to salvage the deal but failed to reach an agreement. North Korea barred IAEA inspectors from the nuclear site and continued to resume work at the Yongbyon nuclear complex. In an effort to save the agreement, Washington removed North Korea from the State Department's list of state sponsors of terrorism, which led to the resumption of the nuclear disabling process.

The agreement on dismantling the nuclear program faced another hurdle because of the lack of an agreed-on process of verification. To evaluate the extent of North Korea's nuclear program, it was crucial to take soil and nuclear waste samples. North Korea did not allow IAEA inspectors to do so, which eventually led to the collapse of nuclear talks.[64]

In 2009, President Barack Obama came to office. During his election campaign, he had indicated his willingness to enter into bilateral talks with Pyongyang, however, his attention after the inauguration focused on the global economic crisis and the ongoing wars in Afghanistan and Iraq. North Korea continued its tough stance and conducted a long-range missile test in April 2009, followed by another nuclear weapons test in May. The Obama administration condemned these acts, and the UNSC issued a statement criticizing North Korea while imposing further sanctions. As a result, North Korea refused to participate in the six-part talks, and further dialogue has been on hold. Recently, however, Pyongyang started sending signals to Seoul and Washington that it is interested in restarting the dialogue. There have been reports that Seoul and Pyongyang and Washington and Pyongyang have been in contact to discuss the resumption of dialogue.

[64] S. Choe, "North Korea Limits Tests of Nuclear Site," *New York Times*, November 12, 2008.

The Policy of Mutual Benefits and Common Prosperity

Because President Lee Myung-bak was critical of the approach employed by the two previous administrations, he introduced a new one: the Policy of Mutual Benefits and Common Prosperity. According to the Vice-Minister of the Unification Ministry Hong Yang-ho, "The policy is designed to settle peace on the peninsula, pursue economic cooperation based on mutual benefits, resolve humanitarian issues and improve the happiness and quality of life for the people of both Koreas."[65] With four guiding principles – pragmatic and result-oriented approaches, strict principles and flexible approaches, national consensus, and balance between inter-Korean cooperation and international cooperation – the policy pursues dialogue, peaceful resolution of the nuclear issues, economic cooperation, social and cultural exchanges, and the resolution of the humanitarian issues such as family separation issues.[66]

Although the Lee administration's Policy of Mutual Benefits and Common Prosperity is similar to the previous administration's North Korea policy with respect to encouraging social, economic, and cultural exchanges, it is significantly different in that it emphasizes reciprocity and does not separate politics and economics. For instance, the Lee administration made it clear that it would speak out against human rights abuses in North Korea and would require the abandonment of the North's nuclear program for further expansion of economic exchanges.[67] The changes in Seoul's policy toward North Korea, however, resulted in harsh rhetoric from the North, deteriorating North-South relations. North Korea threatened to reduce South Korea to ashes and attacked President Lee Myung-bak by calling him a traitor and a U.S. sycophant. Pyongyang also announced that the Lee administration's policy would bring disaster for international efforts to resolve the North Korean nuclear issue.[68] Because the Lee Myung-bak administration abides by the principle of mutual benefits, unconditional aid to the North has largely stopped. As a result, relations between the two Koreas have cooled considerably.

[65] "Seoul Seeks Inter-Korean Benefits, Prosperity," *The Korea Times*, February 25, 2009.

[66] Korean Institute for National Unification, *Policy of Mutual Benefits and Common Prosperity* (Seoul: Korea Institute for National Unification, 2008).

[67] Choe, Sang-hyun, "South Korea Adds Terms Its Aid to the North," *New York Times*, March 27, 2008.

[68] S. Choe, "North Korea Attacks South's President," *New York Times*, April 2, 2008.

Conclusion

The inter-Korean relationship has changed over time as a result of the end of the Cold War and the transition to democracy in South Korea. The end of the Cold War gave way to South Korea's normalization with China and the Soviet Union/Russia. The transition to democracy and the rise of civilian leadership led to South Korea pursuing engagement approaches in dealing with North Korea. These changes, however, did not produce a fundamental change in the relationship between the two Koreas because of the North Korean nuclear crisis. Despite agreements to freeze and dismantle North Korea's nuclear programs, implementation did not occur, and the six-party talks have stalled. The new leadership in South Korea and the United States do not seem to be willing to concede anymore, pointing to difficulties ahead in the inter-Korean relationship and the North Korean nuclear crisis.

7

The South Korea–U.S. Alliance

A crucial element of South Korea's security has been its alliance with the United States. The alliance was formalized in 1953 with the signing of a mutual defense treaty, but the relationship began informally when World War II came to an end. The alliance has had its high and low points, as all long-term relationships do. What began as a patron–client relationship between Washington and Seoul is evolving into one that resembles more of a partnership, although an unequal one. The alliance has been the subject of a multitude of studies in the past fifty years, and the precise nature and future of the alliance remain unknown. It appears likely that the alliance, although shifting in form, will remain an important part of South Korean security and the overall security architecture in East Asia for some time. This chapter will examine the history and components of the alliance, the efforts begun under the George W. Bush administration to restructure the U.S. force presence, and the future direction of the alliance.

An Uncertain Guarantee: 1945–1953

Prior to World War II, Korean ties with the United States were minimal, but the closing days of World War II brought Korea to the attention of U.S. leaders. With Japan's hasty surrender after the dropping of the atomic bombs, U.S. officials quickly crafted a proposal for the United States and the Soviet Union to divide the peninsula at the 38th parallel for taking the Japanese surrender. Moscow agreed to the proposal and accepted Japan's surrender in the North while U.S. forces did so in the South. Washington also made clear its goal that the division was only temporary. For two years, U.S.

and Soviet leaders attempted to negotiate the reunification of the two zones, but Korea was quickly becoming part of the Cold War conflict that was already growing in Europe. It was increasingly clear that a negotiated settlement was unlikely. In November 1947, the United States turned the problem over to the United Nations (UN), which approved a plan that would reunite the peninsula and hold elections. Moscow and Pyongyang refused to comply with the UN resolution, and, after holding its own elections, South Korea, officially known as the Republic of Korea (ROK), came into being on August 15, 1948.

With the official creation of South Korea, U.S. leaders debated the role South Korea should play in U.S. security policy in Asia. In spring 1948, the Truman administration released a report by the National Security Council (NSC 8) that laid out U.S. goals in Korea. The document connected Korea with the Cold War in Europe, noting that "the predominant aim of Soviet policy in Korea is to achieve eventual domination of the entire country." This was a serious threat to U.S. security, as "Soviet control over all of Korea would enhance the political and strategic position of the Soviet Union with respect to both China and Japan, and adversely affect the position of the United States in those areas and throughout the Far East."[1] Consequently, NSC 8 argued that Washington should not abandon South Korea and needed to provide sufficient support to allow Seoul to defend itself. A sudden withdrawal, even after the creation of South Korea, would send a negative signal to the Soviets and to other U.S. allies.

Despite the support demonstrated in NSC 8, others in the United States argued that it was time to leave South Korea. Most Americans were anxious for a reduction in U.S. defense spending and the size of the military, and Congress showed little willingness to oppose this view. The Pentagon was also reluctant, given the likelihood of dwindling resources, to support a large troop presence in Korea. In 1948, the U.S. Joint Chiefs of Staff argued that "the U.S. has little strategic interest in maintaining its present troops and bases in Korea. Moreover, in the event of hostilities in the Far East, these troops would constitute a military liability."[2] A U.S.–Soviet conflict would likely bypass troops in South Korea, and these forces would provide little

---

[1] "Report by the National Security Council on the Position of the United States With Respect to Korea, NSC 8," *Foreign Relations of the United States, 1948*, VI, 1167.
[2] "Report by the National Security Council to the President: NSC 8/2," *FRUS*, 1949, VII, 976.

support for the war effort. General Douglas MacArthur argued that the United States was wise to leave Korea while it could do so of its own volition. He feared that, if war broke out, the United States might be forced to abandon South Korea, a move that would hurt U.S. credibility.[3]

In the end, the fiscal pressures became too great, and, in June 1949, the United States withdrew its last combat troops from South Korea. To compensate for the withdrawal, Washington provided large amounts of military and economic aid along with small arms and defensive weapons. South Korean President Rhee lobbied hard for a formal security guarantee and heavy military equipment, including tanks and combat aircraft. He received none of this, in large part because U.S. officials feared that President Rhee might use the weapons to initiate his own effort to reunify Korea under his rule.

By fall 1949, the Cold War had taken an ominous turn. In August, the Soviets exploded their first atomic bomb, and, in October, China fell to communism. Events in China were particularly troubling, as it had been hoped that Chiang Kai-shek and his Nationalist government would be the chief U.S. ally in Asia. U.S. officials were also dismayed that, despite the massive amounts of aid funneled into Chiang's government, he had been unable to defeat Mao's communist insurgency. As a result, South Korea became even more important to U.S. security interests in the region, and U.S. leaders believed a line had to be drawn there against communist expansion in Asia. U.S. officials believed, however, that this goal could be obtained by building South Korea's capacity to defend itself through economic and military aid. Washington saw how Chiang Kai-shek had wasted huge sums of money and believed South Korea provided a second chance to show how aid could be used as a tool to stop the spread of communism. Consequently, U.S. officials believed they were taking the middle ground between a full, formal defense commitment and abandoning South Korea, fully expecting their approach to be successful in protecting the South.[4]

---

[3] As noted in *FRUS, 1949*, VII, 946. The original document is Department of the Army telegram CX 67198, January 19, 1949, summarized in Robert K. Sawyer, *Military Advisors in Korea: KMAG in Peace and War*, in a volume in the *United States Army Historical Series*, ed. Walter G. Hermes (Washington, D.C.: Government Printing Office, 1962), 37.

[4] See J. Matray, *The Reluctant Crusade* (Honolulu: University of Hawaii Press, 1985), 176, and "Report by the National Security Council to the President-NSC 8/2," *FRUS, 1949*, VII, part 2, 975–8.

Despite these efforts, critics often point to the "defense perimeter" speech given by Secretary of State Dean Acheson as a serious mistake that weakened the U.S. commitment to South Korea. On January 12, 1950, Secretary Acheson addressed the National Press Club and spoke of a defense perimeter that went from Alaska to Japan and on to the Philippines, a line that excluded South Korea. Although the perimeter did not include the South, Acheson maintained that all those outside must be prepared to defend themselves and should appeal to the UN, "which so far has not proved a weak reed to lean on by any people who are determined to protect their independence against outside aggression." When highlighting South Korea, Acheson noted that the United States had invested a great deal in South Korea and would continue to support Seoul as an important interest in Asia.[5] Thus, Acheson had no intent to "write off" South Korea.

Although U.S. leaders did not realize so at the time, the speech helped to convince Kim Il-sung that he could launch an invasion and conquer the South before the United States could come to Seoul's assistance. On June 25, 1950, the Democratic People's Republic of Korea (DPRK) launched its invasion to reunify the peninsula. U.S. officials had believed that subversion and infiltration were the chief threats to ROK security. The invasion, which U.S. leaders were convinced was instigated by Moscow, demonstrated to them that global communism was much more determined to expand in Korea than they had previously believed. Moreover, the U.S. defense commitment had failed to deter communist forces, and a more explicit security guarantee would be needed in the future.

The ROK–U.S. Alliance

When the Korean War ended, U.S. leaders believed they had done a poor job signaling their intent to protect South Korea. Washington was determined to not make this mistake again and proceeded to construct a deterrence strategy to more fully demonstrate its commitment to South Korea's security.

The ROK–U.S. alliance is an example of extended deterrence whereby the United States is attempting to deter an attack on an ally rather than an attack against the U.S. homeland. Resolve is a

[5] D. Acheson, "Crisis in Asia – An Examination of U.S. Policy," *Department of State Bulletin*, XXII, no. 551, January 23, 1950, 116–7.

particularly difficult task in a situation of extended deterrence. No one doubts that a state will respond if its homeland is attacked, but will a defender really back an ally in a crisis? Is the ally sufficiently important to risk war should deterrence fail, especially if nuclear weapons are involved? There is no guarantee that a defender will honor its commitment when that obligation might bring destruction to its own territory. This is particularly problematic if the adversaries possess long-range nuclear weapons. During the Cold War, U.S. allies in Europe often questioned the U.S. commitment, wondering if Washington would really sacrifice Washington for London or Paris. In 1979, Henry Kissinger gave a speech to North Atlantic Treaty Organization (NATO) defense ministers during which he asked European allies to stop "asking us to multiply strategic assurances that we cannot possibly mean, we should not want to execute because if we execute, we risk the destruction of civilization."[6] Washington faced a similar dilemma in implementing a deterrence commitment for South Korea and chose four ways to demonstrate its resolve: a formal security treaty, economic and military aid, deployment of conventional forces, and nuclear weapons.

Formal Security Treaty

Soon after the Korean War, U.S. and ROK officials concluded the Mutual Defense Treaty. The U.S. Senate approved the agreement on January 26, 1954, by a vote of eighty-one to six. According to U.S. Secretary of State John Foster Dulles, the treaty's "primary value consists in giving the Communists notice, beyond any possibility of misinterpretation, that the United States would not be indifferent to any new communist aggression in Korea."[7]

Although the security treaty made the U.S. commitment to defend South Korea explicit, President Rhee was disappointed. He had lobbied hard for an automatic security guarantee with wording similar to that found in the NATO defense treaty that declared, "an attack on one was an attack on all." Instead, the ROK–U.S. treaty noted only that the United States "would act to meet the common danger

---

[6] H. Kissinger, *For the Record: Selected Statements, 1977–1980* (Boston, Mass.: Little, Brown, 1981), 240.

[7] "Progress Report on NSC 170/1, "U.S. 'Objectives and Courses of Action in Korea,'" *FRUS, 1952–1954*, XV, pt. 2, 1767–70.

in accordance with its constitutional processes."[8] The "constitutional processes" clause was inserted in most U.S. treaties after ratification of the NATO agreement to assuage Senate concerns that the "attack on one was an attack on all" wording usurped the congressional power to declare war. Secretary Dulles attempted to reassure Rhee, noting that if South Korea were "subjected to an unprovoked attack you may of course count upon our immediate and automatic military reaction."[9] The security treaty remains in force today.

Economic and Military Aid

In an effort to rebuild a war-torn South Korea and demonstrate U.S. resolve, Washington poured in massive amounts of economic and military aid after the Korean War. From 1955 to 1967, the aid totaled more than $5.8 billion. As the ROK economy improved, support shifted from direct aid to loans, and most military assistance programs were phased out by the 1980s. The only significant security assistance program remaining is the International Military Education and Training program, which provides money for countries to participate in professional military education in U.S. military schools such as the Naval War College.

U.S. Conventional Forces

Treaties and pledges to come to an ally's assistance are easily broken; in a crisis, a defender may decide that an ally is simply not worth the cost of going to war. Thomas Schelling, a pioneer in deterrence theory, once wrote, regarding promises to defend an ally, that "saying so, unfortunately, does not make it true; and if it is true, saying so does not always make it believed. We evidently do not want war and would only fight if we had to. The problem is to demonstrate that we have to."[10] Thus, the best way to demonstrate resolve is to implement a strategy

---

[8] United States Senate, *Mutual Defense Treaty with Korea*, Hearings before the Committee on Foreign Relations, 83rd Congress, 2nd Session, January 13 and 14, 1954 (Washington, D.C.: Government Printing Office, 1954), 51–2.

[9] "Republic of Korea Draft of Mutual Defense Treaty Between the United States and the Republic of Korea," July 9, 1953, *FRUS*, 1952–1954, XV, pt. 2, 1430–1.

[10] T. Schelling, *Arms and Influence* (New Haven, Conn.: Yale University Press, 1966), 35.

that guarantees a response by the defender. Washington attempted to construct an automatic response by stationing U.S. ground forces along the likely invasion routes into South Korea to ensure that any DPRK invasion would confront U.S. troops to act as a "tripwire" to ensure a larger U.S. commitment.[11] From the end of the Korean War until 1971, the United States maintained two combat divisions, the Second and Seventh Infantry Divisions, along the main invasion corridors. Air Force and Navy units were also part of a U.S. presence that totaled approximately sixty-three thousand personnel.

In the years since, the size and location of U.S. forces in South Korea changed on several occasions. In 1971, President Richard Nixon removed the Seventh Infantry Division, reducing U.S. forces by twenty thousand, and shifted the remaining Second Division farther south from its forward positions along the demilitarized zone (DMZ). During his presidential campaign, candidate Jimmy Carter called for the removal of all U.S. ground forces from South Korea. His proposal generated staunch opposition within the United States and South Korea, and once elected, he removed only approximately thirty-four hundred before abandoning his plan. During the Reagan years, troop levels increased, but, with the end of the Cold War, U.S. forces decreased to 37,500 during the Clinton years.

Nuclear Weapons

Nuclear weapons have been an important part of the ROK–U.S. alliance, but in two different ways. First, beginning in the late 1950s, the United States based tactical nuclear weapons along with its conventional forces. U.S. nuclear forces included nuclear-tipped missiles, atomic demolition mines, nuclear artillery shells, and gravity bombs. Nuclear artillery was the chief component of U.S. nuclear forces, intended to thwart a North Korean invasion, particularly the ability to target masses of DPRK troops. Estimates of the number of nuclear weapons that were present in Korea ranged from two hundred fifty to six hundred, depending on the year.[12]

By the late 1980s, support for maintaining nuclear weapons in South Korea began to wane. In 1987, Commander of U.S. Forces

---

[11] T. Roehrig, *From Deterrence to Engagement*, 186.
[12] Ibid., 189.

Korea General Louis Menetrey maintained, "I do not envision any circumstance which . . . would require the use of nuclear weapons,"[13] and, in 1988, Lt. General John Cushman, former commander of I Corps, the troops who protected the approaches to Seoul, agreed that "nuclear weapons are no longer necessary for the defense of Korea."[14] In addition, it became increasingly clear that any use of nuclear weapons in the defense of South Korea would have devastating effects on the South as well as the North and endanger others in the region. Consequently, nuclear weapons were viewed as not worth the problems they caused and not necessary to deter an attack from the North.

In October 1991, the United States began a process of removing all U.S. tactical nuclear weapons from South Korea. Washington hoped this action would also encourage North Korea to abandon its nuclear ambitions and comply with International Atomic Energy Agency (IAEA) inspection requirements. In addition to having implications for Korea, the removal was also tied to the end of the Cold War and the breakup of the Soviet Union. By withdrawing U.S. nuclear weapons, U.S. President George H. W. Bush hoped that Russian President Mikhail Gorbachev would follow suit, helping to lessen the possibility of "stray" Russian nuclear weapons falling into the wrong hands. In December 1991, President Roh Tae-woo announced that all nuclear weapons had been removed from South Korea.[15]

Although no longer based in South Korea, nuclear weapons play another role in ROK security. The United States maintains a large number of nuclear weapons that could be used in a conflict in Korea if needed. Moreover, Washington has consistently stated that South Korea remains under the U.S. nuclear umbrella. In October 2006, Secretary of State Condoleezza Rice raced to Seoul and Tokyo soon after the DPRK's first nuclear weapons test to reassure both allies that the U.S. nuclear umbrella remained in effect. After North Korea's second nuclear test in May 2009, during an ROK–U.S. summit meeting in June 2009, President Barack Obama assured President Lee

---

[13] F. Hiatt, "U.S.: No Use of A-Arms Envisioned in S. Korea," *Washington Post*, December 3, 1987, A54.

[14] J. McBeth, "Withdrawal Symptoms: Americans Ponder the Removal of Nuclear Weapons," *Far Eastern Economic Review*, September 29, 1988, 35.

[15] J. Sterngold, "Seoul Says It Now Has No Nuclear Arms," *New York Times*, December 19, 1991, A3.

Myung-bak of Washington's "continuing commitment of extended deterrence, including the U.S. nuclear umbrella."[16]

The ROK–U.S. Alliance Since 1980

Reinvigorating the Alliance: The Chun–Reagan Years (1981–1989)

For South Korea, the four years under the Carter administration had been a difficult time for the alliance. President Carter had been a vocal critic of South Korea's human rights record and pushed hard for the withdrawal of all U.S. combat troops from the peninsula. When Ronald Reagan came to the White House in January 1981, he was determined to restore the alliance. Reagan was concerned about the spread of communism and the dangers of Soviet domination; South Korea played an important role in addressing these concerns. Reagan's Secretary of State George Shultz noted that "to Ronald Reagan, South Korea was a stalwart ally and a valiant symbol of resistance to communism."[17] Consequently, President Reagan believed the U.S. alliance commitment had deteriorated to unacceptable levels and was adamant to reassert U.S. support for Seoul. President Reagan pledged to retain U.S. ground forces and later increased the number of troops to 43,000, along with providing important upgrades to U.S. and South Korean equipment. In February 1981, President Chun Doo-hwan became the first foreign leader to visit the Reagan White House, an important symbolic show of support for the new South Korean government and the alliance. As noted in Chapter 2, the visit was also a quid pro quo for obtaining a stay of execution and the eventual release of Kim Dae-jung, although this was never announced publicly by either government.

Although all these measures did much to bolster the alliance, they were not without controversy, particularly President Chun's visit. Chun had come to power in a coup followed by the violent crackdown

---

[16] "Joint Vision for the Alliance of the United States of America and the Republic of Korea," June 16, 2009, http://www.whitehouse.gov/the_press_office/Joint-vision-for-the-alliance-of-the-United-States-of-America-and-the-Republic-of-Korea.

[17] G. Shulz, *Turmoil and Triumph: My Years as Secretary of State* (New York: Macmillan, 1984), 90.

of demonstrators at Kwangju. For many South Koreans, the apparent U.S. lack of support for the Kwangju demonstrators in spring 1980 followed by Chun's visit severely damaged the United States's image as an advocate for democracy. U.S. officials at the time believed there was little they could do during Chun's takeover, and South Korean security trumped concerns for political liberalization. Soon after, however, when President Reagan visited South Korea for the first time in 1983, he offered what Secretary of State Shultz described as "our central message: the importance of President Chun's commitment to step aside as president at the end of his term in 1988 and to turn power over to an elected successor."[18] Later, in spring 1987, when it appeared doubtful that President Chun would relinquish power, President Reagan sent Chun a letter "as a friend":

> I believe that political stability based on sound democratic institutions is critical to insuring the long-term security of your country, and you have often expressed the same sentiments. . . . I applaud your commitment to a peaceful transfer of Presidential power next year as a crucial – and, as you say, unprecedented and historic – step in strengthening that institution of democratic government.[19]

Ultimately, President Chun did step down and allow the election to proceed.

The Alliance and the End of the Cold War

President George H. W. Bush followed the Reagan administration and was no less supportive of the ROK–U.S. alliance. Toward the end of his term in 1992, President Bush visited South Korea and reaffirmed, "Let there be no misunderstanding: The United States will remain in Korea as long as there is a need and that we are welcome."[20] Although the alliance remained strong during these years, the global and regional context underwent significant change in the late 1980s and early 1990s. The end of the Cold War, the fall of the Soviet Union, and the demise of global communism altered the international system, creating the possibility of a new security structure in East Asia. China and Russia normalized relations with South Korea, much to

---

[18] Ibid., 977–8.

[19] As quoted in Oberdorfer, *The Two Koreas*, 168.

[20] G. Bush, "The President's News Conference With President Roh Tae Woo," January 6, 1992, *Public Papers of the President, 1992–1993*, Book I, 34.

the chagrin of North Korea. The North Korean economy was forced to stand on its own when Beijing and Moscow removed subsidies and reduced economic and military assistance. Inter-Korean relations appeared to improve as the two Koreas signed non-aggression and denuclearization pacts in the early 1990s, and both were admitted into the UN.

Other important factors generated largely by South Korea's economic and political development were also changing the ROK–U.S. alliance during President Bush's term. First, South Korea was a democracy, having begun its transition in 1987. Seoul and Washington now shared the same political system and commitment to important political values. Second, the economic power of East Asia, including South Korea, was becoming increasingly evident, so many began to speak of the coming century as one likely to be dominated by Asia. These vibrant economies were increasing their ties to the U.S. economy and to others in the region. The economic power of East Asia was growing and becoming more regionally integrated, with South Korea playing a major role in that process. Economic ties and trade links were vital to the region and to U.S. prosperity, making it all the more important that peace and stability continue in East Asia. Moreover, democracy and economic growth were linked, and President Bush declared in his 1992 visit that "the Republic of Korea has stood strong for democracy [and] the Korean people will demonstrate that freedom's way is the way of the future in Asia. Nations which build their prosperity on the freedom of their people know that there is no alternative."[21]

Throughout these four years, South Korea was a consistent ally, providing regular support for U.S. positions in a variety of forums as ROK–U.S. interests aligned. South Korea also provided assistance to U.S. operations during the first Persian Gulf War in 1990–91, sending $500 million in financial assistance along with a medical support unit consisting of 154 personnel, five C-130 aircraft, and 156 ground support personnel.[22] As a result, the alliance was undergoing a subtle change in which ROK prosperity and its transition to democracy made South Korea a more valued ally for the United States. South Korea was no longer simply an interest to protect, but, as President Bush noted,

[21] Ibid., 38.
[22] U.S. Department of Defense, *A Strategic Framework for the Asian Pacific Rim: Looking Toward the 21st Century* (Washington, D.C.: Government Printing Office, February 28, 1991), 6.

the relationship was "more than a military alliance, our countries are moving toward a political, economic and security partnership."[23]

When Bush left the White House, the North Korean nuclear issue was already starting to brew. Intelligence had begun to surface indicating that, despite North Korea's signature to the Nuclear Non-Proliferation Treaty (NPT), it possibly was still pursuing nuclear weapons. When Bush lost the November 1992 election to Bill Clinton, however, the job of addressing this difficult problem fell largely to the next administration.

When President Clinton entered the White House, its dominant campaign theme had been "It's the economy, stupid," and he was determined to focus on a domestic agenda. It was not long before it became evident that such a single-minded focus on issues at home would not survive the multitude of foreign policy problems bombarding his administration. Soon the North Korean nuclear crisis became a major foreign policy headache and the central issue that dominated ROK–U.S. relations. This issue was addressed in the preceding chapter, but it is important to note here that the next eight years posed a difficult challenge in terms of coordinating South Korean and U.S. interests and policy. Although relations were fairly well managed by both sides during these closing years of the twentieth century, the alliance would face more difficult years ahead.

Friction and Questioning the Alliance

Any relationship that lasts for more than fifty years is bound to have some troubled times, and the ROK–U.S. alliance is no different. The alliance began as a highly asymmetric relationship largely requiring South Korea to do Washington's bidding, as it had far less power in the relationship. Of particular concern to South Korean leaders was a fear that the United States might act contrary to ROK interests and that it would do so without consulting South Korean leaders. For example, Nixon's decision to withdraw the U.S. Seventh Infantry Division in the closing months of the Vietnam War greatly worried ROK leaders that it could be the beginning of dismantling the alliance and a U.S. withdrawal from Asia.

---

[23] G. Bush, "Text of Remarks at Camp Casey in Yongsan, South Korea," January 6, 1992, *Public Papers of the President, 1992–1993*, Book I, 43.

Matters worsened when word reached South Korea of Nixon's efforts to open relations with China in 1972. The United States had not given President Park advanced notice or consulted him about the effort. In an off-the-record dinner with the press that followed the revelation of Kissinger's secret visit to China, President Park lamented that, in view of these actions, "How long can we trust the United States?"[24] Later, but before Nixon made his trip to Beijing, Park sent him a letter expressing his concern about the visit and how it might have a negative impact on ROK security. Park also requested a meeting with Nixon before he made the trip. Administration officials dismissed Park's request, and, afterwards, Nixon made a perfunctory announcement that any agreements with China would not be made at South Korea's expense. Several years after Nixon's visit, President Park recalled that "this series of developments contained an unprecedented peril to our people's survival."[25] President Carter's proposal to withdraw all U.S. combat units from South Korea only made matters worse. Despite these difficulties, the alliance remained relatively stable and focused on deterring the threat from the North.

After the turn of the century, alliance relations faced some of their most serious challenges, with some suggesting that the ROK–U.S. alliance might be heading toward its last days. Perhaps the most important source of friction in the alliance was differing views regarding how to deal with North Korea. According to one U.S. official, "If you can't agree on who the enemy is, it raises some pretty fundamental questions about the reasons for your alliance."[26] The United States, as the world's dominant power, has global interests and a foreign policy that since 2001 has been grounded in the "long war" struggle against terrorism. The 2006 U.S. National Security Strategy (NSS) noted:

> defeating terrorism requires a long-term strategy and a break with old patterns. We are fighting a new enemy with global reach. The United States can no longer simply rely on deterrence to keep the terrorists at bay or defensive measures to thwart them at the last moment. The fight must be taken to the enemy, to keep them on the run. To succeed in our own efforts, we need the support and concerted action of friends and allies.[27]

[24] Oberdorfer, *The Two Koreas*, 13.

[25] Ibid., 14.

[26] A. Faiola, "Seoul's Push to Regain Wartime Control from U.S. Divides South Koreans," *Washington Post*, August 29, 2006, A10.

[27] *National Security Strategy of the United States*, March 2006, http://www.whitehouse. gov/nsc/nss/2006/, 8.

U.S. policy in East Asia is viewed as part of this approach, especially through efforts to prevent the proliferation of weapons of mass destruction and keeping these weapons out of the hands of terrorists. Although there is some concern that North Korea might be sufficiently irrational to use a nuclear weapon against the United States, the greater fear in Washington is that Pyongyang, saddled with a destitute economy, might sell a nuclear weapon or related technology to a terrorist group or other U.S. adversaries. Moreover, as noted in the NSS, the support of allies is deemed crucial to this struggle, and Washington has often seen South Korea as providing too little support in this regard. Early in the Iraq War, South Korea provided 3,200 troops to the U.S. effort in Iraq. From the perspective of the Bush administration, this support was minimal and expected, given past U.S. support of South Korea. For Seoul, however, this decision was difficult and contentious but was viewed as the price of maintaining the alliance. Adding further to South Korea's irritation, in his nomination speech for the 2004 Republican nomination, President Bush recognized those who contributed to U.S. efforts in Iraq but neglected to mention South Korea, despite the fact that it was the third-largest contributor of troops in the coalition.[28]

Specific U.S. policy toward North Korea has also been a source of disagreement and tension. Many in the Bush administration entered office deeply skeptical of the U.S. approach during the Clinton years and the 1994 Agreed Framework. North Korea was seen as an enemy that could not be trusted, so the Agreed Framework was viewed as a naïve effort to cap the nuclear ambitions of a despicable regime. Despite some early indications that the administration would continue the Clinton policy, President Bush mandated a review of U.S. policy toward North Korea. Bush was also leery of North Korea's reliability to keep agreements and included North Korea in his now-famous State of the Union address in January 2002 in the "axis of evil." In an interview with Bob Woodward, Bush noted, "I loathe Kim Jong Il,"[29] and, later, during her confirmation hearings, Secretary of State Condoleezza Rice labeled North Korea as an "outpost of tyranny."

---

[28] In the speech, President Bush identified nations "like Great Britain, Poland, Italy, Japan, the Netherlands, Denmark, El Salvador, Australia, and others – allies that deserve the respect of all Americans, not the scorn of a politician." President George W. Bush, "President's Remarks at the 2004 Republican National Convention," September 2, 2004, http://www.whitehouse.gov/news/releases/2004/09/20040902-2.html.

[29] B. Woodward, *Bush at War* (New York: Simon & Schuster, 2002), 340.

Many South Koreans viewed matters differently. For Seoul, North Korea is a regional problem that is not tied to a war on terrorism. North Korea also was not viewed as a proliferation problem and security threat in the same way that Washington saw the dilemma. According to the *2006 Global Strategic Survey* of the International Institute of Strategic Studies, with regard to North Korea,

> where Americans see an increasingly dangerous and repressive regime, South Koreans see a pitiable renegade brother, estranged by an accident of history in which America is culpable. South Koreans do not believe the North Koreans would use their nuclear weapons unless they were forced to do so for regime survival. South Koreans are thus more afraid of a US policy of regime change that could provoke North Korea.[30]

Consequently, a January 2004 poll reported in the *Chosun Ilbo* showed that 39 percent of South Koreans believed the United States was the greatest threat to Korean security compared with North Korea, which came in second at 33 percent. Among respondents in their twenties, 58 percent believed the United States was the greater threat.[31] Some of these views have changed since North Korea conducted its two nuclear tests, with South Koreans becoming far more concerned about the dangers of a North Korean collapse and the costs of reunification.

Concerns also surfaced within the United States that South Korea was slowly drifting toward China, raising the possibility that Seoul would increasingly see its strategic future in the direction of Beijing rather than Washington.[32] In 2003, China became South Korea's largest trading partner. Foreign direct investment between the two countries continues to grow, and the role of China in regional economic integration makes good relations with Beijing important. This reality, coupled with rising anti-Americanism, raised questions about Seoul's future strategic intent, however two South Korean scholars argued that it was incorrect to interpret these events as South Korea drifting away from the United States. "Instead, a combination of South

---

[30] *IISS Strategic Survey 2006* (New York: Routledge, 2006), 298.

[31] "U.S. Is Korea's Adversary," *Chosun Ilbo*, January 12, 2004, http://english.chosun.com/w21data/html/news/200401/200401120029.html.

[32] For an excellent treatment of the impact on China's rise on both Koreas, see S. Snyder, *China's Rise and the Two Koreas: Politics, Economics, Security* (Boulder, Colo.: Lynne Rienner, 2009).

Korean economic development over time, the rise of a new generation in South Korean politics, and changing inter-Korean relations
help explain a Seoul that has become more fundamentally independent
than anti-U.S. or pro-Chinese."[33]

ROK–U.S. relations were further complicated by a series of events
that fueled a rising tide of anti-Americanism. In September 1999, the
Associated Press reported that the U.S. military had opened fire on
Korean refugees at No Gun Ri during the Korean War, believing
some were North Korean spies. The following year, a Korean environmental group accused the USFK of dumping toxic waste into the
Han River. In November 2002, two South Korean middle school
girls were killed by a U.S. military vehicle in a training accident.[34]
When the two Army personnel were acquitted in December, South
Koreans were outraged. Massive demonstrations erupted, calling for
justice and revision of the Status of Forces Agreement that governs
the treatment of U.S. service personnel when they have committed
a crime. Candidate Roh Moo-hyun had already been campaigning
on an anti-U.S. platform that called for greater independence from
Washington. The accident acquittal further inflamed the resentment
that was already building over disagreements regarding North Korean
policy.

Anti-Americanism also had a clear generational character. Many of
those harboring these views were under the age of forty and had little
recollection of the Korean War and U.S. support to protect South
Korea. The "386 generation" furnished an increasing number of the
leaders in ROK politics and society who shared few of the strong,
positive feelings of older generations for the United States and its
protection of South Korea.

A number of U.S. officials and pundits were clearly miffed by the
anti-American sentiment from some in South Korea and saw the
complaints as ungrateful whining. If that was how most South Koreans
viewed the alliance, perhaps it was time for the United States to leave
South Korea. Thus, when President Roh Moo-hyun and President
George W. Bush met on September 14, 2006, for a summit meeting in
Washington D.C., the *Chosun Ilbo*, a major conservative South Korean

---

[33] S. Kim and W. Lim, "How to Deal with South Korea," *Washington Quarterly* 32,
no. 2 (Spring 2007): 72.

[34] See U. Heo and J. Woo, "Changing National Identity and Security Perception in
South Korea," in *Korean Security in a Changing East Asia*, ed. T. Roehrig, J. Seo,
and U. Heo (Westport, Conn.: Praeger, 2007), 197–9.

newspaper, observed, "The Korea-U.S. summit showed, if anything, what an alliance on the brink of divorce looks like."[35]

Some international relations scholars have also contended that the ROK–U.S. alliance is a relic of the Cold War and no longer necessary.[36] According to this argument, South Korea is not vital to U.S. security, and Seoul is more than capable of defending itself. Doug Bandow argues it is time to free "the American people from a commitment that costs far more than it is worth, absorbs valuable military resources, and keeps the Korean people in a dependent relationship that insults their nation hood and puts their destiny in another country's hands."[37] Consequently, there is no need for the alliance or the continued presence of U.S. forces in South Korea.

Despite the anti-American sentiment that continues among some South Koreans, there remains relatively broad support for the alliance, particularly after the wave of missile tests and a second nuclear test. In a 2008 study that used survey data, Chae and Kim compared the attitudes of progressives and conservatives on issues relating to views on North Korea, anti-American sentiment, and support for the ROK–U.S. alliance, among others. The study found that progressives held anti-American views and believed that Seoul and Washington had divergent interests in dealing with North Korea, that the United States did not sufficiently take into account ROK interests, and generally, Washington was an obstacle for improved inter-Korean relations. They also clearly recognized, however, that North Korea was a serious danger, believed the alliance should be strengthened, and opposed a sudden withdrawal of U.S. troops from South Korea.[38] Thus, regarding the ROK–U.S. alliance, Chae and Kim note that both conservatives and progressives in South Korea "essentially agree that the alliance is valuable to South Korea's national interests" and that "anti-American sentiments do not contradict but rather coexist with general support for the alliance."[39]

---

[35] "Getting Ready for Divorce," *Chosun Ilbo*, September 15, 2006, http://english.chosun.com/w21data/html/news/200609/200609150031.html.

[36] For example, see R. Menon, *The End of Alliances* (Oxford: Oxford University Press, 2007), 145–79.

[37] D. Bandow, "Seoul Searching: Ending the U.S.-Korean Alliance," *The National Interest* (Fall 2005): 116.

[38] H. Chae and S. Kim, "Conservatives and Progressives in South Korea," *Washington Quarterly* 31, no. 4 (Autumn 2008): 85–6.

[39] Ibid., 87. For another study of these attitudes, see C. Oh and C. Arrington, "Democratization and Changing Anti-American Sentiments in South Korea," *Asian Survey* 47, no. 2 (March/April 2007): 327–50.

Restructuring the Alliance

Early in the Bush administration, the Defense Department, under Secretary of Defense Donald Rumsfeld, began work on "transformation" to reconfigure the U.S. military into a force that was more agile, expeditionary, and better suited to handle the challenges of the twenty-first century.[40] The U.S. military was structured to deter and, if necessary, fight state adversaries with a traditional army, navy, and air force. Secretary Rumsfeld argued, however, that this no longer applied "to enemies who have no territories to defend and no treaties to honor."[41] Regarding South Korea, Rumsfeld maintained, "our troops were virtually frozen in place from where they were when the Korean War ended in 1953."[42] Although South Korean security remained an important goal, Washington could no longer afford to have troops positioned solely to deter and defend South Korea from an attack by the North. U.S. troops needed to be reduced and reconfigured to allow for use in a broader range of contingencies, providing U.S. forces with "strategic flexibility."

Consequently, in 2003, the United States announced the start of a two-part effort to transform the U.S. troop presence in South Korea.[43] First, the Pentagon stated that it was reducing U.S. forces in Korea to 28,000 by 2008. The first phase of the withdrawal was completed in 2004 with the removal of 5,000 troops, 3,700 of whom were from the Second Brigade of the Second Infantry Division and headed for deployment in Iraq. In 2008, U.S. and South Korean officials agreed to suspend further withdrawals so that the current force structure is at approximately 28,500. To compensate for the withdrawals, Washington committed to spending $11 billion to modernize U.S. forces, including providing Patriot missile batteries.

---

[40] See the *Quadrennial Defense Review Report*, September 30, 2001, and the 2004 *Global Posture Review*.

[41] "Global Posture: Testimony as Prepared for Delivery by Secretary of Defense Donald H. Rumsfeld to the Senate Armed Services Committee," September 23, 2004, www.defenselink.mil/speeches/2004/sp20040923-secdef0783.html.

[42] Ibid.

[43] See T. Roehrig, "Restructuring the U.S. Military Presence in Korea: Implications for Korean Security and the U.S.-ROK Alliance," in *On Korea*, vol. 1, Academic Paper Series (Washington, D.C.: Korea Economic Institute, 2007), 132–49, and C. Nam, "Relocating the U.S. Forces in South Korea: Strained Alliance, Emerging Partnership in the Changing Defense Posture," *Asian Survey* 46, no. 4 (July/August 2006): 615–31.

The second part of the reconfiguration is the relocation of U.S. forces from their forward-deployed positions north of Seoul to two hub locations south of the capital. In June 2004, U.S. and South Korean officials agreed to move U.S. forces to Osan Air Base and Camp Humphreys near Pyeongtaek. The consolidation into two hubs means that the U.S. military will return fifty-nine bases totaling more than 36,000 acres to South Korea. Relocating U.S. forces to these two locations allows the United States to reduce its footprint and lessen some of the friction that occurs from the presence of these troops on ROK soil. These installations include U.S. Forces Korea (USFK) headquarters at Yongsan, which is valuable real estate in the heart of Seoul. Some of the bases have already been returned to South Korea, and additional land has been purchased for the necessary expansion of Camp Humphreys and Osan Air Base. Although completion of the two facilities and the transfer of U.S. forces had been slated for 2008, construction delays have pushed the completion of the project back to possibly 2013.

As these two efforts progressed, they were joined by the issue of operational control (OPCON) of South Korean forces. During the Korean War, the United Nations Security Council created the United Nations Command (UNC) to coordinate the efforts of the sixteen countries that came to South Korea's assistance. The Security Council designated a U.S. commander to lead the UNC, and, in July 1950, President Rhee placed ROK forces under UN OPCON. After the war, OPCON of South Korean forces shifted from the UNC to the U.S. military command during both war and peacetime.

In 1978, Seoul and Washington altered the command relationship to integrate South Korea more extensively into the command structure. The new arrangement, called the Combined Forces Command (CFC), consisted of fourteen sections, each headed by a "chief" and a "deputy" as the second-in-command. U.S. officers hold the positions of chief for eight of these sections, including the most important position of commander-in-chief, the top position in the structure.[44] South Korean officers hold the "chief" position in the remaining six sections. For each section, if a U.S. officer holds the position of chief, a South Korean holds the position of deputy, and vice

---

[44] In addition to being the commander-in-chief of the CFC, the U.S. commander is also the commander of the UNC and USFK.

versa. The CFC is an integrated command structure that supports joint planning, training, and operational exercises. The CFC commander, a U.S. four-star general, reports to both the ROK and the U.S. president. In the event that war breaks out, the CFC would assume operational control (OPCON) over ROK and U.S. forces along with any U.S. forces sent to the region to help coordinate the responses of ground, air, and naval units in the defense of South Korea.

In 1990, President Roh Tae-woo began discussions to alter this relationship, and, in 1994, Seoul and Washington agreed to have the United States return peacetime OPCON to South Korea. As a result, the ranking South Korean commander assumed the day-to-day management of the ROK armed forces, but these troops remained under U.S. OPCON during wartime.

In 2002, Seoul and Washington began talks to return wartime OPCON to ROK commanders. The following year, newly elected President Roh Moo-hyun pushed the return with great enthusiasm. After two years of talks, defense officials agreed to make the change. When South Korea had demonstrated its desire for returning OPCON, the Pentagon was happy to comply. The only remaining issue was the precise date of the transfer, and this was the cause of some disagreement. Washington wished to make the change by 2009, fearing that a longer timeline might allow ROK authorities to change their mind. South Korea wanted the transfer to occur by 2012 to have more time to make the necessary preparations to assume full OPCON. In the end, U.S. officials acceded to South Korean wishes, and the transfer is set for April 17, 2012.

Defense planners continue to work on the details of the new command structure, but the precise nature of the plan is not yet finished. Most likely, the CFC will be deactivated and replaced with some type of parallel command structure with an independent U.S. Korea Command (KORCOM) and ROK command that will collaborate through a military cooperation center to coordinate joint operations in a crisis. South Korea will be in the lead for operations, however, and the United States will be in support, the reverse of the previous command relationship. Both forces will continue with high levels of integration and training and will continue to operate a joint intelligence center after the OPCON transfer. Moreover, exercises such as Key Resolve/Foal Eagle and Ulchi Freedom Guardian, formerly named Ulchi Focus Lens,[45] will continue to ensure that both sides maintain the proper capabilities and necessary coordination for South Korean security.

The chief driver behind South Korea's desire for the return of wartime OPCON was President Roh Moo-hyun. In an interview, President Roh remarked,

> Korea is the sole country that does not have complete operational control (OPCON) of its own troops. The country is the 11th largest economic powerhouse and has the sixth-largest military forces but it does not have wartime OPCON. OPCON is the basis of self-reliant national defense. The point is that self-reliant national defense is the essence of sovereignty for any nation.[46]

The South Korean military had grown in size and capability, so it could begin to assume the primary responsibility of defending the country. Moreover, U.S. leaders were also convinced that the transfer would not jeopardize South Korea's security. General Burwell B. Bell, the USFK commander when the intention to transfer wartime OPCON was announced, maintained that the three ROK armies "are powerful fighting forces. They're very, very capable."[47] In addition, General Bell assured South Koreans that the ability to deter, and if necessary, defeat North Korea remained the primary goal of the alliance, "and nothing will be done, in transferring any command relationships, that jeopardizes that fundamental."[48] Throughout the transfer, the United States will help South Korea make the necessary transition and will continue to provide the necessary capabilities, such as missile defense or intelligence-surveillance-reconnaissance (ISR) capabilities, until South Korea is ready to assume these roles so that there is no increased risk to South Korean security. The United States will continue to provide naval and air assets in a supporting role for the defense of South Korea, but ROK troops will be in the lead on the ground. In

---

[45] *Ulchi* refers to Korean General Eulji Mundeok, a famous leader during the Koguryo Dynasty in the Three Kingdoms Period who helped defend the kingdom from China.

[46] Roh Moo-hyun, as quoted in "Regaining Wartime Operational Control," *Vantage Point*, September 2006, 23.

[47] General B. B. Bell, "News Transcript: U.S. Forces Korea Media Roundtable," September 29, 2006, 8, www.usfk.mil/org/FKPA/sptr/contents/9_29_06_USFK%20Media%20Roundtable.pdf.

[48] Ibid.

November 2009, the successor to General Bell, USFK Commander
Walter Sharp, reiterated that the South Korean military is one of the
world's strongest, and, regarding the OPCON transfer, noted that "we
are on track. By 2012, the Republic of Korea military leadership will
be ready to take over."[49]

Despite President Roh's determination and assurances from the
United States that the OPCON transfer would not endanger ROK
security, many in South Korea were unhappy with this plan. Criticism
came from both the left and the right in South Korea, but for different
reasons. One of Washington's goals in restructuring its force presence
in South Korea was to provide "strategic flexibility" so that U.S. forces
there could respond to a variety of contingencies throughout Asia if
the need arose, including a possible conflict with China regarding
Taiwan. For those on the left, this was a dangerous scenario; South
Korea could be dragged into a conflict with China as U.S. aircraft used
their bases in South Korea to conduct missions against Chinese forces.
In January 2006, U.S. and ROK officials reached an understanding
in which Seoul acknowledged "the rationale for the transformation
of the U.S. global military strategy, and respects the necessity for
strategic flexibility." In turn, Washington agreed to respect "the ROK
position that it shall not be involved in a regional conflict in Northeast
Asia against the will of the Korean people."[50] Later, President Roh
proclaimed that South Korea retained the right to veto the use of
U.S. forces based in South Korea for operations outside the Korean
Peninsula.[51]

For conservatives, the transfer of wartime OPCON, along with the
reduction and relocation of U.S. forces in Korea, was an ominous signal
that pointed to a complete dismantling of the alliance. They believed
Washington was punishing Seoul for being an ungrateful ally in the
wake of the outbursts of anti-Americanism in ROK society and within
the Roh administration. Moreover, these critics maintained that South
Korea was simply not ready to take over this responsibility and were
particularly concerned about South Korea's continued reliance on the

[49] "Scheduled 2012 Transfer of OPCON on Track: U.S. Commander," *Seoul
Times*, November 5, 2009, http://theseoultimes.com/ST/?url=/ST/db/read.
php?idx=8908 (accessed November 17, 2009).

[50] U.S. Department of State, "United States and the Republic of Korea Launch
Strategic Consultation for Allied Partnership," January 19, 2006, www.state.
gov/r/pa/prs/ps/2006/59447.htm.

[51] L. Niksch, "Korea: U.S.-Korean Relations – Issues for Congress," (Washington,
D.C.: Congressional Research Service, July 21, 2006), 15.

U.S. military for intelligence. Without the careful coordination and sharing of intelligence gathering, as had occurred under the CFC, the South Korean military would have a serious gap in its capability. Conservatives were also concerned that the elimination of the CFC and the relocation of U.S. troops to positions south of Seoul would remove the "tripwire" function of U.S. troops and weaken deterrence. Given the prospects of horrendous destruction should deterrence fail, they believed that any measure that weakened deterrence was a huge mistake. Finally, many also feared the increased defense expenditures that would be necessary to upgrade the ROK military to take over wartime OPCON in a relatively short time; these costs could have a disastrous impact on the economy. In short, conservatives believe that maintaining the CFC structure is absolutely necessary for maintaining the ROK–U.S. alliance and South Korean security and continue to hope the OPCON transfer can be reversed or delayed.

Conservative opponents have done their best to reverse the decision. In August 2006, sixteen former South Korean defense ministers released a statement that condemned the turnover, lamenting, "We are thunderstruck that the president, who is responsible for safeguarding national defense and the nation's survival, takes national security so lightly."[52] Opponents gathered in a protest rally of five thousand people, including five hundred retired generals and admirals, to criticize the Roh administration for pursuing such a dangerous policy and called on officials to stop the dismantling of the CFC and the transfer of wartime OPCON. In November 2009, twenty former Korean deputy commanding generals of CFC sent a letter to President Barack Obama and President Lee Myung-bak requesting that they reconsider the transfer of wartime OPCON scheduled for April 2012.[53]

Despite these concerns and efforts to overturn the decision, the OPCON transfer and other elements of restructuring continue and are unlikely to be reversed. It is possible that there will be further delays in the relocation of U.S. troops and extending the date for final OPCON transfer. Both administrations are now committed to the moves, however, and too much effort and money have already gone

[52] "Roh Turns Deaf Ear to 16 Former Defense Chiefs," *Chosun Ilbo Online*, August 10, 2006, http://english.chosun.com/w21data/html/news/200608100032.html.

[53] Ashley Rowland and Hwang Hae-rym, "Ex-S. Korean generals: Unify Wartime Commands," *Stars and Stripes*, November 12, 2009, http://www.stripes.com/article.asp?section=104&article=66025 (accessed November 17, 2009).

into the changes. The United States remains committed to South
Korea's defense, including the continued extension of the U.S. nuclear
umbrella. Furthermore, North Korea is becoming increasingly isolated, and, although it has made improvements in some areas of its
military capabilities, most notably nuclear weapons, ballistic missiles,
and special operations forces, the overall power of the DPRK continues to deteriorate. Moreover, Seoul has developed its own strong
and capable military, particularly its ground forces, and has a large
economy to support its national security needs. The OPCON transfer creates some significant challenges and will necessitate the creation
of a new command structure. Despite these changes, U.S. and ROK
forces will continue their extensive cooperation and conduct exercises to ensure their coordination, but with the United States in a
supporting role.

From North Korea's perspective, these changes are unlikely to generate any calculation that they have an opportunity to test the U.S.
commitment to South Korea. The alliance and some level of U.S.
force presence will remain in place for some time, and U.S. and ROK
leaders regularly stress the importance of the alliance. In June 2009,
the ROK–U.S. joint vision concluded after the Lee–Obama summit
maintained, "Our open societies, our commitment to free democracy
and a market economy, and our sustained partnership provide a foundation for the enduring friendship, shared values, and mutual respect
that tightly bind the American and Korean peoples."[54] It is difficult
to imagine that North Korea would see the restructuring as a serious
opportunity to test the alliance.

The restructuring also helps to lessen the U.S. footprint on the
peninsula and treats South Korea more as a partner while still supporting ROK security. Rather than endangering ROK security and the
ROK–U.S. relationship, these measures may actually help to ensure
the long-term viability of the alliance, which increasingly has a broader
role to play beyond security on the Korean Peninsula. Moreover, signs
indicate that ROK public opinion is returning to a more favorable
view of the United States. In 2003, a Pew Research poll indicated
that only 46 percent of South Koreans held a favorable view of the

---

[54] For the complete text, see www.whitehouse.gov/the_press_office/Joint-vision-
for-the-alliance-of-the-United-States-of-America-and-the-Republic-of-Korea/.

United States, but, by 2007, that number had climbed to 58 percent, and by July 2009 it had reached 78 percent.[55] Thus, these changes are part of a constant evolution of an important relationship that helps the alliance to be more of a partnership rather than the patron–client relationship of old.

On June 16, 2009, President Barack Obama and President Lee Myung-bak met in Washington, D.C., to discuss, among other things, the future of the ROK–U.S. alliance. At the conclusion of their talks, the two leaders issued a joint vision that outlined in broad terms how the alliance has evolved and how it might proceed in the years ahead. The document declares:

> The United States-Republic of Korea Mutual Defense Treaty remains the cornerstone of the U.S.-ROK security relationship, which has guaranteed peace and stability on the Korean Peninsula and in Northeast Asia for over fifty years. Over that time, our security Alliance has strengthened and our partnership has widened to encompass political, economic, social and cultural cooperation. Together, on this solid foundation, we will build a comprehensive strategic alliance of bilateral, regional and global scope, based on common values and mutual trust. Together, we will work shoulder-to-shoulder to tackle challenges facing both our nations on behalf of the next generation.[56]

Many of the details of this joint vision will require further discussion, but it is an important starting point for developing a direction for the future of the alliance. North Korea will continue to be a problem that will require collaboration and policy coordination between the two allies. ROK–U.S. economic ties will also continue to be an important part of the alliance; Seoul and Washington will need to work out their differences to conclude the Korea–U.S. Free Trade Agreement (KORUS FTA) to deepen the economic relationship. Subsequent administrations in both countries must continue to dialogue and work on developing what both have called a "comprehensive strategic alliance."

---

[55] Pew Global Attitudes Project, "South Korea" 2009, http://pewglobal.org/database/?indicator=1...country=116.

[56] "Joint Vision for the Alliance of the United States of America and the Republic of Korea," June 16, 2009.

Conclusion

The alliance emerged from the confrontation of the Cold War and has endured for more than fifty years. During this time, the alliance has experienced some hardships and tense relations, but South Korean and U.S. leaders have continued to affirm the importance of the relationship to address important national interests. These years also witnessed significant changes to the force structure, responsibilities, and command relationships of the alliance.

With the end of the Cold War, many challenged the fundamental premise of the alliance, as the global struggle against communism had ended. Moreover, South Korea's economic and military power increased dramatically since the 1950s, allowing Seoul to take over a greater share of alliance responsibilities. Despite the end of the Cold War and past tensions, the alliance remains strong. With more changes under way and a fluid security environment in Asia in the years ahead, the South Korea–U.S. alliance is likely to remain an important relationship to ensure regional peace and security.

8

South Korea and the Regional Powers

On many occasions, Korea's history has been impacted by the relationships it has had with the three regional powers on its border: China, Japan, and Russia/Soviet Union. In the past, Korea was often weak in comparison to these contenders and was forced to survive as best as it could. Increasingly, Republic of Korea (ROK) economic, political, and military power is making it an important player in the region and a sought-after partner. Moreover, South Korea has ambitions to be an even more significant actor and is seeking to build its blue-water naval capabilities, allowing it (a) to be less dependent on others to protect its commercial interests and (b) to have the ability to project power and influence more broadly. As a result, an understanding of South Korea's relations with the major powers in the region is crucial to assess Seoul's current position and where it is headed in the future.

China

For many years, Korea existed as a kingdom under the suzerainty of the Chinese Empire. China and Korea maintained a big brother–little brother relationship wherein Korea paid tribute to Chinese emperors as a sign of respect to its big brother. Korea's historical and cultural ties to China are extensive, as a great deal of Korean culture came to the peninsula from China, including art, education, and the legacy of Confucius. This relationship lasted until the end of the nineteenth century, when China became weak and the Korean peninsula fell under Japanese control.

With the end of World War II, it was not long before Chinese–South Korean relations were dominated by the Cold War. After a protracted civil war, China became communist in October 1949 and, under the leadership Mao Zedong and the Communist Party, proceeded to implement a harsh, totalitarian system. When the Korean War began in June 1950, China did not initially join the conflict. When U.S./United Nations (UN) troops crossed the 38th parallel in October 1950, however, anxiety in Beijing increased, and China issued warnings that continuing to advance north was unacceptable. As U.S./UN troops moved closer to the Yalu/Amnok River in November 1950, Chinese "volunteers" poured across the border and pushed back the advance. The Korean War ended with a ceasefire and relatively little ground exchanging hands, but the sides of the Cold War were now clear. For the next four decades, Republic of Korea (ROK)–Chinese relations were frosty. China remained one of Pyongyang's most important allies, providing political and economic support along with a formal security guarantee, whereas South Korea was staunchly anti-communist and a treaty ally of the United States.

Sino–Korean Relations and the End of the Cold War

In 1978, Chinese leader Deng Xiaoping began an extensive reform of China's economy that opened markets and deregulated prices, laying the groundwork for its phenomenal economic rise. Deng once remarked that it doesn't matter if the cat is black or white, so long as it catches mice, signaling a willingness to abandon ideology for a more pragmatic approach. As a result, China began the evolution to establish its hybrid system of a capitalist economy and communist political system, with leaders believing they could grow the Chinese economy while maintaining central political control.

As the years passed, Chinese trade ties with South Korea began to grow, although often informally, through third parties such as Hong Kong and Japan.[1] Beijing was very cautious, however, in pursuing any further openings with South Korea, fearing these actions would damage its ties with the North. Mao Zedong once remarked that China's relationship with the North was as close as lips and teeth, and more than nine hundred thousand Chinese died protecting the Democratic People's Republic of Korea (DPRK) in the Korean War. In addition,

---

[1] N. Kristof, "China-South Korea Trade: Boom, Yes, but a Quiet One," *New York Times*, November 25, 1988, http://www.nytimes.com/1988/11/25/business/china-south-korea-trade-boom-yes-but-a-quiet-one.html.

Seoul still formally recognized Taiwan, creating an important obstacle to improved relations.

By the 1990s, South Korea's economic strength was too important for Beijing to keep Seoul at arm's length. In 1980, total Sino–ROK trade was only $41 million, but, by 1991, trade increased to $4.4 billion. In 1987, Chinese trade with North Korea had reached only a paltry $513 million, and much of this was subsidized by Beijing.[2] Chinese leaders also believed they could coax South Korea into ending its diplomatic ties with Taiwan in exchange for formal recognition. When Moscow began its move to improve ties with Seoul in the early 1990s, Beijing was more comfortable developing ties with the South.[3] As a result, China began to pursue formal relations with South Korea, although with much more concern for how it would be perceived in the North than was the case in Moscow. In May 1991, following a similar announcement by Russia in April, China stated that it would not veto a South Korean application to join the United Nations (UN). With both Russia and China making their intentions clear, North Korea acquiesced and applied for admission as well. After South Korea was in the UN, China opened more formal channels to begin normalizing relations.

For South Korea, the push to open ties with China came in earnest from President Roh Tae-woo's *Nordpolitik*, which sought to improve relations with the communist world. As the chief target of *Nordpolitik*, Roh exerted great effort to establish relations with China. For example, following the Tiananmen Square crackdown in 1989, President Roh worked behind the scenes to convince President Bush, British Prime Minister Margaret Thatcher, and other leaders to refrain from a harsh response, making certain that Chinese leaders were aware of his efforts.[4] To reassure China regarding its concerns for how Pyongyang might react, President Roh told Chinese Foreign Minister Qian Qichen,

> we fully understand China's loyal relationship with North Korea that was forged through the Korean war, [but] I believe that China, [South] Korea and North Korea can build a relationship without betraying that loyalty. As I have stated several times, we are not thinking, not even

[2] Korea International Trade Association, Trade Statistics, http://global.kita.net.
[3] Oberdorfer, *The Two Koreas*, 231.
[4] Ibid., 242–3.

in dreams, of a German style unification by absorption, which North
Korea is worried about. What we want to do with North Korea, who
are of the same nation, is to abandon hostility and restore confidence
and to establish a cooperative relationship. It is not our position to
dominate them based on our economic power.[5]

After several rounds of talks, in August 1992 South Korea and
China established formal diplomatic relations. In return, South Korea
dropped its recognition of Taiwan, an important political goal for
China in addition to the economic opportunities that lay ahead.

Economic Ties and the North Korean Nuclear Crisis

Since Seoul and Beijing established formal diplomatic ties, their relationship has been dominated by two phenomena: efforts to solve the
North Korean nuclear problem and continued growth of ROK–Sino
trade and investment. Since the six-party talks began in 2003, South
Korea and China have been in agreement about the goal of denuclearization of the Korean Peninsula. China's chief fear is that a nuclear
North Korea, particularly one that is belligerent, would push Japan and
South Korea to acquire nuclear weapons, creating a possible nuclear
arms race in East Asia. During the early rounds of these talks, China
and South Korea, under President Roh Moo-hyun, agreed on a softer
line that promoted diplomatic and economic engagement instead of
exerting more pressure. South Korea was committed to the Policy of
Peace and Prosperity, President Roh's version of the sunshine policy,
while China was North Korea's chief ally and largest trade partner.
As the two countries that share the longest border with North Korea,
both had a lot to lose should the North implode. Moreover, for South
Korea, the costs of reunification under these circumstances would be
high. Most estimates indicate that Korean reunification will be significantly costlier than German reunification. Moreover, the South
Korean economy is much smaller than West Germany's, making the
burden even more difficult. Regional instability and the likely refugee
flows that would head both north and south in the wake of North
Korea's collapse is a horrible scenario that both countries seek to avoid.

When the conservative Lee Myung-bak administration came to
power, it took a harder line on North Korea, maintaining that it

[5] Ibid., 244–5.

would remain committed to engagement and provide aid but would not simply give away political and economic concessions without reciprocal actions from North Korea, a criticism often leveled against the sunshine policy. After a round of missile tests in April 2009 and a second nuclear test the following month, China also shifted further toward a hard line against the DPRK, finally having had enough with the North's provocative behavior. Beijing was furious that North Korea, despite multiple warnings to the contrary, had conducted the tests and voted in favor of a more extensive UN Security Council resolution that imposed further sanctions on the North. Despite this initial outrage, China retreated a bit, calling for a more measured response to the North Korean actions, noting that the goal was to bring Pyongyang back to the negotiating table. In October 2009, Chinese Premier Wen Jiabao visited North Korea, bringing a large aid package and statements of support for the DPRK.[6] Chinese patience continues to wear ever thinner, however, and there are signs that Chinese leaders are rethinking their policy toward Pyongyang. Both Seoul and Beijing remain committed to dialogue and the six-party talks, but the future of these negotiations is in grave doubt.

The second important dimension of ROK–Sino relations is the significant and growing web of economic ties between the two countries. Prior to normal relations between South Korea and China in 1991, Beijing purchased 1.4 percent of Seoul's exports; by 2003, that share climbed to 18.1 percent, more than the 17.7 percent share bought by the United States.[7] In 2003, China became South Korea's largest trading partner, surpassing the United States in a position Washington had held since the 1960s. In 2007, exports to China represented 22.1 percent of South Korea's total, and 17.7 percent of South Korea's imports came from China.[8] ROK–Sino trade increased from $2.9 billion in 1990 to $168.4 billion by 2008, with South Korea holding more than a $14 billion surplus (see Table 14). The global economic crisis is likely to cause a significant decrease in these trade levels, however. South Korea and China have held talks to conclude a free trade agreement (FTA) but have been unable to reach a final deal.

---

[6] Choe Sang-hun, "China Aims to Steady North Korea," *New York Times*, October 6, 2009, http://www.nytimes.com/2009/10/07/world/asia/07korea.html (accessed November 5, 2009).

[7] S. Kim and W. Lim, "How to Deal with South Korea," *Washington Quarterly* 30, no. 2 (Spring 2007): 78.

[8] CIA World Factbook, www.cia.gov.

Table 14. *1990–2008: South Korea and China trade*

	Total bilateral trade	Exports from South Korea to China	Imports to South Korea from China
1990	$2.9 B	$584.9 M	$2.3 B
1995	$16.5 B	$9.1 B	$7.4 B
2000	$31.3 B	$18.5 B	$12.8 B
2005	$99.6 B	$61.0 B	$38.6 B
2008	$168.4 B	$91.4 B	$77 B

Source: Korea International Trade Association, http://global.kita.net.

Foreign direct investment (FDI) is another important part of the relationship. China is the number-one destination of South Korean foreign investment, reaching almost $6.5 billion in 2007, or 23.5 percent of South Korea's total FDI. There are more than forty thousand South Korean companies that have investments in China with a total accumulated value of $100 billion.[9] One of the first major investors in China after the two countries normalized relations was LG, which invested $3.5 million to open a factory that produced digital electronics. China's investment in South Korea is less extensive but still significant. In January 2009, officials from China and South Korea announced an agreement on the largest joint development project between the two countries valued at $1.28 billion, of which Chinese investors will cover a little more than 44 percent. The project will build the Muan Corporate City in South Cholla province and include the construction of 22,000 housing units, an industrial park for information technology and biotechnology, an international college, and a Chinese exclusive economic zone.[10] In 2010, China will be hosting the Shanghai Expo, a six-month event that will allow South Korea to showcase its culture, technology, and business opportunities to an estimated 70 million visitors, 95 percent of whom will be Chinese. The Chinese government has pledged to spend $586 billion in 2010 for investment in infrastructure and other construction projects. South Korean officials are hopeful that this funding will create opportunities for further bilateral economic cooperation.[11]

[9] "South Korea Investment Grows Together in China," *China Daily*, June 23, 2008, http://chinadaily.com.cn/bizchina/2008-06/23/content_6787090.htm.
[10] H. Lee, "Korea-China Project Gets Go-Ahead," *Joong-Ang Ilbo*, January 21, 2009, http://joongangdaily.joins.com/article/view.asp?aid=2900088.
[11] "Shanghai Expo Could Showcase Korea," *Yonhap*, March 24, 2009, http://joongangdaily.joins.com/article/view.asp?aid=2902629.

Although economic cooperation with China has created a host of prospects for both countries, ROK–Sino relations are complex, and there is also the potential for antagonism as the two become economic competitors. Friction could arise in several areas. Competition in manufacturing will increase as Chinese capacity and quality continue to improve. Beijing has already expressed a desire to challenge South Korea's ranking as the world's largest shipbuilder. Both countries are also in great need of energy resources and raw materials to fuel their economic growth. China's consumption of resources and its methods of dealing with developing countries that supply the resources, often referred to as the "Beijing consensus," could be a problem for South Korea. A report by the South Korean Ministry of Strategy and Finance noted, "The increasing influence of China could put Korea's diplomatic efforts to secure natural resources in peril. Korea needs to come up with economic policies in response to the expanding Beijing Consensus."[12] Finally, South Korean exports will confront increasing competition from Chinese producers in markets in the developing world and in Chinese domestic markets. All of these issues could lead to serious friction and dampen enthusiasm for this relationship.

As ROK–Sino economic ties grew, some in the United States express concern that South Korea is slowly drifting not only toward an economic relationship but also a strategic relationship with China that could lead to an eventual dissolution of the ROK–U.S. alliance. According to these concerns, South Korea would increasingly see that its economic and political future is linked to China's rise and eventually lead ROK officials to choose Beijing over Washington. For those in Washington who fear that South Korea is moving away from its close relationship with the United States, Sunhyuk Kim and Wonhyuk Lim argue that "these concerns are overblown. The emergence of a confident and self-assertive South Korea implies more independent thinking in South Korea's foreign policy, not a shift to China at the United States' expense."[13] Moreover, China's efforts to turn its economic integration with South Korea into political leverage have not taken place. According to Scott Snyder, China's rise has increased Beijing's influence on the Korean Peninsula, and ROK–Sino relations have improved, "but not to the extent that Seoul is likely to pursue strategic realignment with Beijing or willingly

[12] G. Moon, "Ministry: The 'Beijing Consensus' Poses Risk," *Joong-Ang Ilbo*, April 14, 2009, http://joongangdaily.joins.com/article/view.asp?aid=2903556.
[13] Kim and Lim, "How to Deal with South Korea," 78.

forego the security benefits of the alliance with the United States."[14] For most in South Korea, the benefits of a relationship with the United States are far more important for maintaining South Korean security than is a relationship with China.

Although economic ties continue to grow, South Korea also remains wary of China's rise and the implications this could have for the future of the region. Moreover, there are potential sources of tension that could complicate relations. One example is a dispute about the history of the ancient kingdom of Koguryo, or Gaogouli to the Chinese.[15] The Kingdom of Koguryo controlled the northern portion of the Korean Peninsula along with much of Manchuria from 37 B.C. to 668 A.D. The remainder of the Korean Peninsula was controlled by Baekje (18 B.C.–660 A.D.) in the southwest and Silla (57 B.C.–935 A.D.) in the southeast. In 668 A.D., Silla conquered Koguryo and Baekje to control the entire peninsula until Silla fell in 935 A.D. For all Koreans, the unification of these three kingdoms under Silla rule is the precursor to the modern state of Korea and an important part of Korean history and identity.

In the 1980s, some Chinese historians began to assert that Koguryo's history was actually more closely affiliated with China's past but distinct from the "Three Kingdoms" period in Korean history. Korean historians responded, and the dispute remained largely one among academics. In 2002, Chinese historians at the Chinese Academy of Social Sciences started the Northeast Asia Project, a five-year, $2.5 million, state-funded effort, to examine these historical issues. In 2003, China applied to the United Nations Educational, Scientific and Cultural Organization (UNESCO) to have its Koguryo tombs included on the UN list of "World Heritage Sites." North Korea had applied to the list in 2001 for its Koguryo tombs, and Koreans suspected that China applied to maintain its "claim" on the kingdom.

In 2004, the Chinese Foreign Ministry created an uproar by removing content on Koguryo from its Web site. When South Korea protested, Chinese authorities responded by removing all references

---

[14] Snyder, *China's Rise and the Two Koreas: Politics, Economics, Security*, 4.
[15] For a detailed discussion of the issue, see T. Roehrig, "History as a Strategic Weapon: National Identity and the Korean Dispute over Koguryo," *Journal of African and Asian Studies* 45, no. 1 (February 2010): 5–28, and P. Hays Gries, "The Koguryo Controversy, National Identity, and Sino-Korean Relations Today," *East Asia* 22, no. 4 (2005): 3–17.

of Korean history prior to 1948 in an effort to assuage South Korean anger. The issue had become a sore spot between the two governments and a serious concern for many Koreans.

Why is South Korea so concerned about this issue? The dispute about Koguryo is less about history and more about the political and economic ramifications of the issue for the present and future. South Koreans saw these Chinese moves as a formal government action to alter Korean history. Moreover, according to a South Korean history professor at Yonsei University in Seoul, "Koreans trace their roots to Koguryo; the name Korea stems from Koguryo. The Chinese claim shakes the core of Koreans' national identity."[16] At first, the South Korean government responded cautiously, fearful of damaging relations with China; however, domestic pressure and continued Chinese actions pushed the Roh Moo-hyun administration to respond more strenuously.

Chinese motivations here are unclear and complex. One possibility is that China may be preparing a historical argument for seizing North Korean territory should the DPRK collapse. China has also expressed concern about the claims by some South Koreans that there is land in Manchuria that belongs to Korea. China's historical claims may be an effort to address these issues. A second argument focuses on China's ethnic diversity and the government's fears of ethnic separatism. Numerous Chinese of Korean descent live along the border with North Korea, and there is fear that, in the chaos of a North Korea collapse, the Korean-Chinese community might break off from China and join its sisters and brothers in a unified Korean state. Chinese leaders may fear that any concession to Korean pressure could spark demands from other ethnic groups, leading to unrest, instability, and the possible disintegration of the Chinese state.[17]

Despite these concerns, South Korea's relations with China are important and growing. The Chinese economy provides many important opportunities for trade and investment for South Korea and everyone else in the region, yet South Korea will remain watchful to ascertain the future direction of a rising China and its goals in Asia.

---

[16] S. Choe, "Tussle over a Vanished Kingdom," *International Herald Tribune*, October 13, 2006, http://www.iht.com/articles/2006/10/12news/history.php.

[17] M. Byington, "The War of Words Between South Korea and China Over An Ancient Kingdom: Why Both Sides are Misguided," *History News Network*, George Mason University, September 6, 2004, http://hnn.us/articles/7077.html.

Japan

South Korea's relations with Japan have long existed in the shadow of the Japanese Occupation (1910–45). It was a brutal period in Korean history during which Japan sought to eliminate Korean culture and language, assimilate Korea into Japan, and exploit the Korean economy for the sake of the Empire. After World War II, the United States concluded alliances with both countries, but relations between Tokyo and Seoul were strained.[18] South Korea and Japan normalized relations in 1965, but resentment from the occupation lingers below the surface, even when formal relations between the two governments are good. Koreans, along with others who were victims of Japanese aggression during World War II, believe that Tokyo has been insufficiently apologetic for its past actions. Despite formal apologies from the emperor and several past prime ministers, there is lingering resentment that Japan has not fully come to terms with its past, as evidenced by its treatment of World War II in Japanese history books and periodic statements by Japanese conservatives. For example, General Toshio Tamogami wrote in an essay that Japanese actions were not aggressive and that Japan was tricked by President Franklin Roosevelt into attacking Pearl Harbor. General Tamogami was removed from his position as Air Force chief of staff and Japanese Prime Minister Taro Aso dismissed the essay, but these events continue to raise questions about Japan's remorse. Also, in March 2007, then Prime Minister Shinzo Abe said that "comfort women" were not coerced into sexual slavery during World War II.[19] Abe later apologized for the statement, but the damage had been done.

ROK–Japanese relations during the 1980s were tentative, although economic ties continued to grow. In 1984, Japanese Prime Minister Yasuhiro Nakasone made an effort to improve relations by making an unprecedented visit to South Korea and approving a long-term loan for South Korean defense spending.[20] Together, he and President Chun Doo-hwan exerted considerable effort to build a better relationship between the two countries. In 1996, South Korea and

[18] See K. Cooney and A. Scarbrough, "Japan and South Korea: Can These Two Nations Work Together?," *Asian Affairs* 35, no. 3 (Fall 2008): 173–92.

[19] C. Joyce, "Japanese PM Denies Wartime 'Comfort Women' Were Forced," *Telegraph*, March 3, 2007, http://www.telegraph.co.uk/news/worldnews/1544471/Japanese-PM-denies-wartime-comfort-women-were-forced.html (accessed November 5, 2009).

[20] K. Pyle, *Japan Rising: The Resurgence of Japanese Power and Purpose* (New York: Public Affairs, 2007), 272.

Japan received word that they would jointly host the 2002 World Cup Soccer Championship. Although there was initially some tension, both sides worked hard to improve cooperation to hold a successful event.

In 2001, with the beginning of the Koizumi administration in Japan, relations between Seoul and Tokyo took a decided turn for the worse. Several of the problems were rooted in the legacies of World War II. In April 2005, the Japanese Ministry of Education approved a junior high school social studies textbook that critics maintained did not fully account for Japanese actions in the war, either omitting or downplaying sensitive topics such as the Annexation of Korea, the Nanjing Massacre, chemical and biological weapons units, and "comfort women" that projected a negative image of Japan or arguing that the Japanese occupation of Asia had been beneficial for the region. As had been the case when previous textbooks were released in 1983 and 1998, others in East Asia who believed Japan was whitewashing its history lodged vehement protests, and thousands in South Korea, China, and elsewhere in the region hit the streets to protest.

Another irritant that escalated tensions was Prime Minister Koizumi's regular visits to the Yasukuni Shrine in Tokyo that honors Japanese war dead. The shrine is not owned or affiliated with the government, and there are no bodies entombed there; however, among the 2.5 million honored at the shrine are fourteen Class A war criminals, including General Hideki Tojo, who were convicted at the Tokyo war crimes trials after World War II. Prime Minister Koizumi always insisted that he visited the shrine as a private citizen. He made six such trips while in office, and each time protests raged throughout East Asia. In comparison, former Prime Ministers Nakasone and Ryutaro Hashimoto visited the shrine only once while in office. Koizumi's successor, Shinzo Abe, refrained from visiting Yasukuni and made it a point to improve relations between Seoul and Tokyo, visiting the South Korean capital within months of coming to office. His successor, Yasuo Fukuda, was also determined to improve Japan's standing in the region and did not visit Yasukuni. When Taro Aso, a strong conservative, assumed the office in 2008, some expected a return to the difficult Koizumi years. Instead, he also worked to improve South Korean–Japanese relations and did not visit Yasukuni. Japan's current prime minister, Yukio Hatoyama, has pledged not to visit Yasukuni. Moreover, in a meeting with South Korean President Lee at the G-20 meeting in September 2009, Prime Minister Hatoyama noted that his party had to be "courageous enough" to "look straight in the face

Table 15. *1990–2008: South Korea and Japan trade*

	Total bilateral trade	Exports from South Korea to Japan	Imports to South Korea from Japan
1990	$31.2 B	$12.6 B	$18.6 B
1995	$49.6 B	$17.0 B	$32.6 B
2000	$52.3 B	$20.5 B	$31.8 B
2005	$72.4 B	$24.0 B	$48.4 B
2008	$98.3 B	$28.3 B	$70.0 B

Source: Korea International Trade Association, http://global.kita.net.

of history" to build a "constructive and future-oriented" relationship with South Korea, remarks that are hopeful signs of improved relations between Seoul and Tokyo.[21]

Despite these historical issues that lie below the surface, South Korea and Japan share several important interests that encourage the growth of a more robust relationship. Both countries are vibrant democracies that maintain a free press, civil rights and liberties, and the rule of law. Seoul and Tokyo also have formal security alliances with the United States and are part of Washington's "hub and spoke" alliance system that helps maintain peace and security in the region. Finally, both are powerful players in the global economy, with Japan ranking second and South Korea thirteenth in total gross domestic product (GDP). Their trade links are extensive (see Table 15). In 2008, Japan was South Korea's third most important destination for exports at $28.3 billion, behind China and the United States, and the second most important source of imports at $70 billion, behind only China. In 1990, ROK–Japanese trade was approximately $31 billion, but by 2008 it had increased to more than $98 billion, a 216 percent increase. Although South Korea's exports to Japan are dwarfed by the amount sold to China ($91.4 billion), imports from Japan are relatively close to the amount bought from China ($76.9 billion). Despite the global economic downturn, trade between Seoul and Tokyo grew at a rate of 7 to 8 percent throughout 2008.

In addition to trade relations, FDI from Japan grew significantly in 2008 and 2009. Fueled in large part by the 60 percent increase in the value of the Japanese *yen* compared to the South Korean *won* along

[21] "Hatoyama Vows to Look Squarely at History," *Chosun Ilbo*, September 25, 2009, http://english.chosun.com/site/data/html_dir/2009/09/25/2009092500404 (accessed November 6, 2009).

with the drop in South Korean real estate prices, Japanese tourists and investors have been flocking to South Korea for bargains. In the first half of 2009, Japanese FDI to South Korea increased by 82 percent, while investment from the United States and the European Union (EU) fell during the same period. In particular, Japanese investment in manufacturing rose 151 percent to $1.1 billion. A Japanese private equity fund, Vana World, decided to invest $3 billion in a free economic zone to the west of Seoul, and Hyundai Oil Bank of Korea and Cosmo Oil of Japan have entered into a joint venture worth $1.2 billion to expand petroleum production lines in Seosan, South Korea.[22]

In June 2009, President Lee and Prime Minister Aso held another round of summit meetings focused largely on resuming the six-party talks, without North Korea if necessary, so that the remaining five countries could discuss, according to President Lee, "how to convince North Korea to give up its nuclear ambitions."[23] The leaders also agreed to resume and upgrade efforts to achieve an economic partnership agreement, a pact that is a level below a formal FTA, and to begin discussions on nuclear energy cooperation.

One of the contentious issues that complicates ROK–Japanese relations is the dispute regarding Dokdo, which consists of two small islands and numerous surrounding reefs. The islands are located midway between South Korea and Japan in the East Sea (Sea of Japan). Koreans call the islands Dokdo, meaning "lone island," but Japan refers to them as Takeshima ("bamboo island"). Most in the West, including the United States, refer to the islands as the Liancourt Rocks, named for a French whaling ship that narrowly avoided crashing into the islands in 1849. Although the islands themselves are too small and rocky to be of much value, the sea around them contains valuable fishing grounds and possibly offshore deposits of oil and natural gas. Under the United Nations Convention on the Law of the Sea, states are entitled to a two-hundred-nautical-mile exclusive economic zone, and these islands would play an important role in determining these lines.

---

[22] See H. Kim, "Japanese Investment in Korea Rises by 82%," *Korea Times*, July 2, 2009, http://www.koreatimes.co.kr/www/news/biz/2009/07/123_47860.html, and "Hyundai Oil Bank of Korea and Cosmo Oil of Japan Form a Joint Venture," *Yonhap News*, June 9, 2009.

[23] Y. Makino and J. Tabushi, "Aso, Lee Seek Resumption of Six-Party Talks," *Asahi Shimbun*, June 29, 2009, http://www.asahi.com/english/Herald-asahi/TKY 200906290011.html.

In June 1952 during the Korean War, President Rhee issued the "Proclamation of Sovereignty over the Adjacent Seas," establishing a line of sovereignty that included Dokdo for South Korea. Seoul has formally occupied the islands since 1954 and maintains a lighthouse, watchtower, wharf, and a Coast Guard unit on the island. Dokdo has only two permanent residents, an octopus fisherman and his wife who live with forty government personnel who maintain and administer the facilities on the island.

Despite South Korea's possession of Dokdo, the status of the islands remains a matter of serious dispute between South Korea and Japan. In the mid-1990s, both countries made unambiguous declarations that the islands were integral parts of their territory. According to a pamphlet authored by Japan's Ministry of Foreign Affairs, "10 Issues of Takeshima," Japan maintains that, since the seventeenth century, it has used the islands as a stopover for Japanese fisherman and for travel to other islands, thereby establishing Japanese sovereignty. In 1905, the document maintains, Japan reestablished sovereignty by incorporating the islands into Shimane Prefecture, the closest government entity on the main island of Honshu in western Japan. The islands remained in Japanese hands throughout the colonial period and World War II. In September 1951, the Allied powers and Japan signed the San Francisco Peace Treaty, which brought a formal end to World War II. The relevant portion of the document, Chapter II, Article 2, states that "Japan recognizing the independence of Korea, renounces all right, title and claim to Korea, including the islands of Quelpart, Port Hamilton and Dagelet."[24] According to Japan, ROK officials petitioned the United States during the drafting of the agreement to include a specific reference to Dokdo as one of the included islands but were rebuffed. After President Rhee drew the maritime line in 1952, Japan proposed on several occasions to have the matter decided by the International Court of Justice (ICJ), but South Korea refused to comply.[25]

South Korea maintains that Dokdo has long been a part of Korea, having first been incorporated into the Silla dynasty in the sixth century. Numerous Korean documents after this period note that Dokdo

[24] "Treaty of Peace with Japan," signed September 8, 1951, and entered into force April 29, 1952, http://www.international.ucla.edu/eas/documents/peace1951.htm.
[25] Ministry of Foreign Affairs of Japan, "10 Issues of Takeshima," February 2008, http://www.mofa.go.jp/region/asia-paci/takeshima/pamphlet_e.pdf.

was a Korean possession. South Korean sources maintain that, in 1696, a Korean named Ahn Yong-bok received written affirmation from the Tokugawa Shogunate in Japan recognizing Korean sovereignty over Dokdo. The South Korean government points to an 1877 document issued by the Meiji era's (1868–1912) Grand Council of State indicating that Dokdo and the neighboring Ulleungdo were not part of Japan.[26]

For South Korea, a crucial part of the dispute is Japan's incorporation of Dokdo on February 22, 1905. Japan considered the land *terra nullius* – belonging to no one – and believed it was included in its eventual annexation of Korea, making all of Korean territory Japanese. Koreans argue, however, that these events did not establish Japanese sovereignty and were not done voluntarily. The process of Korea becoming a protectorate in 1905 and its later annexation into the Japanese Empire were agreements forced on Korea under duress. The Korean government protested to the fullest extent possible, with the Korean State Council issuing Directive No. III on April 29, 1906, denouncing Tokyo's claims.[27] Under the Protectorate Treaty, however, Japan was responsible for Korean foreign affairs and had little recourse for further action. Moreover, an argument that Japan held sovereignty prior to 1905 based on discovery and *terra nullius* is problematic because, as one author notes, "Korea did not intentionally relinquish title to Japan.... Furthermore, Japanese claims to sovereignty based on the annexation treaties negate any claim to have discovered Takeshima because the treaties concede a lack of initial ownership."[28]

South Korea also maintains that documents written after World War II by U.S. occupation authorities support its claim. The Supreme Commander of Allied Powers (SCAP) issued an instruction memo (SCAPIN No. 677) that excludes Dokdo from Japanese territory but also contains a caveat that "nothing in this directive shall be construed as an indication of Allied policy relating to the ultimate determination of the minor islands referred to in Article 8 of the Potsdam Declaration." Article 8 of the Potsdam Declaration notes, "The terms of the Cairo Declaration shall be carried out and Japanese sovereignty

[26] "Korea's sovereignty over Dokdo," http://www.korea.net.

[27] S. Fern, "Tokdo or Takeshima?: The International Law of Territorial Acquisition in Japan-Korea Island Dispute," *Stanford Journal of East Asian Affairs* 5, no. 1 (Winter 2005): 86.

[28] Ibid., 87.

shall be limited to the islands of Honshu, Hokkaido, Kyushu, Shikoku and such minor islands as we determine."[29] South Korea also points to another occupation document, SCAPIN 1033, that prohibits Japanese vessels and personnel from coming closer than twelve nautical miles to Dokdo. Thus, in the San Francisco Peace Treaty that ended World War II, Japan acknowledged Korean independence and renounced claims to Korean lands, noting three islands but not specifically mentioning Dokdo. This does not appear to be intended as a complete listing of all possible islands, however. The South Korean government maintains that Japan lobbied U.S. officials to exclude Dokdo, leading to omission from the treaty, and that the earlier documents demonstrate the intent to return territory that was seized by force.[30]

In January 2009, a South Korean researcher with the Korea Maritime Institute reported finding two Japanese documents supporting Seoul's position that Dokdo is Korean. The two ordinances – prime ministerial ordinance No. 24 (June 6, 1951) and financial ministerial ordinance No. 4 (December 13, 1951) – state that Dokdo, Ulleungdo, and Chejudo are not Japanese territory.[31] According to an official from the South Korean Foreign Ministry, "This is the first time it has been disclosed that Japan excluded Dokdo from its territorial space in accordance with its own laws. They are materials that are of great help to proving Dokdo is Korean territory."[32] The official also noted, however, that these documents may not be "100 percent decisive" because Japan was still under U.S. occupation at the time and more research would be necessary. In February 2010, Yuji Hosaka, a Japanese professor at South Korea's Sejong University, announced the discovery of two more Japanese maps from 1877 and 1889 that do not include Dokdo as part of Japan's territory.[33]

From time to time, the Dokdo/Takeshima issue flares up, as occurred in 2004 when the South Korean postal service issued commemorative stamps of the islands, followed soon after by a local Japanese

---

[29] See "Potsdam Declaration," http://international.ucla.edu/eas/documents/potsdam.htm.

[30] "Korea's Sovereignty over Dokdo," http://www.korea.net.

[31] "Japan Must Give Up False Claims to Dokdo," *Chosun Ilbo*, January 5, 2009, http://english.chosun.com/w21data/html/news/200901/200901050031.html.

[32] "Korea Gets Boost from Japanese Dokdo Papers," *Chosun Ilbo*, January 5, 2009, http://english.chosun.com/w21data/html/news/200901/200901050020.html.

[33] "More Maps Weaken Japan's Claim to Dokdo," *Chosun Ilbo*, February 18, 2010, http://english.chosun.com/site/data/html_dir/2010/02/18/2010021800465.html.

government celebrating Takeshima Day, which it continues to do every February 22. In 2007, the South Korean Navy commissioned its first amphibious assault ship named the ROKS *Dokdo*. The following year, Japan's Ministry of Education published a pamphlet for middle school teachers that encouraged them to remind their students of Japan's claim to Takeshima. Finally, in 2009, the Japanese Ministry of Defense published a White Paper that claimed Takeshima as its own territory.[34] All of these instances generated a strong rebuke from the other side. This dispute is likely to remain active for some time, but South Korea will continue to occupy the islands, and Japan will likely continue to assert its claim but take few actions beyond that.

The U.S. position on the dispute between its two allies has been neutrality and that it is up to South Korea and Japan to settle the dispute. In July 2008, the Bush administration was unexpectedly thrust into the controversy when the U.S. Board of Geographic Names (BGN), part of the U.S. Geological Survey, changed the listing of the islands from "South Korean" to "undesignated sovereignty," creating a firestorm in Seoul. Apparently, the BGN was attempting to standardize its treatment of certain listings but failed to check with senior levels of the government. President Bush quickly reversed the name change through an executive order but not before these events rattled South Korean nerves.

Soviet Union/Russia

From the end of World War II through the 1980s, relations between Seoul and Moscow were also shaped by the Cold War. South Korea, led by stalwart, anti-communist governments, was allied with the United States in the struggle against communist expansion. The Soviet Union had important economic and security ties, including a formal security treaty, with North Korea. Given the DPRK's insistence on the

---

[34] In an interview with the *Chosun Ilbo*, Professor Kazuhiko Kimijima, a professor of history from Tokyo Gakugei University and part of a joint research project between Japanese and Korean historians, maintained that the government should refrain from teaching that Dokdo/Takeshima is Japanese until the dispute is resolved. He went on to say that, although he is not a Dokdo expert, "I think it is right to say that Dokdo is Korean territory. The opposite view is unconvincing." "Japanese Academic Slams Tokyo Over Dokdo," *Chosun Ilbo*, July 25, 2008, http://english. chosun.com/w21data/html/news/200807/200807250013.html.

illegitimacy of the South Korean regime, Moscow had no formal relationship with Seoul.

By the 1980s, South Korea's relations with the Soviet Union had changed little. There were few points of contact between Seoul and Moscow, and Pyongyang worked hard to ensure it stayed that way. In 1981, the Reagan administration assumed office with a characterization of the Soviet Union as the "evil empire" and a strong focus on anti-communism that fueled a major increase in U.S. defense spending. In December 1979, Soviet forces invaded Afghanistan and raised concerns regarding a more aggressive Soviet foreign policy. South Korea under President Chun Doo-whan shared these concerns about the Soviet threat.

ROK–Soviet relations hit their low point on September 1, 1983, when a Soviet fighter shot down Korean Airline (KAL) flight 007 over the East Sea/Sea of Japan, just west of Sakhalin Island. The flight was headed from New York to Seoul with a stop to refuel in Alaska. All 269 passengers and crew died in the crash. Moscow initially denied the action but later admitted to shooting down the plane, arguing that it had violated Soviet airspace over a sensitive military facility. Furthermore, Soviet authorities blamed the United States and its South Korean ally for conducting a spy mission but claimed the order to shoot down the plane had come from a local Soviet commander on the ground. The plane was more than three hundred and fifty miles off course because of unintentional navigation errors of which the KAL pilots were likely unaware.

ROK–Soviet relations had been improving prior to the KAL flight 007 tragedy, as Moscow had begun to allow Soviet companies to trade with South Korean firms through third parties. North Korean officials complained strenuously about these actions but to no avail. Soviet delegates were also scheduled to travel to Seoul for a meeting of the International Parliamentary Union, but the visit was cancelled in the wake of the KAL flight 007 tragedy.[35]

By the end of the 1980s, the Cold War confrontation that formed much of international relations was beginning to change. First, Soviet leader Mikhail Gorbachev came to power, determined to reform the economic and political system of the Soviet Union. The economic reforms and restructuring of the Soviet economy, known as *perestroika*, were difficult and slow to generate the prosperity necessary for the

[35] Oberdorfer, *The Two Koreas*, 140.

public to support the changes. The Soviet Union was headed in a new direction, and, although most could not conceive of the end of the Cold War and the breakup of the Soviet Union, it was clear that times and relationships were on the verge of change.

Second, by the late 1980s, the South Korean economy had become a world player and was impossible for Moscow to ignore. The opportunities available with ties to a vibrant ROK economy, despite Pyongyang's protests, provided important benefits to Moscow to help it weather the turmoil of its economic transition. Slowly, Soviet authorities allowed increased economic contacts through third parties along with increased cultural and sports exchanges. In November 1988, the Politburo decided that it was time to begin improving formal relations with South Korea. Gorbachev, now at the height of his power, believed that South Korea could provide the necessary loans and investment to help it through the difficult economic transition. In his memoirs, Gorbachev recalled that "we could not . . . continue opposing the establishment of normal relations with [this] country, which showed an exceptional dynamism and had become a force to be reckoned with, both in the Asia-Pacific region and in the wider world."[36]

By 1988, Moscow had removed travel restrictions on ROK citizens to visit Russia and reopened postal, telegraph, and telephone links. South Korean officials also concluded a business cooperation agreement with the Soviet Chamber of Commerce and set up a trade affairs office in Moscow in July 1988 that did a brisk business upon opening its doors. Although most Russian officials favored increased ties with South Korea, some were concerned with the speed of these efforts, fearing they might upset North Korea and other old Soviet allies. Gorbachev continued to push hard for a rapid buildup of ties, however, knowing that any economic support he could get from South Korea was desperately needed to prop up the struggling economy.[37]

President Roh Tae-woo was only too happy to work with Gorbachev in establishing economic and political links. A formal relationship with Moscow gave the South Korean government international standing and was a huge coup in its struggle with the North. Pyongyang had long maintained that it was the rightful authority on the peninsula and that any recognition of the government in Seoul

---

[36] M. Gorbachev, *Memoirs* (New York: Doubleday, 1996), 544.
[37] Oberdorfer, *The Two Koreas*, 210.

propped up an illegitimate regime while cementing the division of the Korean Peninsula. Formal ties undermined these claims and made it likely that similar measures would follow from China. President Roh also made it clear, however, that South Korea would provide significant aid and investment, but only in the case that Seoul and Moscow established formal diplomatic relations. These efforts, part of President Roh's *Nordpolitik*, were also designed to nudge North Korea into being more flexible. A senior South Korean official noted that the North's nonrecognition of the South was the last remnant of the Cold War, "the last island in a sea of change," and that improved Russian–South Korean relations "would give North Korea a chance to rethink their position and become more reasonable in accepting change."[38] In September 1990, South Korean and Russian Foreign Ministers Choi Ho-joong and Eduard Shevardnadze signed an Agreement on the Establishment of Diplomatic Relations between the two countries while at a UN General Assembly to formalize diplomatic ties.

As expected, North Korea did not react well when informed of Moscow's change in policy to a "Two Koreas" approach that sought good relations with both Pyongyang and Seoul. Moscow had given Pyongyang assurances that it would continue to hold South Korea at arm's length, but this was only a temporary measure to placate the North. When informed of the change, North Korea protested vehemently, threatening to put greater effort into a nuclear weapons program and possibly recognize former states from the old Soviet Union, such as Kazakhstan. Russian leaders were already committed to better relations with the South, however, and North Korean protests fell on deaf ears.[39] Increasingly, economic ties with North Korea became a liability that the deteriorating Russian economy could no longer afford to prop up. Russia was North Korea's largest trading partner, but Pyongyang was unable to pay for even heavily subsidized goods, building ever more debt. Eventually, North Korea defaulted on most of these obligations.

In November 1992, Presidents Roh Tae-woo and Boris Yeltsin signed a treaty that further established formal relations between South Korea and Russia. Although political ties had become established, South Korean businesses were reluctant to follow, much to Moscow's

[38] J. Gross, "After the Summit; Gorbachev, Ending U.S. Trip, Meets South Korea Leader, Who Sees a Renewal of Ties," *New York Times*, June 5, 1990.
[39] Oberdorfer, *Two Koreas*, 215–6.

disappointment. First, the Russian economy was still struggling and offered few lucrative opportunities for South Korean companies. Second, Russian politics remained chaotic, raising concerns for the country's domestic political stability. Finally, in the transition from its old communist system that was hostile to foreign investment, Russia possessed a questionable legal infrastructure to promote commerce. For all of these reasons, there was simply too much uncertainty for the safety and profitability of ROK business investments. As these dimensions of the Russian economy and legal infrastructure improved, however, South Korean–Russian economic ties grew as well.

Eventually, South Korea provided Russia with a financial package that totaled close to $3 billion. Since 1994, Russia has tried to pay off a significant part of the debt through arms sales that included armored personnel carriers, battle tanks, antitank missiles, antiaircraft missiles, helicopters, and spare parts.[40] These sales reached their peak in 1997. Both North Korea and the United States were unhappy with these transactions. For Pyongyang, these sales represented another dimension of Russian betrayal. In addition, these deals provided South Korea with T-80 tanks, a more advanced model than the T-72 that Pyongyang purchased from Moscow, and S-300PMU antitactical ballistic missiles that could be used against North Korean SCUDs. Washington was also not happy with the sales, especially ROK proposals to buy sophisticated Russian weapons systems. The United States pressured Seoul to scale back the purchases and threatened to restrict the sale of future technology to South Korea. In 2003, South Korea eventually wrote off $660 million of the debt from approximately $2.24 billion that remained. The remaining $1.58 billion was to be paid off over the next twenty-three years, including through more arms deals.[41]

South Korean–Russian Relations: Potential, Expectations, and Cooperation

In many respects, South Korean–Russian relations are in their infancy, and, although there is much potential for greater economic and political ties, it remains to be seen whether this relationship will reach the

[40] See S. Ahn, "Understanding Russian-South Korean Arms Trade: A Nontraditional Security Approach?" *Armed Forces and Society* 35, no. 3 (April 2009): 421–36.
[41] "South Korea Forgives $660 Million of Russia's Debt," *Korea Now* 32, no. 13 (June 28, 2003): 18.

heights many hope it will. For Russia, improved ties hold out the possibility of an important economic relationship. Russian officials hope that South Korean companies will be key players in construction projects for the facilities Moscow must build for the 2012 Asia-Pacific Economic Cooperation (APEC) meeting to be held in Vladivostok and the 2014 Winter Olympics scheduled for Sochi. Moscow has also begun to turn its attention to developing the untapped potential of Siberia and the Russian Far East. If Russia fails to develop its Far East, some estimates indicate that Russian population in the region will drop from 32 million to 8 to 10 million as Russians migrate to the West for better economic opportunities.[42] Gleb Ivashentsov, Russian ambassador to South Korea, noted, "An economic, technological and social upsurge in Siberia and the Far East is needed, if Russia is to have a future as a great power. The national leadership has set some grandiose tasks for this huge region, whose attainment is due to yield a powerful payoff."[43]

South Korean companies have already invested heavily in the European side of Russia. In December 2007, Hyundai Motors announced that it would build a $400 million plant in St. Petersburg. Hyundai is already the third-leading exporter of automobiles to Russia. Lotte, LG, and Samsung, major South Korean *chaebol*, already have operations in the Moscow area. South Korean investment and loans shifted eastward could be an important engine to help Russia develop its Asian lands. The South Korean and Russian economies are complementary, with South Korea providing most of the technology and investment, while more than 90 percent of Russian exports to South Korea are primary products such as oil, gas, timber, fish, and minerals.[44] Finally, ties with South Korea help Moscow bridge over to states that were once Cold War adversaries.

Many of these arguments also work for South Korea, but in a different way. Russia presents several economic opportunities, particularly in the energy sector, and the complementary economies are a benefit to South Korea as well. Other areas of economic cooperation

[42] E. Yoon, "Russian Foreign Policy and South Korean Security," in *Korean Security in a Changing East Asia*, ed. T. Roehrig, J. Seo, and U. Heo (Westport, Conn.: Praeger, 2007), 146–7.

[43] Gleb Ivashentsov, "Russia and the Republic of Korea: New Horizons of Partnership," *International Affairs* 55, no. 1 (2009): 87–8.

[44] V. Denisov, "Moscow-Seoul: Partnership Based on Trust," *International Affairs* 51, no. 3 (June 2005): 131.

Table 16. *2008 Trade with South Korea*

	Total bilateral trade	Exports from South Korea	Imports to South Korea
China	$168.4 B	$91.4 B	$77 B
Japan	$98.3 B	$28.3 B	$70 B
Russia	$18.0 B	$9.7 B	$8.3 B

Source: Korea International Trade Association, http://global.kita.net.

include climate change, fishing, construction, science and technology, energy, and space exploration, among others. South Korean–Russian economic ties are growing slowly and are relatively small (see Table 16), especially when compared to Seoul's relationships with Beijing and Tokyo. There is a belief, however, that the potential for greater financial cooperation is significant and likely to grow, especially if some of the North Korean problems can be solved.

Relations with Moscow also help South Korea craft a more independent foreign and economic policy that is less reliant on ties to the United States or China. A relationship with Moscow helps to provide a counterweight to the power of China, the United States, and Japan in the region. Russia can also act as a valuable intermediary with North Korea, and joint development projects can help to bring economic growth to the DPRK while integrating the North with the regional economy.[45] Finally, for South Korea and Russia, improved relations allow them to address several other common interests, including counterterrorism, stopping the spread of weapons of mass destruction, piracy, cyber crime, and solving the North Korean nuclear problem.

There is a broad range of cooperative activities, but three may be the most significant for South Korea: oil and gas pipelines; connecting the Trans-Korean railway to the Trans-Siberian railroad; and cooperation in space exploration.

Oil and Gas Reserves

South Korea consumes large amounts of energy yet has almost no domestic sources of oil and gas, relying heavily on imports to sustain its economic growth.[46] Seoul already imports natural gas via tanker

[45] Yoon, "Russian Foreign Policy and South Korean Security," 136–7.
[46] Ibid., 146–50.

from Russian reserves on Sakhalin Island. In 2008, the state-owned companies Gazprom and KOGAS began cooperation on a natural gas pipeline that would allow larger amounts of Russian gas to be shipped to South Korea. The chief obstacle to the project is that the pipeline would require North Korean cooperation. When the agreement was made, both sides were hopeful that DPRK participation would be forthcoming, particularly if Russia were to help North Korea modernize its energy infrastructure. At the moment, however, Pyongyang's cooperation is unlikely. In the meantime, South Korean companies have concluded a number of contracts to build equipment for the Russian energy industry and tankers for oil and liquefied natural gas.

Railroad Deal

In September 2008, Presidents Lee Myung-bak and Dmitry Medvedev signed a deal that will reconnect the Trans-Korean railway with the Trans-Siberian rail line. The "Iron Silk Road," Russia's name for the project, would provide a huge boost to its Far East economy and help build valuable transportation infrastructure. When completed, the rail links will allow South Korea to ship products to markets in Central Asia, Europe, and the Middle East, greatly reducing shipping costs. The railway would connect Busan, already the world's tenth-largest port, with Seoul, then across North Korea and on to Russia, with connections to the Trans-Siberian railroad. Again, the project would require North Korean cooperation along with repairs to its dilapidated rail net that are estimated to cost more than $2.5 billion. As with the pipeline project, trains traveling through North Korea raise serious security concerns and make the route vulnerable to North Korean provocations. Pyongyang stands to gain much from the project, however, through charging tolls and other fees; an improved transportation infrastructure, especially for the goods it produces for export at Kaesong; and the likely amounts of assistance South Korea and Russia will provide to build and repair the DPRK railroad. Although North–South relations are often uncertain, it is hoped that Russian participation will allow Moscow to act as an intermediary to help facilitate the projects.

Space Program Cooperation

An area that has been of particular interest to South Korea is cooperation with Russia to develop Seoul's satellite launch and space capability.

South Korea began work on a Korean Space Launch Vehicle (KSLV) in 2000, and, in 2004, President Roh Moo-hyun traveled to Russia to sign an ROK-Russian space cooperation agreement.[47] Russia agreed to train South Korean astronauts at Russian facilities and to help the South build the KSLV-1. South Korea's first astronaut, Yi So-yeon, went into space in April 2009 aboard a Russian spacecraft traveling to the International Space Station. Russian authorities also provided the core of the propulsion system and a liquid fuel rocket for the KSLV-1 but were reluctant to provide further technology for the program. In June 2009, South Korea finished construction of the Naro Space Center in Goheung along the southwestern tip of the peninsula. The space center was built from a Russian design but was modified to fit South Korean needs. South Korea has expressed a strong interest in further cooperation, but Russian officials have been less enthusiastic. The Korea Aerospace Research Institute that heads the South Korean space program plans to produce a KSLV-2 based purely on indigenous designs but has had to delay these plans because of difficulties in obtaining the necessary technology from Moscow.

After several delays, on August 25, 2009, South Korean officials launched the KSLV-1, also called the Naro-1, in a bid to make South Korea the tenth country to place a satellite in orbit from its home territory. The Russian-made rocket had a smooth takeoff but traveled beyond the required trajectory to successfully place the satellite in the proper orbit. Seoul does have satellites in orbit that have been launched from other countries and intends to continue its satellite launch and space programs.[48]

Conclusion

As debate continues regarding Asia's geopolitical and economic future along with the potential for conflict in the years ahead, South Korea once again finds itself in the middle of this unfolding story. Compared with its role in the late nineteenth and early twentieth centuries, South Korea is now a thriving, mid-range power with ambitions to play a

---

[47] See D. Pinkston, "South Korea, Russia Seek to Accelerate Development of South Korean Space Launch Vehicle," May 2007, Monterey Institute of International Studies, http://cns.miis.edu/other/wmdi0705c.htm.

[48] D. Kirk, "S. Korea's Failed Satellite Launch Sets Back Space Effort," *Christian Science Monitor*, August 25, 2009, http://www.csmonitor.com/2009/0825/p06s12-woap.html (accessed November 6, 2009).

greater role in the region than it did in the past.[49] South Korea has important economic ties to China and Japan as well as plans to develop its more modest relationship with Russia in the future. Seoul also has plans to grow its naval capability to protect its expanding commercial interests and to increase its influence in the region. South Korea's future is tied to a settlement of the North Korea nuclear issue and possible reunification along with China's rise and the future of East Asia more broadly. These are all difficult issues, and it is unclear how they will resolve in the years ahead. South Korea's increasing political, economic, and military power make it likely that Seoul will play an increasing role in determining the future of the region and in helping to maintain peace and stability in East Asia.

[49] For a more detailed discussion, see T. Roehrig, "Korean Security and Big Power Relations," in *Korean Security in a Changing East Asia*, ed. Roehrig et al., 95–113.

Selected Bibliography

Ahn, C. "Financial and Corporate Restructuring in Korea: Accomplishments and Unfinished Agenda." *The Japanese Economic Review* 54 (2001):252–70.

Ahn, S. "Understanding Russian-South Korean Arms Trade: A Nontraditional Security Approach?" *Armed Forces and Society* 35, no. 3 (April 2009): 421–36.

Amsden, A. *Asia's New Giant: South Korea and Late Industrialization*, Oxford: Oxford University Press, 1989.

Bedeski, R. *The Transformation of South Korea: Reform and Reconstruction in the Sixth Republic under Roh Tae Woo 1987–1992*. London: Routledge, 1994.

Brazinsky, G. *Nation Building in South Korea: Koreans, Americans, and the Making of a Democracy*. Chapel Hill: University of North Carolina Press, 2007.

Cha, V. "Korea Unification: The Zero-Sum Past and Precarious Future." In *Two Koreas in Transition: Implications for US Policy*, I. Kim, ed., 63–92. St. Paul, MN: Paragon House, 1998.

Chae, H. and Kim, S. "Conservatives and Progressives in South Korea." *Washington Quarterly* 31, no. 4 (Autumn 2008): 77–95.

Cho, M. "Roh Moo-hyun Government's Peace and Prosperity Policy: Prospects and Tasks." *Unification Policy Studies* 12, no. 1 (2003): 1–27.

Connaughton, R. *Rising Sun and Tumbling Bear Russia's War with Japan*. London: Cassell, 2004.

Conroy, H. and Patterson, W. "Duality and Dominance: A Century of Korean-American Relations." In *Korean-American Relations, 1866–1997*, Y. Lee and W. Patterson, eds., 1–10. Albany: State University of New York Press, 1999.

Cooney, K. and Scarbrough, A. "Japan and South Korea: Can These Two Nations Work Together?" *Asian Affairs* 35, no. 3 (Fall 2008): 173–92.

Cotton, J. *Politics and Policy in the New Korean State*. New York: St. Martin's Press, 1995.

Creekmore, M. Jr. *A Moment of Crisis: Jimmy Carter, the Power of a Peacemaker, and North Korea's Nuclear Ambitions*. New York: Public Affairs, 2006.

Cumings, B. *Korea's Place in the Sun: A Modern History*. New York: W. W. Norton, 1997.

——— ed. *Child of Conflict: The Korean-American Relationship, 1943–1953*. Seattle: University of Washington Press, 1983.

Dudden, A. *Japan's Colonization of Korea: Discourse and Power*. Honolulu: University of Hawaii Press, 2005.

Duus, P. *The Abacus and the Sword: The Japanese Penetration of Korea, 1895–1910*. Berkeley: University of California Press, 1998.

209

Eckert, C. J., Lee, K., Lew, Y., Robinson, M., and Wagner, E. *Korea: Old and New, A History*. Cambridge, MA: Harvard University Press, 1990.

Emery, R. *Korean Economic Reform: Before and Since the 1997 Crisis*. Aldershot, UK: Ashgate, 2001.

Fern, F. "Tokdo or Takeshima?: The International Law of Territorial Acquisition in Japan-Korea Island Dispute." *Stanford Journal of East Asian Affairs* 5, no. 1 (Winter 2005): 78–89.

Fowler, J. "The United States and South Korean Democratization." *Political Science Quarterly* 114, no. 2 (Summer 1999): 265–88.

Gleysteen, W. Jr. *Massive Entanglement, Marginal Influence: Carter and Korea in Crisis*. Washington, DC: Brookings Institution Press, 1999.

Goldstein, M. *The Asian Financial Crisis: Causes, Cures, and Systemic Implications*. Washington, DC: Institute for International Economics, 1998.

Jesse, N., Heo, U., and DeRouen, K. Jr. "A Nested Game Approach to Political and Economic Liberalization in Democratizing States: The Case of South Korea." *International Studies Quarterly* 46 (2002): 401–22.

Ha, Y. "South Korea in 2000: A Summit and the Search for New Institutional Identity." *Asian Survey* 41(2001): 30–39.

Haggard, S., Kim, B., and Moon, C. "The Transition to Export-Led Growth in South Korea: 1954–1966." *Journal of Asian Studies* 50 (1991): 850–73.

Haggard, S. and Moon, C. "Institutions and Economic Policy: Theory and a Korean Case," *World Politics* 42 (1990): 210–37.

Han, S. *The Failure of Democracy in South Korea*. Berkeley: University of California Press, 1974.

Hane, M. *Modern Japan: A Historical Survey*, 2nd ed. Boulder, CO: Westview Press, 1992.

Hays, Gries, P. "The Koguryo Controversy, National Identity, and Sino-Korean Relations Today." *East Asia* 22, no. 4 (2005): 3–17.

Henderson, G. *The Politics of the Vortex*. Cambridge, MA: Harvard University Press, 1968.

Heo, U. "South Korea: Democratization, Financial Crisis, and the Decline of the Developmental State." In *The Political Economy of International Financial Crisis*, S. Horowitz and U. Heo, eds., 151–64. Lanham, MD: Rowman & Littlefield Publishers, 2001.

Heo, U. and Stockton, H. "Elections and Parties in South Korea Before and After Transition to Democracy." *Party Politics* 11 (2005): 675–89.

Heo, U. and Kim, S. "Financial Crisis in South Korea: Failure of the Government-Led Development Paradigm." *Asian Survey* 40 (2001): 492–507.

Heo, U., Jeon, H., Kim, H., and Kim, O. "The Political Economy of South Korea: Economic Growth, Democratization, and Financial Crisis." University of Maryland School of Law, 2008.

Heo, U. and Woo, J. "South Korea's Experience with Structural Reform: Lessons for Other Countries." *Korean Social Science Journal* 33 (2006):1–24.

Heo, U. and Hyun, C. "The 'Sunshine Policy' Revisited: An Analysis of South Korea's Policy Toward North Korea." In *Conflict in Asia: Korea, China-Taiwan, and India-Pakistan*, U. Heo and S. Horowitz, eds., 89–103. Westport, CT: Greenwood, 2003.

Heo, U. and Woo, J. "South Korea's Response: Democracy, Identity, and Strategy." In *Identity and Change in East Asian Conflicts: The Case of China, Taiwan and the Koreas*, S. Horowitz, U. Heo, and A. Tan, 149–64. New York: Palgrave Macmillan, 2007.

"Changing National Identity and Security Perception in South Korea," In *Korean Security in a Changing East Asia*, T. Roehrig, J. Seo, and U. Heo, eds., 192–205. Westport, CT: Praeger, 2007.

Kang, C. "Segyehwa Reform of the South Korean Developmental State." In *Korea's Globalization*, S. Kim, ed., 76–101. New York: Cambridge University Press, 2000.

Kang, K. and Walker, S. "The 2000 National Assembly Elections in South Korea." *Electoral Studies* 21 (2002): 480–5.

Kihl, Y. *Transforming Korean Politics: Democracy, Reform, and Culture*. Armonk, NY: M. E. Sharpe, 2004.

Kim, C. *The Korean Presidents: Leadership for Nation Building*. Norwalk, CT: EastBridge, 2007.

Kim, D. "The Korean Labor Market: The Crisis and After." In *Korean Crisis and Recovery*, D. Coe and S. Kim, eds., 261–92. Washington, DC: International Monetary Fund and Korea Institute for International Economic Policy, 2002.

Kim, H. "The 2000 Parliamentary Election in South Korea." *Asian Survey* 40 (2000): 894–913.

Kim, S. *The Politics of Military Revolution*. Chapel Hill: University of North Carolina Press, 1971.

Kim, S. "State and Civil Society in South Korea's Democratic Consolidation." *Asian Survey* XXXVII, no. 12 (December 1997): 1135–44.

   The Politics of Democratization in Korea: The Role of Civil Society. Pittsburgh, PA: University of Pittsburgh Press, 2000.

   "Civil Society in South Korea: From Grand Democracy Movements to Petty Interest Groups?" *Journal of Northeast Asian Studies* 15, no. 2 (Summer 1996): 81–97.

Kim, S. and Lim, W. "How to Deal with South Korea." *Washington Quarterly* 32, no. 2 (Spring 2007): 71–82.

Kirk, D. *Korean Crisis: Unraveling of the Miracle in the IMF Era*. New York: St. Martin's Press, 2000.

Lee, H. "South Korea in 2002: Multiple Political Dramas." *Asian Survey* 43 (2003): 64–77.

Lee, K. (E. Wagner and E. Shultz, tr.). *A New History of Korea*. Seoul: Ilchokak Publishers, 1984.

Lee, N. *The Making of Minjung: Democracy and the Politics of Representation in South Korea*. Ithaca, NY: Cornell University Press, 2007.

Lee, Y. *The State, Society and Big Business in South Korea*. London: Routledge, 1997.

Levin, N. and Han, Y. *Sunshine in Korea: The South Korean Debate over Policies toward North Korea*. Santa Monica, CA: RAND, 2002.

Lie, J. and Park, M. "South Korea in 2005: Economic Dynamism, Generational Conflicts, and Social Transformations." *Asian Survey* 46 (2006): 56–62.

Matray, J. *The Reluctant Crusade*. Honolulu: University of Hawaii Press, 1985.

Mo, J. "Political Culture and Legislative Gridlock: Politics of Economic Reform in Pre-crisis Korea." *Comparative Political Studies* 34 (1999): 467–92.

Mo, J. and Moon, C. "Business-Government Relations under Kim Dae-jung." In *Economic Crisis and Corporate Restructuring in Korea*, S. Haggard, W. Lim, and E. Kim, eds., 127–49. New York: Cambridge University Press, 2003.

Moon, C. "Understanding the DJ Doctrine: The Sunshine Policy and the Korean Peninsula." In *Kim Dae-jung Government and Sunshine Policy: Promises and Challenges*, C. Moon and D. Steinberg, eds., 31–45. Washington, DC: Georgetown University Press, 1999.

Nahm, A. *Korea: Tradition and Transformation: A History of the Korean People*. Elizabeth, NJ: Hollym International, 1988.

Nam, C. "Relocating the U.S. Forces in South Korea: Strained Alliance, Emerging Partnership in the Changing Defense Posture." *Asian Survey* 46, no. 4 (July/August 2006): 615–31.

Oberdorfer, D. *The Two Koreas: A Contemporary History*. New York: Basic Books, 1997.

Oh, J. *Korean Politics: The Quest for Democratization and Economic Development*. Ithaca, NY: Cornell University Press, 1999.

Paine, S. *The Sino-Japanese War of 1894–1895: Perceptions, Power, and Primacy.* Cambridge: Cambridge University Press, 2005.

Park, T. "South Korea in 1997: Clearing the Last Hurdle to Political-Economic Maturation." *Asian Survey* 38 (1997): 1–10.

  "South Korea in 1998: Swallowing the Bitter Pills of Restructuring." *Asian Survey* 39 (1999): 133–44.

Pirie, I. *The Korean Developmental State: From Dirigisme to Neo-Liberalism.* London: Routledge, 2008.

Pyle, K. *Japan Rising: The Resurgence of Japanese Power and Purpose.* New York: Public Affairs, 2007.

Rhee, Y., Ross-Larson, B., and Pursell, G. *Korea's Competitive Edge: Managing the Entry into World Markets.* Baltimore: Johns Hopkins University Press, 1984.

Roehrig, T. "History as a Strategic Weapon: The South Korean and Chinese Struggle for Koguryo." *Journal of Asian and African Studies* 45, no. 1 (February 2010): 5–28.

  The Prosecution of Former Military Leaders in Newly Democratic Nations: The Cases of Argentina, Greece, and South Korea. Jefferson, NC: McFarland, 2002.

  From Deterrence to Engagement: The U.S. Defense Commitment to South Korea. Lanham, MD: Lexington, 2006.

  "Assessing North Korean Behavior: The June 2000 Summit, the Bush Administration, and Beyond." In *Conflict in Asia: Korea, China, and India-Pakistan,* U. Heo and S. Horowitz, eds., 67–88. Westport, CT: Praeger, 2003.

  "North Korea and the US State Sponsors of Terrorism List" *Pacific Focus* 24, no. 1 (April 2009): 85–106.

  "'One Rogue State Crisis at a Time!': The United States and North Korea's Nuclear Weapons Program." *World Affairs* 165, no. 4 (Spring 2003): 155–78.

  Korean Dispute over the Northern Limit Line: Security, Economics, or International Law? Baltimore: University of Maryland School of Law, 2008.

  "Restructuring the U.S. Military Presence in Korea: Implications for Korean Security and the U.S.-ROK Alliance," In *On Korea,* vol. 1, Academic Paper Series, 132–49. Washington, DC: Korea Economic Institute, 2007.

  "Korean Security and Big Power Relations." In *Korean Security in a Changing East Asia,* Roehrig et al. (ed.), 95–113. Westport, CT: Praeger, 2007.

Scott-Stokes, H. and Lee J. eds. *The Kwangju Uprising: Eyewitness Press Accounts of Korea's Tiananmen.* New York: M. E. Sharpe, 2000.

Shim, Y. *Korean Bank Regulation and Supervision: Crisis and Reform.* Hague: Kluwer Law International, 2000.

Shin, G. *Ethnic Nationalism in Korea: Genealogy, Politics, and Legacy.* Stanford, CA: Stanford University Press, 2006.

Shin J. and Chang, H. *Restructuring Korea Inc.* London: Routledge, 2003.

Snyder, S. *China's Rise and the Two Koreas: Politics, Economics, Security.* Boulder, CO: Lynne Rienner, 2009.

Stetz, M. and Oh, B. eds. *Legacies of the Comfort Women of World War II.* Armonk, NY: M. E. Sharpe, 2001.

Steuck, W. *Rethinking the Korean War: A New Diplomatic and Strategic History.* Princeton, NJ: Princeton University Press, 2002.

Yoon, E. "Russian Foreign Policy and South Korean Security." In *Korean Security in a Changing East Asia,* T. Roehrig, J. Seo, and U. Heo, eds., 136–54. Westport, CT: Praeger, 2007.

Yoshimi, Y. *Comfort Women.* New York: Columbia University Press, 2001.

Youn, Y. "South Korea in 1999: Overcoming Cold War Legacies." *Asian Survey* 40 (2000): 164–71.

Index